THE CHRISTIAN YEAR

ITS PURPOSE
AND
ITS HISTORY

Rev. Walker Gwynne, D.D.
Author of
"Manual of Christian Doctrine," "The Gospel in the Church," etc.

HERITAGE BOOKS
2024

HERITAGE BOOKS
AN IMPRINT OF HERITAGE BOOKS, INC.

Books, CDs, and more—Worldwide

For our listing of thousands of titles see our website
at
www.HeritageBooks.com

A Facsimile Reprint
Published 2024 by
HERITAGE BOOKS, INC.
Publishing Division
5810 Ruatan Street
Berwyn Heights, MD 20740

Copyright © 1915 Longmans, Green, and Co.
First Edition, February, 1915
Reprinted, August, 1917

— Publisher's Notice —
In reprints such as this, it is often not possible to remove blemishes from the original. We feel the contents of this book warrant its reissue despite these blemishes and hope you will agree and read it with pleasure.

International Standard Book Number
Paperbound: 978-0-7884-2987-3

INTRODUCTION

THE lack and the need of a popular manual on the Christian Year were forced on the attention of the writer when he undertook to teach a class in the Newark Diocesan Training School for Teachers. His aim in the present volume is to provide such a book as an intelligent teacher would desire, giving, not merely the bare facts concerning the different festivals and fasts, but also some account of the practical and devotional reasons which the whole Catholic Church has had from the beginning for adopting the system of her Christian Year and Calendar.

So far as defence or *apologia* is concerned, Hooker with his lofty philosophical treatment of the subject is of course unexcelled. But Hooker is not accessible to the average student, and his somewhat antiquated style, in spite of its nobility and charm, is not likely to attract the ordinary reader of to-day. There are only a few monographs in English on the Christian Year, intended chiefly for candidates for Holy Orders, of which the latest and most useful are " The Church Year and the Calendar " by the late Bishop Dowden of Edinburgh, and " The Liturgical Year " by the Rev. Vernon Staley. Of the latter there is an abridgment entitled " The Seasons, etc., of the Christian Year." " Heortology, a History of the Christian Festivals from their Origin to the present Day," by Professor Kellner of the University of Bonn,[1] is probably the most complete monograph on the subject, but its treatment is almost wholly technical and historical. As its author is a Roman Catholic it occasionally shows, as might be expected, some marked leanings. For the rest, the writer was compelled to search in encyclopædias, and books on liturgics, most of which, however, contain only dry-as-dust information as to dates and authorities and origins, which are chiefly of interest to the liturgical student or archæologist. In this respect, however, he would single out as of especial value Chapter VIII of " Origines du Culte Chrétien," by Duchesne, of which an English translation by M. L. McClure is published by the S.P.C.K. (London, 1903); the 20th and 21st books of Bingham's "Antiquities of the Christian Church," and chapters 6, 7, and 8, in " The Ministry of Grace " by Bishop John Wordsworth of Salisbury.

It may be well to mention here for the ordinary reader that the original sources of information on the Church Year are to be found in early Church historians, missals, and other service books, decrees of Church councils, official documents, sermons preached on festival days, early calendars, and hymnaries.

For much that the author has written on the Calendar he is indebted to an excellent volume on " The Theory and Use of the Church Calendar in the Measurement of Time," by his former preceptor, the late Professor Samuel Seabury, D.D., of the General Theological Seminary, New York, a grandson of the first American Bishop.

Of the many devotional books on the Christian Year probably the best and most useful modern volume is that of the late Arthur Cleveland Coxe, Bishop of Western

[1] English translation, 1908, Kegan Paul & Co.

INTRODUCTION vii

New York, entitled "Thoughts on the Services," a new issue of which, edited by Bishop Whitehead of Pittsburgh, is published by the Lippincott Co. of Philadelphia. Of poetry it is needless to say that Keble's "Christian Year" and "Lyra Innocentium," and Mrs. Alexander's "Hymns for Little Children," take the lead in charm and devotional feeling. Bishop Ken's "Hymns for All Festivals of the Christian Year,"[1] amid much that is dull, contains a few poems of real worth. In George Herbert, Spenser, Wordsworth, Tennyson, and the "Lyra Apostolica" (containing poems by Newman, Keble, and others), the "Lyra Messianica" by Orby Shipley, "Lyra Catholica" by E. Caswall, "Lyra Sanctorum" (for the Minor Festivals), "The Cathedral" by Isaac Williams, and Palgrave's "Treasury of Sacred Song," besides the Hymnals, much illustrative poetry may also be found.

While the author makes no pretensions to original liturgical lore, he believes that his treatment of the various subjects has the support of the latest and best scholarship. He hopes, moreover, that the little book may be found useful, not only in his own communion, but also in other bodies of English-speaking Christians, whose growing tendency is to return to the ancient and well-tried methods of the historic Church in matters of worship and festival. It has been wisely said that, "By the changes of day and night, of seasons and years, Creation calls upon man to raise his mind to God at stated times, and to enter into communion with Him."[2] It may be that the observance together of the great immemorial days and seasons of the Christian Year which, through all the centuries, have made Christians

[1] 1721; new ed. by Pickering, 1868.
[2] Kellner's *Heortology*, p. 1.

to kneel together before their common Lord, in a common worship, will prove the most effective method, above mere argument, for bringing about that visible unity for which, with dying breath, the Lord Jesus pleaded with the One God and Father of us all.

CONTENTS

INTRODUCTION
PAGE

The Need of a Popular Manual—Hooker's defence of the Christian Year—Bishop Dowden—Vernon Staley—Professor Kellner—Duchesne—Professor Seabury—Original Sources—Devotional and Poetical Aspects.............. v

CHAPTER I
WHY THE CHURCH HAS A CHRISTIAN YEAR

The System "broad-based" on Human Reason and Experience—Pagan Religions, Modern Christian Bodies, and Civil Governments all Alike in their Use of Anniversaries and Commemorations—Bishop Arthur Cleveland Coxe on the Value of the Christian Year—Hooker's Judgment........ 1

CHAPTER II
PURITAN OBJECTIONS

Hooker's Philosophic Defence of the Church's System—Action of the Puritan Parliament in 1644—Abuse of Good Customs no Reason for their Destruction—Even the Sabbath Perverted and Abused by Ancient Jews, as Sunday is by Modern Christians.................................. 7

CHAPTER III
THE CHURCH YEAR A GROWTH

Its "Root" in the Divinely Appointed Ritual Year of the Church of Israel—Its "Branch" in the Incarnate Life of

CONTENTS

PAGE

Christ—A Full Account not to be expected in the New Testament—Continuity and Fulfilment of the Church of Israel in the Church of Christ.......................... 11

CHAPTER IV

THE RITUAL YEAR OF THE CHURCH OF ISRAEL

The Sabbath not Jewish, but Universal—The other Sacred Festivals Historical—Passover, Pentecost, Tabernacles, Feast of Trumpets, or New Year, Purim, Dedication, or Feast of Lights, Great Day of Atonement—Names of the Jewish Months—Dr. Edersheim on the Effect of the Ritual Year on the Imagination of Jewish Children............. 15

CHAPTER V

THE JEWISH YEAR AND THE APOSTOLIC CHURCH

Under this System Christ and His Apostles were Trained from Childhood—To these Laws and Customs our Lord was Supremely Loyal—He Chooses Two of the Great Feasts of Israel with which to associate His Death and Resurrection, the Coming of the Holy Ghost and the Establishment of His Church........................... 22

CHAPTER VI

THE BEGINNINGS OF THE CHRISTIAN YEAR IN THE APOSTOLIC CHURCH

The First Christians were all Jews who faithfully observed the Ancient Festivals and Fasts, but saw in them the "Body" where formerly there was but a "Shadow of Good Things to Come"—Passover and Pentecost—"The First Day of the Week," being the Day of the Resurrection, observed in Addition to the Sabbath as a "Sister Day"... 28

CHAPTER VII

THE VALUE OF CUSTOM AND TRADITION IN THE CHURCH

S. Paul's Valuation of Customs and Traditions—The Worth of Customs and Traditions to a Nation and to Individuals—

CONTENTS xi

PAGE

All Traditions not of Equal Obligation—The Test "from the Beginning"—"Sursum Corda"—The Holy Scriptures and the Sacred Ministry Supreme Examples of Tradition—What then is the Purpose of Holy Scripture?—Archbishop Alexander, Scott Holland, Dean Hook, Dr. E. Hawkins... 35

CHAPTER VIII

The Church Calendar and Its Use

Greek and Roman Calendars—*Anno Domini*, or the Year of Our Lord—Why not adopted till the Year 541—Dionysius Exiguus—What we owe to Julius Cæsar—Error of the Calendar in A. D. 1582—"New Style" adopted by Churches in Communion with Rome—Not adopted by England till 1752—Greek and Russian Churches retain the "Old Style."... 43

CHAPTER IX

Technical Words in the Calendar

Lunar Cycle, Metonic Cycle, Golden Number, or Prime, Paschal Moon, Epact, Dominical Letter, Bissextile or Leap Year, Ferial and Festal, Vigil and Eve, Octave, Movable and Immovable Feasts...................... 47

CHAPTER X

The Beginning of the Church Year—Advent and Christmas

Great Variety in Details of Calendars, but One Central Principle, the Incarnation—The Purpose of Advent—Other Names for Christmas—The Meaning and History of "Mass"—Why December 25?......................... 53

CHAPTER XI

Other Immovable Feasts of Our Lord

Circumcision, Epiphany, Presentation in the Temple, Annunciation, Transfiguration............................... 58

CONTENTS

CHAPTER XII

The Movable Feasts—Easter and Ascension

Why Easter not Immovable like Christmas—(For Origin of Easter see Chapters IV and V; for Origin of Sunday see Chapter VI.) Great Importance attached to Easter seen in the Quartodeciman Controversy—How finally settled in the Church at the Council of Nice, A.D. 325—Why the British and Irish Rule for Easter differed from that of Italy—Ascension Day—"The Pilgrimage of Silvia".... 64

CHAPTER XIII

Other Movable Feasts—Whitsunday and Trinity

The Coming of the Holy Ghost and the Birthday of the Church—The Name Whitsunday—The calling of Sundays "after Trinity" instead of "after Pentecost, or Whitsunday," peculiar to the English Church, and to the German Churches founded by the English 70

CHAPTER XIV

The Saints' Days

Hooker on their Observance—Red-letter and Black-letter Days—The Special Value of Black-letter Days—Why a Saint's Day is called *Dies natalis*, or Birthday—Appropriateness of the Time of the Nativities of the Baptist and of Our Lord—Also the Days given to S. Andrew, S. Thomas, S. Stephen, S. John the Evangelist, and the Holy Innocents—The Origin of Saints' Days—Bishop Westcott, Bishop Ellicott, and Dr. Newman on Saints' Days........ 75

CHAPTER XV

The Feast of S. Michael and All Angels

Only Two Angels mentioned by Name in the Canonical Scriptures—Two also in "the Books Called Apocrypha"—The Prominence given by Our Lord and the Holy Scriptures to Angels—The Great Practical Purpose of the Revelation of the Ministry of Angels—Hooker on the Angels 82

CONTENTS xiii

CHAPTER XVI

The Feast of All Saints

PAGE

All Hallows and Hallowe'en—The Great Need of such a Day of Remembrance—Paradise not Heaven—The Intermediate State only a Place of Preparation for Heaven—The American Day of National Thanksgiving...................... 87

CHAPTER XVII

The Black-letter Days

The Revision of the Old English Calendar in 1661 imperfect—The Present English Calendar, with Notes on the Black-letter Days... 92

CHAPTER XVIII

The Fasts of the Christian Year

Fasts equally with Festivals open to Abuse—Yet the New Testament as well as the Old full of Accounts of Fasting—The Example of Christ and His Apostles—The True Purpose of Fasting—The English-speaking Church lays down no Hard and Narrow Rules for Fasting............ 101

CHAPTER XIX

Lent and Pre-Lent

The Words Lent and Quadragesima—Meaning of the Names of the Pre-Lenten Sundays—Early Origin of the Fast in Preparation for Easter—Blunt on the Original Object of Lent—Ash-Wednesday and Shrove-Tuesday—Mid-Lent, or Refreshment Sunday.............................. 106

CHAPTER XX

Holy Week

Not "Passion Week"—The Events of Palm Sunday, and the four following Days—Maundy Thursday, why so called... 110

CONTENTS

CHAPTER XXI

GOOD FRIDAY AND EASTER EVEN

PAGE

Good Friday kept at first as a Feast Day in connection with Easter—After the Decision of the Church to observe Easter always on a Sunday, Good Friday naturally acquired its Present Character—Consecration of the Eucharist, but not Reception, began early to be omitted on Good Friday—Called the "Mass of the Pre-Sanctified"—Blunt on the Disuse of this Custom in the Church of England—The practice of Bishop King of Lincoln, Dean Church, Dean Gregory, and Dr. Liddon—Easter Even.... 114

CHAPTER XXII

OTHER DAYS OF FASTING

Ember and Rogation Days—Fridays—Vigils and Eves.... 120

CHAPTER XXIII

VARIATIONS AND REVISIONS OF CALENDARS

The Use of Liturgies Universal in the Primitive Church—Leading Features Common to All, yet Many Variations in Detail—Meaning of the Word "Use"—Various Revisions of the Liturgies of Rome and England—Need of Revision also in the Calendars, especially of Black-letter Days—Some Peculiarities of the Roman and Oriental Calendars.. 124

APPENDIX

THE LITURGICAL COLORS................................. 131
LEADING QUESTIONS FOR REVIEW OR EXAMINATION.......... 133
INDEX... 137

THE CHRISTIAN YEAR
ITS PURPOSE AND ITS HISTORY

CHAPTER I

WHY THE CHURCH HAS A CHRISTIAN YEAR

"The way before us lies
Distinct with signs, through which in set career,
As through a zodiac, moves the ritual year."
—*Wordsworth,* "*Eccles. Sonnets,*" **XIX**.

"Our festival year is a bulwark of orthodoxy as real as our confessions of faith."—*Archer Butler.*

THE question of the age or origin of particular festivals or fasts is not so important as the practical and historical grounds on which the Christian Year is founded. No apology in the modern sense of the word is needed for its use, but rather an *apologia* or *rationale* to show how the system is "broad based" on reason and human experience as well as on the divine will. It has been well said indeed that "The foundations and heart of the whole festal system of the Church were given by a Higher Hand, and only the development—the much less important part of the whole—is to be attributed to the thoughts of men."[1]

The Christian Year may then be described (1) as a

[1] Kellner's *Heortology,* p. 203.

scheme which provides a dramatic method of commemorating, at special seasons and on special days, the chief events of the Incarnate Life of our Lord. (2) It provides for the worshipper a well-rounded system of Scripture lessons, epistles and gospels, and selected psalms and hymns, for the purpose of securing what S. Paul calls "the proportion (*analogia*) of the faith",[1] that is, a symmetrical framework invaluable to preacher and people alike, saving them from the evils of sensationalism and distorted teaching, and from the exaggeration or over-emphasis of one set of truths at the expense of others equally important. (3) It recalls the main features of some noble lives recorded in the New Testament besides that of our Lord; also the lives of notable men and women in the Church's history after these first days; showing how Christlike were many of His servants all through the centuries. It thus testifies also to the historic continuity of the Church from the Apostles' days, while proclaiming the fact that real sainthood or imitation of Christ is not an impossibility, but is within the reach of all. Moreover (4), true to the experience of our daily life, it provides for variety of devotional tone in alternate fast and festival, which it makes manifest also to the eye by means of ecclesiastical colors adapted to the seasons.

The Christian Year is thus the skeleton on which the Prayer Book and the whole system of the Church's teaching are framed. It is true a skeleton in itself is not a thing of delight, yet nevertheless there can be neither life nor beauty without it in flower, or tree, or man. It is the necessary framework on which to lay the flesh and blood and color of the living man or the living plant.

[1] Rom. xii. 6.

It is important therefore at the outset to understand that in the observance of a ritual year there is nothing forced or artificial. Such a plan is strictly in accordance with human nature as testified to by all history, pagan, Jewish, and Christian alike. Egyptians and Assyrians, Greeks and Romans, all had their festivals and fasts. The people of Israel had a ritual year by divine direction and particular ordinances. Nor are such observances confined to religious systems. Even civil governments, modern as well as ancient, have always found it necessary to have their national anniversaries and commemorations. When the revolutionary and infidel government of France rejected the ancient ritual year of the Church, and even the old civil year which took its date from the birth of Christ (*Anno Domini*), it was forced to coin new names for the months, to each of which it gave thirty days uniformly, and it ordained a system of five festival days wherewith to fill out the year, placing them from September 17th to 21st. These it devoted respectively to "The Virtues, Genius, Labor, Opinion, and Rewards." Moreover, instead of the weekly Sunday it made only one day in ten a holiday. But human nature at length rebelled, and the scheme lasted less than fourteen years, namely, from Sept. 22, 1792, the date of the establishment of the Republic, till Jan. 1, 1806. So likewise, without formally rejecting the Christian Year, America has its Fourth of July or Independence Day, its Washington's and Lincoln's birthdays, its Columbus Day, its Thanksgiving, Decoration, Labor, and Arbor Days.

Even those religious bodies whose forefathers rejected the Christian Year, have their "Flower Sunday," their "Hospital," "Children's," "Peace," and "Temperance" Sundays, their "Rally Day," and "Week of Prayer," and are ever coining other special days of observance. Moreover, along with this, most happily, they are almost universally adopting much which they once rejected. Easter Day is now observed by nearly all of them. They are beginning to keep Holy Week, if not Lent, and they observe Christmas socially, if not yet on its religious side. All which goes to show how deeply rooted in human nature and in human need is this principle of associating great truths with times and seasons. It is the principle in fact laid down by God in the Fourth Commandment of the moral law, where the Sabbath is made the commemoration of God's rest from the work of creation, and the pledge of that future " Sabbath rest " which " remaineth for the people of God." [1]

Bishop Coxe is writing concerning the Christian Year when he says: " Look at this majestic system of claiming all time for Christ, and filling every day in every year with His Name, and His Worship. See how vast and rich the scheme, as a token of, and a provision for, the Second Advent. . . . God is the real author of this scheme, and it is revealed, in its substance, as part of His Wisdom for perpetuating His Truth. . . . And yet because all this is but part of our inestimable inheritance as Churchmen, we hardly think of it as, even on popular grounds, a conclusive reason for being what we are, and as furnishing an irresistible argument against those who oppose themselves. Of course we are Churchmen on higher grounds, and for independent reasons: yet it is a fact that the mind of our countrymen is too much perverted and prejudiced to appreciate these higher principles. We can hardly refer to them without wounding their feelings, and exciting their antagonism. But might we not safely and charitably direct their attention to our Liturgic System, first of all, as something

[1] Heb. iv. 9; Rev. Ver.

WHY THE CHURCH HAS A CHRISTIAN YEAR 5

which they ought to examine; and then leave them to their own conclusions, when once they shall have discovered that this inestimable possession is only to be found in its completeness among those who have preserved all the other Apostolic institutions of the Gospel in their purity and integrity?"[1]

"The Judicious" Hooker, as he was well named, the contemporary of Shakespeare and Bacon, with his keen philosophic mind and balanced judgment, sets the question of a ritual year on the highest plane of practical wisdom and necessity. It is not a question of personal preference or æsthetics. It is a matter which has the stamp and approval, not only of nature in its best estate, but of the Holy Scriptures, and the Church in all the ages. "All things whatsoever having their time," he writes, "the works of God have always that time which is seasonable and fittest for them. His works are some ordinary, some more rare, all worthy of observation, but not of all like necessity to be remembered; they all have their times, but they do not add the same estimation and glory to the times wherein they are. For as God by being everywhere yet doth not give unto all *places* one and the same degree of holiness, so neither [does He give] one and the same dignity to all *times* by working in all. For if all, either places or times, were in respect of God alike, wherefore was it said unto Moses by particular designation, 'This very place wherein thou standest is holy ground'?[2] Why doth the Prophet David choose out of all the days of the year but one whereof he speaketh by way of principal admiration, 'This is the day which the Lord hath made'?[3] No doubt, as God's extraordinary presence hath hallowed

[1] *Thoughts on the Services*, pp. 17, 18.
[2] Ex. iii. 5.   [3] Psalm cxviii. 24.

and sanctified certain *places*, so they are His extraordinary works that have truly and worthily advanced certain *times*, for which cause they ought to be, with all men that honour God, more holy than other days." [1]

He then quotes from that uncanonical but wonderfully wise book, "Ecclesiasticus, or the Wisdom of Sirach, the Son of Jesus," [2] "Why doth one day excel another, when as all the light of every day in the year is of the sun? By the knowledge of the Lord they were distinguished; and He altered seasons and feasts. Some of them hath He made high days, and hallowed them, and some of them hath He made ordinary days."

Hooker sums up his account of the festal system of the Church in these eloquent words: " Well to celebrate these religious and sacred days is to spend the flower of our time happily. They are the splendor and outward dignity of our religion, forcible witnesses of ancient truth, provocations to the exercise of all piety, shadows of our endless felicity in heaven, on earth everlasting records and memorials, wherein they who cannot be drawn to hearken to what we teach, may, only by looking on what we do, in a manner read whatsoever we believe." [3]

[1] *Ecc. Polity*, V. lxx., pp. 489, 490, Keble's ed.
[2] xxxiii. 7, 8, 9.
[3] *Ecc. Polity*, V. lxxii, pp. 518, 519, Keble's ed.

CHAPTER II

PURITAN OBJECTIONS

"If these beautiful arts—architecture, painting, music, and the like—detain men on their own account, to wonder at their own intrinsic charms, down among the things of sense,—if we are thinking more of music than of Him whose glory it heralds, more of the beauty of form and color than of Him whose temple it adorns,—then, be sure, we are robbing God of His glory; we are turning His temple into a den of thieves. No error is without its element of truth, and jealousy on this point was the strength of Puritanism, which made it a power notwithstanding its violence,—notwithstanding its falsehood."—*H. P. Liddon*, Sermon on *Intruders in the Temple*.

IN spite of the natural fitness of the Christian Year to men's spiritual needs, as we have remarked in the preceding chapter, the Church of England met with great and bitter opposition in regard to its observance from the Puritans in the sixteenth and seventeenth centuries. Hooker, in his splendid defence of the Church against these narrow views, speaks of "the difference in days" as being "natural and necessary." "Even nature," he says, "hath taught the heathens, and God the Jews, and Christ us, that festival solemnities are a part of the public exercise of religion."[1] He quotes S. Augustine as saying, "By festival solemnities and set days we dedicate and sanctify to God the memory of His benefits, lest unthankful forgetfulness thereof should creep upon us in course of time."[2] And Hooker further adds: "The very law of nature itself, which all

[1] *Ecc. Pol.*, V. lxx., pp. 490–494. [2] Pp. 495, 6.

men confess to be God's law, requireth in government no less the sanctification of times, than of places, persons, and things, unto God's honor." [1] It was God who said to Moses at the Bush, "The place whereon thou standest is holy ground," and it was God also who said, "Ye shall keep My Sabbaths, and reverence My Sanctuary." [2]

To all this reasoning the Puritans objected strenuously, though with great inconsistency, as being themselves sticklers for their own self-appointed fast-days, and their own severe and unscriptural view of the Sabbath. In 1644 the Puritan Parliament passed an ordinance strictly forbidding the observance of all holy days, and appointed a solemn fast to be held on Chrismas Day, alleging that that festival was originally of heathen origin. The law required every one to go to work, and that every keeper of a closed shop should be brought before the judge and punished. This condition of things lasted for sixteen years.

Referring to one of the petty objections of the Puritan party to the proper day for the observance of Easter, Dr. Samuel Seabury in his valuable treatise on "The Church Calendar" says, "On such occasions, and even in anticipation of them, the Puritans, whom God seems to have created to try the patience of the saints, were seized with inward spasms." "They were a class of men," he adds, "who stood more in need, as Dr. South somewhere says, of Luke the Physician than of Luke the Evangelist." [3] The Late Bishop Huntington of Central New York, himself of devout Puritan ancestry, expressed a similar opinion when he described Puritanism in this aspect of its character as "a disturbed biliary duct."

If Puritan objections had been confined to the abuse

[1] p. 497.   [2] Ex. iii, 5; Lev. xix. 20.   [3] Pp. 114, 116.

PURITAN OBJECTIONS

of the Christian Year, to the multiplication of saints' days and other festivals, and to many superstitious practices that had grown up about their observance, they would have been listened to respectfully. We know that the very best of customs are liable to abuse, and have been abused. In fact these very Puritans turned the Lord's Day into a very different kind of day from God's appointment of it; burdensome, hard, and unlovely, very unlike that "delight" which Isaiah says it was meant to be.[1] That, however, is a poor reason for their descendants in this generation making it a day of revelry such as many Church people also, alas, both in England and elsewhere had done, and are doing to-day. So too of Christmas and other holy days. All had been abused, just as similar days among the Jews had been. Isaiah had told the people in the Name of God: "The new moons and sabbaths I cannot away with. It is iniquity, even the solemn meeting."[2] The same was true of their sacrifices and their incense, all of them nevertheless of divine obligation. But perversion and abuse are grounds for destruction only to fanatics, and not to true reformers. All good things have been abused, the Bible, the Prayer Book, the ministry, the sacraments, the altar, the pulpit, the church. The Sabbath was woefully perverted in our Lord's day, but that only gave Him reason for restoring it to its rightful place, not for repealing the law that ordained it.[3]

Even in Apostolic days Jews who had become Christians had to be warned against the perversion of such good customs as they had inherited from their forefathers. "Ye observe days, and months, and times, and years," writes S. Paul to the Jewish Christians of Galatia. "I am afraid of you," he adds, "lest I have

[1] Isaiah lviii. 13. [2] Isaiah, i. 13. [3] S. Matt. xii. 8.

bestowed upon you labor in vain."[1] Their old purely Jewish customs were no longer necessary for Christians. They were only "shadows" and "beggarly rudiments," he says.[2] They could indeed lawfully use them, as he himself did, but not impose them as of necessity. All Christian Jews kept Saturday, their old day for keeping the Sabbath, as well as Sunday. We find the Apostle himself on one occasion offering the ancient Jewish sacrifices in the Temple,[3] and this was twenty-five years after his conversion. But all these things had ceased to be of obligation to Jewish Christians, and were purely voluntary.[4] "The body is of Christ."[5] Here is the reality, in feast, and ministry, and sacrament, for which all these "shadows" had prepared the way.

[1] Gal. iv. 10, 11.
[2] Heb. x. 1; Gal. iv. 9, Rev. Ver.
[3] Acts xxi. 20-27.
[4] See Col. ii. 16; Rom. xiv. 4, 5, 6.
[5] Col. ii. 17.

CHAPTER III

THE CHURCH YEAR A GROWTH

"There shall come forth a shoot out of the stock of Jesse, and a branch out of His roots shall bear fruit."—*Isaiah* ii. 1., *Rev. Ver.*

As we proceed to examine the system of the Church's Year we shall see that it is not a completely developed plan from the beginning, but a growth or evolution from a single root, to which many nations and many generations have contributed their special gifts, just as the soil does to the vine. It had its "root" in the ritual year of the Church of Israel. It had its "Branch" in the Incarnate Life of our Lord out of "the root of Jesse."[1] He is the Alpha and the Omega, the Beginning and the Ending, the First and the Last, the Light and the Life, of all her worship and her work.

When we trace it historically we find that, just as surely as our modern fruit trees and vines, peach, apple, plum, grape, have been developed from early wild species with less succulent and palatable fruit, so the Christian Year has its origin in the ritual year of the Patriarchs and of Israel. That was the "root" as well as the "shadow." The "Branch" and the "Body" are "of Christ." It is this "mystery of the Holy Incarnation" which the Church by her Christian Year, with marvellous practical wisdom, has planned century after century to illustrate in dramatic form, by season and day, by lesson and prayer, by hymn and

[1] Is. xi. 10.

color, and in well-rounded proportion, for the edification of all her children.

We must not therefore expect a full account of the Church's ritual year in the New Testament. We must be content if we get only glimpses of it here and there, and allusions to what S. Paul calls the "traditions," and "customs," and "ways" of the Church in Apostolic days, which are not to be lightly disregarded by any man calling himself a Christian.[1] Nor must we expect to find the system of the Christian Year fully developed even in the later days of the Primitive Church. Like the liturgy, and Christian architecture, and art, and hymnology, it took on form and beauty by slow degrees century after century; just as beautiful cathedrals and parish churches, with altars, organs, music, painting, sculpture, trained and vested choirs, took the place of a bare room or a burial chamber in the catacombs; or just as some of the same things to-day take the place of a hired hall, or a disused foundry, or an old railway car in an American or Canadian mining town.

Let us first consider in some detail the immediate source and pattern of the Year of the Church of Christ. One of S. Augustine's many epigrammatic sayings was that the Gospel was "latent in the Old Testament, and patent in the New." That, however, is only another way of expressing the great assertion of our Lord that He came "not to destroy the law or the prophets, but to fulfil."[2] And as Christ Himself was the fulfilment of all the foreshadowing and the promises of "The Gospel preached before" in the Old Testament,[3] so His Church is the fulfilment of the Church of Israel.

This organic continuity, as of a tree from its root, is

---

[1] 2 Thes. ii. 15; iii. 6; 1 Cor. xi. 2, margin, and 16; iv. 17.
[2] S. Matt. v. 17.   [3] Gal. iii. 8.

THE CHURCH YEAR A GROWTH 13

forcibly and beautifully illustrated in those magnificent prophecies in the 52d, 53d, 54th and 60th chapters of Isaiah, where the new and the old are, in the prophet's vision, indistinguishable one from the other, each growing into and blending with the other. The Church of the promised Christ or Messiah is not a different Church, but the fruition, and enlargement, and glorification of the earlier Church of Israel. Though Israel is in the immediate foreground of Isaiah's vision, it is the glorious Church which is to have its new birth on the Day of Pentecost, and its preachers and priests in "all the world," among "all nations," and "unto the end of the world;"[1] it is this great society and "kingdom of God" that the prophet addresses when he exclaims, "Awake, awake; put on thy strength, O Zion, put on thy beautiful garments, O Jerusalem. . . . How beautiful upon the mountains are the feet of him that bringeth good tidings, that publisheth peace." Or again, after describing the sorrows and the shame of the Cross and Passion, he utters the wonderful apostrophe beginning, "Sing, O barren, thou that didst not bear. . . . Enlarge the place of thy tent, and let them stretch forth the curtains of thine habitation. . . . Thy seed shall inherit the Gentiles. . . . O thou afflicted, tossed with tempest, and not comforted, I will lay thy foundation with sapphires. . . . No weapon that is formed against thee shall prosper; and every tongue that shall rise against thee in judgment thou shalt condemn." And once more in the splendid vision of the 60th chapter he exclaims, "Arise, shine, for thy light is come. . . . And the Gentiles shall come to thy light, and kings to the brightness of thy rising." None of these prophecies ever had any fulfilment in the ancient and literal Church of Israel as it stood

[1] S. Mark xvi. 15; S. Matt. xxviii. 19, 20.

alone. But all history proclaims the great vision realized in the Church of Christ, "My Church,"[1] the "Holy Catholic and Apostolic Church" of the creeds.

And again, just as we find all the ancient sacrifices fulfilled in the "one perfect and sufficient sacrifice" of the Cross, so we see its perpetuation and its commemoration in that holy sacrament instituted in the Upper Room out of the very materials of bread and wine which remained over and above from the Paschal feast, the greatest of all the sacrifices of Israel. And again, as we find the Mosaic or Aaronic priesthood in three sacred orders of high priest, priest, and Levite fulfilled in the one great "Apostle and High Priest, Jesus Christ,"[2] so we see this ancient ministry fulfilled in and merging into the new apostleship and priesthood which our Lord Himself ordained to speak and act for Him on earth.[3] The hereditary and physical descent of the sons of Aaron finds its counterpart and fruition in the spiritual descent of the apostolic succession of the three "Orders of Ministers in Christ's Church,—Bishops [or Apostles], Priests, and Deacons."[4] And in like manner we find the ritual year of Israel dying and blending into the dawn of a more glorious year, just as the Jewish Sabbath, on the primal Easter, "began to dawn toward the first day of the week,"[5] telling in unmistakable accents that those things which prophets foresaw, and "kings desired to see," and the whole world languished for,[6] had indeed come at last in all their fulness.

[1] S. Matt. xvi. 18.
[2] Heb. iii. 1.
[3] S. John xx. 21, 22, 23; Acts i. 8; 2 Cor. v. 20; 1 Cor. iv. 1; and compare Mal. iii. 3 with Acts vi. 7.
[4] Preface to Ordinal in the Prayer Book.
[5] S. Matt. xxviii. 1.
[6] S. Luke x. 24; Haggai ii. 7.

CHAPTER IV

THE RITUAL YEAR OF THE CHURCH OF ISRAEL

"He appointed the moon for seasons."—*Psalm* civ. 19.
"These are the feasts of the Lord, even holy convocations, which ye shall proclaim in their seasons."—*Lev.* xxiii. 4.

LET us now think of some of the details of that ancient Messianic year which was "latent in the Old Testament, and patent in the New."

The Sabbath, one of its most essential parts, was of course not of Israel but was part of the primal and universal law of morals; "made for man," as our Lord expresses it,[1] that is, for all mankind. But even this universal Sabbath had an added meaning and purpose for Israel after its Exodus from Egypt, as 1500 years later it had a still greater added meaning and purpose for Christians. For in addition to the reason which all the world had for keeping the Sabbath, Israelites had now, they are told, another reason, inasmuch as it also commemorated their deliverance from the labor and bondage and death sentence of Egypt.[2]

It must be remembered that there was no Jewish character whatever in the Sabbath of the Ten Commandmandments, nothing which was inapplicable to "man," that is, to all the world. So far as one day in seven was concerned, it demanded only that it should be kept "holy," and that "no manner of work," except of course such as was necessary, should be done upon it. The Mosaic law indeed added much in the matter of the worship required for the day, in sacrifices and ritual

[1] S. Mark ii. 27.   [2] See Ex. xi., xii. 14, 17; Deut. v. 14, 15.

observances; and all this, which was not of the essence of the commandment, was sadly perverted when our Lord was on earth. Yet even the Mosaic observance of the day was meant to be " a delight " as Isaiah had said.[1] It was only the traditions of the Pharisaic school that had turned the day into a time of gloom, and of burdensome, and frequently most absurd, precepts which drew down the indignant condemnation of the Lord Jesus.[2]

The other sacred days of the Church of Israel, and which were peculiar to it, were all historical. They were commemorations of some great event in the nation's history, and were also for the most part connected with the agriculture of the nation, the chief source of its wealth, and the visible token of its direct dependence on God. The three greatest of these were the feasts of the Passover, of Pentecost, and of Tabernacles, held respectively in the spring, the summer, and " the end of the year."

The original purpose of the Passover was to keep in memory year after year the great deliverance of the nation from the bondage of Egypt.[3] It received its name (Hebrew *Pesach*) from the fact that the angel of death had " passed over "[4] the houses of the Children of Israel, whose lintels and door posts were marked with the blood of the Paschal Lamb. It was observed from the 14th to the 21st day of the month Abib (the older name of the month Nisan), the month in which the Children of Israel made their escape. The time was chosen for their hasty journey when the moon was at its full after the vernal equinox, the best season for such a flight. Henceforth, for this reason, this month

[1] Isaiah lviii. 13.
[2] S. Mark ii. 4, 5, 23, etc.; S. Luke xiv. 5; S. John v. 10, etc.
[3] Ex. xii.   [4] Ex. xii. 27.

THE RITUAL YEAR OF ISRAEL 17

was to be the first month of the year to them instead of Tishri at the time of the autumnal equinox (September-October).[1]

The lamb was to be carefully chosen on the 10th day of Abib, and on the 14th it was to be killed in sacrifice, roasted, and eaten, with bitter herbs and unleavened bread, the worshippers all standing with robes girded, and staff in hand, tokens of their haste and readiness for the journey that was to give them freedom. The feast was to continue for seven days until the 21st day at even, during which time there was to be no leaven found in all their houses. Hence the name, the **Feast of Unleavened Bread.** Moreover, though there is no explicit statement to that effect, Jewish scholars tell us that the lamb was roasted whole on two wooden spits of pomegranate. Justin Martyr (second century) and Tertullian (third century) tell us that these were passed through the body like a cross. A cup of red wine also, mingled with water, formed part of the sacred supper.[2]

Besides this historic association of the feast, the Passover had also, as did the other great feasts, a character connected with the agricultural life of the people. "A sheaf of the firstfruits of the harvest" is to be brought to the priest, who is to "wave it before the Lord" in thankful token of their dependence upon Him for their care.[3]

Pentecost, the Greek for *Fiftieth*, is the name given by the Grecian Jews, and the Greek versions of Tobit [4] and 2 Maccabees,[5] to the second great feast, which

---
[1] See Ex. xxiii. 4–15; xxxiv. 18.
[2] See Edersheim's *Life and Times of Jesus*, Vol. II., pp. 480–9, for an interesting account of the feast as celebrated by our Lord and His Apostles.
[3] Lev. xxiii. 10, 11.   [4] Tobit ii. 1.   [5] 2 Maccabees xii. 32.

celebrated the giving of the Law from Sinai fifty days after the departure from Egypt.[1] Its original name was the **Feast of Weeks;**[2] also the **Feast of Harvest,** when "two wave loaves of fine flour," the firstfruits of the harvest, are to be offered unto the Lord.[3]

The Feast of Tabernacles was to be held "in the end of the year," on the 15th day of the seventh month (Tishri), when the people were to dwell in tents or booths for seven days in memory of their journey to the land of Promise.[4] Like the other great feasts it was connected also with the harvest, and was called the **Feast of Ingathering.**[5]

On all these great festivals the first day, and the last day, or octave, were to be marked by "a holy convocation," a great act of united worship. A great fast was also prescribed by the divine law, the **Day of Atonement,** to be held on the 10th day of the seventh month (Tishri).[6]

In addition to these festivals and fasts prescribed by the Law of Moses, and ordained by God, there were others of a minor character, such as the **Feast of Trumpets** (the civil **New Year's Day**), the first of Tishri the seventh month,[7] and the **New Moons.**[8] Chief among those established by the authority of the Church were the **Feast of Purim,** and **The Dedication, or Feast of Lights.**

Purim was observed on the 14th and 15th of the month Adar (part of December and January). It commemorated the deliverance of the Jews (509 B.C.) during their captivity in Persia, when Haman, the Agagite, plotted

---

[1] Ex. xix., xx.   [2] Deut. xvi. 9, 10.
[3] Ex. xxiii. 16; Lev. xxiii. 15, 16, 17.
[4] Lev. xxiii. 34 to end.   [5] Ex. xxiii. 16.
[6] See Lev. xvi. and xxiii. 27. Compare Heb. ix. 12, 25.
[7] Lev. xxiii. 24.   [8] 1 Sam. xx. 5; Psalm lxxxi. 3, etc.

THE RITUAL YEAR OF ISRAEL 19

to destroy them, and Esther the Queen, a Jewess, by her intercessions delivered them.[1] **The Feast of the Dedication, or of Lights,** was held on the 25th of the ninth month, Chisleu (Nov.-Dec.), in memory of the cleansing and rebuilding of the Temple and altar after their desecration by the armies of Antiochus Epiphanes, when the Jews won a great victory over their enemies under the generalship of the patriot Priest, Judas Maccabeus in 166 B.C.[2] Compare S. John x. 22, where our Lord is present at the feast.

Besides the great fast of the Day of Atonement, other fasts were prescribed by ecclesiastical authority. Chief among these was that which commemorated the destruction of the Temple and city by fire, 586 B.C., on the 7th of the fifth month, Ab (July-August).[3] Other fasts in the fourth, seventh, and tenth months are mentioned by Zechariah.[4] The 2d and 5th days of the week (Monday and Thursday) were also fast days.[5]

The names of the months according to the Church Calendar of Israel are as follows: (1) *Abib* or *Nisan*,[6] (corresponding to parts of March and April); (2) *Iyyar* (April-May); (3) *Sivan*[7] (May-June); (4) *Tammuz* (June-July); (5) *Ab* (July-August); (6) *Elul*[8] (August-September); (7) *Tishri* (September-October); (8) *Marchesvan* (October-November); (9) *Chisleu*[9] (November-December); (10) *Tebeth*[10] (December-January); (11) *Shebat*[11] (January-February); (12) *Adar*[12] (February-

---

[1] Esther ix. [2] 1 Macc. iv. 36 to end.
[3] See 2 Kings xxv. 8, and compare Zech. vii. 3, 4, 5.
[4] Zech. viii. 19. [5] S. Luke xviii. 12.
[6] Ex. xiii, 4; Neh. ii. 1; Esther iii. 7.
[7] Esther viii. 9. [10] Esther ii. 16.
[8] Neh. vi. 15. [11] Zech. i. 7.
[9] Zech. vii, 1: Neh. i. 1. [12] Esther iii. 7; Ezra vi. 15.

March). Only the names of the first, third, sixth, ninth, tenth, eleventh and twelfth months are found in the Old Testament. None are recorded in the New.

Dr. Edersheim, a clergyman of the Church of England, of Jewish parentage and early education, gives the following vivid picture of the effect of all this system of festival and fast upon the opening mind and imagination of a Jewish child:

"There could not be national history, nor even romance, to compare with that by which a Jewish mother might hold her child entranced. And it was his own history—of his tribe, clan, perhaps family; of the past, indeed, but yet of the present, and still more of the glorious future. Long before he could go to school, or even Synagogue, the private and united prayers and the domestic rites, whether of the weekly Sabbath or of festive seasons, would indelibly impress themselves upon his mind. In midwinter there was the festive illumination in each home. In most houses, the first night only one candle was lit, the next two, and so on to the eighth day; and the child would learn that this was symbolic, and commemorative of the **Dedication of the Temple,** its purgation, and the restoration of its services by the lion-hearted Judas the Maccabee. Next came, in earliest spring, the merry time of **Purim,** the feast of Esther and of Israel's deliverance through her, with its good cheer and boisterous enjoyments. Although the **Passover** might call the rest of the family to Jerusalem, the rigid exclusion of all leaven during the whole week could not pass without its impressions. Then, after the **Feast of Weeks,** came bright summer. But its golden harvest and its rich fruits would remind of the early dedication of the first and best to the Lord, and of those solemn processions in which it was carried up to Jerusalem.

As autumn seared the leaves, the **Feast of the New Year** [Trumpets] spoke of the casting up of man's accounts in the great Book of Judgment, and the fixing of destiny for good or for evil. Then followed the Fast of the **Day of Atonement**, with its tremendous solemnities, the memory of which could never fade from mind or imagination; and, last of all, in the week of the **Feast of Tabernacles**, there were the strange leafy booths in which they lived and joyed, keeping their harvest-thanksgiving, and praying and longing for the better harvest of a renewed world." [1]

It was amid such surroundings, and under such influences, that our Lord, and His Apostles, and first disciples, and the first Christians, grew from infancy to manhood and womanhood.

[1] *The Life and Times of Jesus the Messiah*, vol. I, pp. 228, 229.

CHAPTER V

THE JEWISH YEAR AND THE APOSTOLIC CHURCH

"Thus saith the Lord, stand ye in the ways, and see, and ask for the old paths, where is the good way, and walk therein, and ye shall find rest for your souls."—*Jer.* vi. 16.

IN considering the Jewish Year as it affected the religious lives of the early Christians, it is important to remember that it was only part of a great system of what we call churchly ways and customs in which our Lord and His Apostles, and all the first converts, had been trained from childhood. They knew no other kind of religious life. Their buildings for worship, especially their Temple, had not been merely " meeting-houses," but sacred places, " houses of God " and " of prayer."[1] Their worship had not been left to individual taste or haphazard. It was liturgic, dignified, largely musical as rendered by trained and vested choristers, with well-known and accustomed prayers, and a set form and order of service both in Synagogue and Temple. They had been ministered to by a priesthood in three sacred orders, not appointed or instituted by the people, but ordained by the special command and authority of God, so that " no man " dare assume the office, " take this honor unto himself," as the author of the epistle to the Hebrew Christians puts it,[2] but must have the

---
[1] S. Matt. xii. 4; S. John ii. 16.   [2] Heb. v. 4.

THE JEWISH YEAR 23

lawful call of God in His appointed way. These priests and other ministers were accustomed also to wear an official vestment in their public ministrations.

To these customs and traditions our Lord as a true Israelite was supremely loyal. While He was open in His condemnation of hypocrisy and greed in the rulers of the Church, never once was He charged by His enemies with disloyalty to the priesthood itself. While He condemned freely the formalism of the Pharisees and their followers, He was never accused by them of despising or neglecting the Church's solemn worship or her festivals and fasts. He had been brought up in a godly home; admitted as a member of the Church when only eight days old; presented as an offering to God in His Temple when He was only six weeks old.[1] When he was twelve years He was "confirmed," as we might express it, and admitted to all the sacred privileges of the Church, her sacrifices and other ordinances. When thirty He submitted to a form of baptism, "the baptism of repentance,"[2] which had no divine authority, but only the sanction of the later Church of Israel as an appropriate ordinance for receiving converts (proselytes) from heathenism and repentant Jews, the former of course receiving circumcision also.[3] Even to the last day of His life He submitted Himself to all the lawful authority of the priesthood, in spite of the fact that it was the ruling members of this very priesthood who hounded Him to His death.[4] Always and everywhere He was a true Israelite, faithful even in the "mint, anise, and cummin" as well as in "the weightier matters of the

[1] Lev. xii; S. Luke ii. 21-25.
[2] S. Mark. i. 4.
[3] S. Luke ii. 41, 42; S. Matt. iii. 13-16.
[4] S. Luke v. 14; xvii. 14; S. Matt. xxiii. 2, 3.

law "; " in all the commandments and ordinances of the Lord blameless." [1]

But it is perhaps in His loyalty to the ritual year of Israel that we have the most striking illustration of this feature of our Lord's life of " obedience." [2] As we see Him when a boy of twelve careful to observe the feast of the Passover; then sitting at the feet of the doctors in the Temple listening submissively to their teachings; then "subject" to His parents in Nazareth,[3] so we find Him continuing to do even to the close at that last Passover which He glorified by His death and resurrection. Nor were the feasts of divine appointment the only ones which He honored. We find Him keeping at least one which had only the authority of the Church for its observance, the feast of the Dedication, which had been instituted by Judas Maccabeus 200 years before, to commemorate the restoration of the Temple and altar after their desecration by the heathen invaders.[4]

And the most remarkable thing in this connection is the fact that our Lord deliberately made choice of the two greatest feast days of the ancient Church with which to associate the chief events of His life, and of the life of His Church. Let us not forget that the time of His death was wholly in His own keeping. "No man taketh it from Me" He had said of His life; and again He asserted, "My time is not yet full come." [5] And this chosen time and hour of His was the great feast of the Passover. When the day approached He prepared for it in the most exact and careful way.[6] On the very day, and probably at the very hour, when the lamb of the Passover should have been offered up—for in their

---

[1] S. Matt. xxiii. 23; S. Luke i. 6.   [2] Heb. v. 8.
[3] S. Luke ii. 41 to end.   [4] S. John x. 22; 1 Macc. iv. 52–59.
[5] S. John x. 18; vii. 8.   [6] S. Matt. xxvi. 18.

eagerness for His blood the priests seem to have neglected the proper time—at this moment the true "Lamb slain [in intention] from the foundation of the world"[1] was actually offered in sacrifice upon the cross.

And when we come to the next supreme event in our Lord's work for the world, the case is perhaps still more remarkable. During forty days the risen Lord remained on earth to instruct His Apostles how to set about the establishing of His Church, and to give them proofs of the reality of His resurrection.[2] But why, after the forty days were ended, and He had ascended into heaven, did He oblige them to wait ten days longer as "orphans," "comfortless," without His visible presence, and also without the promised Comforter? To us as to them it seems at first incomprehensible that He should not have sent the Holy Ghost at once. But whatever other reason there may have been besides this trial of their faith and patience, the peculiar significance of His *not* sending the Holy Ghost until the feast of Pentecost, the fiftieth day after His resurrection, is beyond a question. Pentecost, coming as it did in the early summer, was doubtless chosen also for the very practical reason that travel by sea and land was then safer and easier, and vast numbers of worshippers from distant countries were then able to come to Jerusalem; "Parthians, and Medes, and Elamites, and the dwellers in Mesopotamia," and all the other foreign Jews who are named by S. Luke in the second chapter of the Acts as being present there on the Church's birthday. Nevertheless it still remains a striking testimony to our Lord's valuation of the ritual year of Israel as an instrument of witness and of popular instruction, that it was not, as S. Luke expresses it, until "the day of Pentecost was

[1] Rev. xiii. 8.   [2] Acts. i. 3.

fully come" that the promised Paraclete came indeed with visible and audible signs to give life and power to the little anxious flock of "about one hundred and twenty" souls[1] who on that day constituted the Holy Catholic and Apostolic Church of Christ.

Our Lord had not told them at what particular time His promise of the Comforter should be fulfilled. They had asked Him when His great work of "restoration of the kingdom" should begin, but His only reply was that they must wait patiently in Jerusalem.[2] Nevertheless they seem to have had some assurance that the day of the next great feast which commemorated the giving of the law from Sinai, and celebrated God's continual care of His people in the gathering of the firstfruits of the harvest, should be the time of His coming. For we are told that on that day they "were all with one accord in one place" in evident expectation.[3]

It was then in such an atmosphere, and with such examples before them, that the Apostles and first Christians were born and bred. Could it be possible, we may well ask, that, under the plea that henceforth the worship of God is to be "in spirit and in truth," they would cast aside as useless or worse all these sacred customs and traditions of their race and Church, so honored by their Lord Himself all His life long? That is the incredible thing which most of the sects of modern Protestantism would have us believe. Was there henceforth to be no sacred order of priesthood in the new Church as there had been in the old, though Christ had taken such pains to train and teach, not only twelve, but seventy men, choosing them and separating them from the multitude and especially commissioning the twelve in the most solemn way, to act for Him on earth "unto

[1] Acts. i. 15. [2] Acts. i. 4–8. [3] Acts ii. 1.

the end of the world "? Were there henceforth to be no ordered worship, no dignified official robes, no ritual year of festival and fast to commemorate the infinitely greater events of those " good tidings of great joy," of which the old feasts and fasts were but the dim foreshadowings? Knowing the atmosphere in which our Lord and His Apostles lived and moved, we are now in a position to see what importance the whole Church in the earliest days would naturally attach to these things as they were developed and carried over into the Church of Christ.

CHAPTER VI

THE BEGINNINGS OF THE CHRISTIAN YEAR IN THE APOSTOLIC CHURCH

"Christ our Passover is sacrificed for us, therefore let us keep the feast."—1 *Cor.* v. 7, 8.

"I must by all means keep this feast that cometh in Jerusalem."—*Acts* xviii. 21.

"He hasted, if it were possible for him, to be at Jerusalem the day of Pentecost."—*Acts* xx. 16.

CONFINING ourselves now to the single question of the ritual year, it would at the outset seem most natural that the first converts, instead of rejecting, would Christianize the old sacred festivals when, as we have seen, they were not only religiously observed by their Lord, but also actually and deliberately connected by Him with the greatest events of His own life and work. Let us see then what glimpses we can get in the New Testament concerning how the Apostles actually regarded these ancient hallowed festivals from the standpoint, not of Judaism, but of the Church of Christ.

1. First of all we find S. Paul, twenty years after the descent of the Holy Ghost, telling his Jewish fellow countrymen in Ephesus, when they urged him to remain longer with them, that he " must by all means keep this feast that cometh [namely, Pentecost] in Jerusalem." [1] Four years later we find S. Luke telling concerning him that he " hasted, if it were possible for him, to be at

[1] Acts xviii. 21.

BEGINNINGS OF THE CHRISTIAN YEAR 29

Jerusalem the day of Pentecost."[1] So too S. Paul himself, in his first letter to the Corinthians, writes, "I will tarry at Ephesus until Pentecost."[2] Now what was the thought uppermost in the mind of a man like S. Paul in the keeping of this feast of Pentecost? The older reason for its observance, namely, the giving of the law from Sinai and the birth of the Mosaic Church, was doubtless not forgotten. As a Jewish feast the day had still many sacred associations for him, " a Hebrew of the Hebrews."[3] But the new and greater reason for his " keeping the feast " as a Christian lay elsewhere. The marvellous giving of the Holy Ghost on this day some twenty years before, that He might " write the Law on men's hearts,"[4] and gather in the " firstfruits of the harvest "[5] of which our Lord Himself was the chief Sower, and bring to its birth the Church of the new Israel and new Jerusalem—this must have been the dominant thought in the Apostle's mind. It could not have been otherwise.

2. As regards the observance of **Easter** as a Christian festival by the Apostolic Church we have fewer intimations given us in the New Testament. The word occurs only once in our Authorized Version, where it is said of Herod that he " intended after Easter " to put S. Peter to death.[6] But the word here in the original is simply " Pascha " or "Passover," and nothing can be inferred from it concerning the Christian observance of the day. It is very probable, however, that S. Paul is referring to the Christian observance of Easter when, writing to the Church in Corinth concerning a shameful scandal in that Church, he urges them to " purge out the old leaven " of sin, " for," he adds, " Christ our Passover is sacri-

[1] Acts xx. 16.   [2] 1 Cor. xvi. 8.   [3] Phil. iii. 5.
[4] Heb. viii. 10.   [5] Ex. xxxiv. 22.   [6] Acts xii. 4.

ficed for us, therefore let us [us Christians] keep the feast."[1]

But however that may be, we know that the time of the Crucifixion and the Resurrection was kept as a great annual feast of the Church from the beginning. In fact so early and so universal was its observance, and so important was it regarded as a witness to the resurrection, that a difference in regard to the proper day for its observance was the occasion of the first schism in in the Church, some Eastern Churches holding that it should be kept on any day of the Paschal week, and others that it should be always on a Sunday as the first Easter had been.[2] This controversy will be explained more in detail later on.[3]

3. And the observance of **Sunday** or "the first day of the week," instead of Saturday which the Jews reckoned as "the seventh," rests upon exactly the same authority as that of Pentecost and Easter, namely, the early and universal custom and tradition of the Church. Here the New Testament is perfectly clear. It is true we have nowhere the record of a command for, the change by our Lord, though such a direction may have been given among those "things pertaining to the kingdom of God," that is, the Church, of which He spoke to the Apostles during the great Forty Days between His resurrection and His ascension.[4] But the absence

---

[1] 1 Cor. v. 7, 8.
[2] S. Mark xvi. 2.   [3] See Chapters XII and XX.
[4] Our Lord, so far as we have any record, uses the word "Church" only on two occasions and that in private (S. Matt. xvi. 18; xviii. 17) while He employs the phrase "kingdom of heaven" (S. Matthew only) or "kingdom of God" constantly. In the mouth of the Apostles after the Church is set up this proportion is entirely reversed. "The Church" now becomes the common designation; "the kingdom" uncommon. In the Acts, Epistles, and the Rev-

BEGINNINGS OF THE CHRISTIAN YEAR 31

of such a record makes the change all the more remarkable. Here was a provision, not of the ritual but of the moral law, the Fourth Commandment, requiring six days for labor, and a seventh for rest and worship; and for 1500 years or more the whole nation had been keeping what we call Saturday as the Sabbath. It was therefore most natural that Jews would come to think that Saturday and " the seventh day " must necessarily mean the same thing. To change to another "seventh" day would seem a breach of the moral law itself. But the Church in the New Testament and ever after, until the "Seventh Day Baptists" appeared 1600 years later, never showed the faintest hesitation on the subject. Sunday, or " the first day of the week," was adopted apparently at once as the weekly festival day commemorating and witnessing to the resurrection, just as Easter does as the annual festival day which witnesses to the same fact.

This does not imply that Saturday was no longer observed by Jews who became Christians. It was most natural, and we know it to be the case from early historians, that devout Jewish Christians observed both days, as they also continued to observe other customs of Jewish worship. These, however, were purely voluntary matters with them. They were not to be regarded

elation "kingdom" occurs 25 times, "the Church" 111 times. Our Lord's unequal use of the words is easily accounted for by the fact that while it was under the figure of a kingdom that the prophets foretold the new order, "Church," either in Hebrew (Aramaic) or in the Greek of the Septuagint, was the word in common use among the Jews for their present "household of faith." See Acts vii. 38 and Heb. ii. 12. Christ would therefore avoid all unnecessary clashing with Jewish prejudice, and only employs "Church" in speaking privately to His Apostles. But once the Church is set up openly, the day for consulting prejudice is past as obligatory or perpetual any more than the circumcising of their children, or the rule about "clean" and "unclean" meats, or the offering of the accustomed sacrifices in the Temple while it stood. S. Paul himself, as we have already seen, on one occasion offered sacrifice along with other Christian Jews, and he caused Timothy to receive circumcision even after he became a Christian, in order to meet the prejudices of other Jewish Christians, because though his father was a Gentile his mother was a Jewess.[1]

The observance of "the first day of the week" or Sunday instead of Saturday as the Christian fulfilment of the Fourth Commandment (in which as the primal law there is no trace of Judaism) is evident from the account of the celebration of the Holy Communion on that day in Troas when S. Paul preached, and from the same apostle's direction to the Church in Corinth concerning a special weekly offering on the day for the poor Christians in Jerusalem.[2] It may also be inferred from the account which S. John gives us of the place and the day when he first received his "Revelation." It was "the Lord's Day," he writes, though this might also mean Easter Day.[3]

But all this change of days came very gradually in deference to the very natural prejudices and devout feelings of Jewish converts. The "beggarly elements," as S. Paul calls the old customs and ceremonies of Israel, were allowed to continue for a time, even after the realities of which they were but the shadows and the husk had actually come.[4] The Lord's Day was therefore necessarily slow in supplanting entirely the Saturday Sabbath. In fact the two days continued side by side

[1] Acts xxi. 18, etc.; xvi. 4; Col. ii. 16, 17.
[2] Acts xx. 7; 1 Cor. xvi. 2.   [3] Rev. i. 10.   Gal. iv. 9.

BEGINNINGS OF THE CHRISTIAN YEAR 33

for several centuries as "sister days," as Gregory the Bishop of Nyssa in the fourth century calls them. The Apostolic Constitutions, so-called, which probably represent even an earlier period than the fourth century, have this exhortation: Christians must "gather together especially on the Sabbath, and on the Lord's Day, the day of the Resurrection "[1]; and again they say, "Keep the Sabbath and the Lord's Day as feasts, for the one is the commemoration of the Creation, and the other of the Resurrection."[2] This was a common rule in the East, though curiously enough at Rome the Saturday Sabbath was a fast day in the time of S. Augustine, and the same is true of some other places in the West, though the majority of Western Churches did not so regard it. At Milan, for instance, the day was not treated as a fast; and S. Ambrose, in reply to a question put by Augustine at the instance of his mother Monica, stated that he regarded the matter as one of local discipline, and gave the sensible rule to "do in such matters at Rome as the Romans do."[3]

Another fact to be borne in mind in regard to the observance of Sunday as well as other festivals of the Church in the early days is that, during the first three centuries throughout the Roman Empire, Christianity was an illegal religion (*religio illicita*), and therefore frequently the subject of persecution by the State. Judaism on the other hand was a legal religion, and had its weekly Sabbath, but the Roman law recognized no weekly rest day for other nations. Gentile Christians therefore would naturally feel it doubly difficult to observe the Lord's Day as a complete day of

[1] *Apos. Con.* ii. 59. [2] *Apos. Con.* vii. 23.
[3] *The Church Year and Kalendar*, by Bp. Dowden, p. 8. The quotation from Augustine is from Ep. liv. 3, ad Bonifacium.

rest and worship. This would be particularly true of slaves, who formed the majority of the population in most parts of the Empire, and of the working classes generally. This will probably account for the night service which we have seen at Troas, and may serve as an excuse for the sleep of the young man Eutychus after a day of hard toil either as a slave or a free laborer. (It should be remembered also that the Jewish day began at sunset, and not at midnight.) The day was not a legal holiday until the conversion of the first Christian emperor, Constantine, in the beginning of the fourth century, when toleration was first proclaimed, and Christianity became the religion of the state.[1]

[1] It was in A.D. 321 that Constantine gave leave to the Christian soldiers in his army to be absent from duty in order that they might attend divine service on Sunday. The heathen soldiers had to assemble and offer prayers for the Emperor and his family. At the same time Constantine forbade the law courts to sit on Sunday. See Eusebius, *Vita Const.*, 4. 19, 20; and Sozomen, *His. Eccles.*, i. 18.

CHAPTER VII

THE VALUE OF CUSTOM AND TRADITION IN THE CHURCH

"The keeping or omitting of a Ceremony, in itself considered, is but a small thing; yet the wilful and contemptuous transgression and breaking of a common order and discipline is no small offence before God."—*Preface to the English Prayer Book: Of Ceremonies.*

THERE is nothing strange or unreasonable or unscriptural in this resting of the observance of these festival days merely on custom or tradition, instead of on a recorded command of our Lord or His apostles. It is remarkable, though too often overlooked, how frequently the words "tradition," "custom," and "way," or their equivalents, occur in the New Testament. Three times "The Way" is used as a name or designation of the Church itself.[1] S. Paul in writing to correct certain evils in the Church in Corinth gives as a sufficient reason for some things his own "ways in Christ."[2] As a sufficient argument against another practice in the same Church he writes, "We have no such custom, neither the Churches of God";[3] and he says in the same chapter, "Hold fast the traditions, even as I delivered them unto you."[4] To the Thessalonian Church he says, "Stand fast, and hold the traditions which ye have been taught, whether by word, or our epistle"; and again, "We command you in the name of our Lord Jesus Christ, that ye withdraw yourselves from every brother that walketh

---

[1] Acts xix. 9, 23; xxiv. 14, Rev. Ver.   [2] 1 Cor. iv. 17.
[3] 1 Cor. xi. 16.   [4] 1 Cor. xi. 2, Rev. Ver.

disorderly, and not after the tradition which he received of us." [1]

Few of us realize how much the fulness and richness of our common everyday life is dependent on customs and ways handed on to us and by us by tradition, sometimes written, but far more frequently not written. The characteristic, the most valuable features in fact of families and nations alike are these unwritten customs and traditions. They are things not wrought out by each generation, or each set of individuals for themselves, but are inherited and handed on to others. How much a nation or a family would have to give up, how much poorer it would be, if it abandoned all except what is inscribed in its laws or its records, the things "written in the bond." The great bulk of a nation's customs, the pith and heart of its character, is not found recorded in its histories or literature. It could not be described in words; it could not be transferred to another nation by means of written documents alone. If acquired at all by others, it must be acquired by close contact, almost by a new birth and a new life, an engrafting of one into the other, a suffusion of blood.

Now if one will only give the matter a moment's thought it is evident that very much of the life of the Church must necessarily be of this same description. Even to-day, when missionaries go out to heathen lands, there are a thousand things they teach by word and act and "ways" that could not be conveyed by writing. When S. Columba set sail from Ireland to convert the heathen Picts and Scots he took with him many companions, not all ecclesiastics or teachers or preachers, but living examples of what the Christian faith had done, and therefore could do, for men. The business man

[1] 2 Thess. ii. 15; iii. 6.

THE VALUE OF CUSTOM AND TRADITION 37

knows this when he travels hundreds of miles to have only five minutes' talk with some correspondent. He knows that that five minutes' conversation face to face will accomplish more than whole quires of writing.

And in the Church it is no different. Human nature is alike everywhere. And what a host of such "traditions," "customs," "ways" acquired, not from writings, but from the words and acts of the apostles and first Christian missionaries themselves, must have existed in the early Church, nay, must in a large measure still exist throughout the whole historic Church to-day. Tradition means literally something handed on, like the lighted torch in the torch-race of the ancient Greeks, one runner bearing it to a certain point where it is handed to another and another until the goal is attained. And Christian tradition is simply this lighted torch, handed on in the Church from age to age, from generation to generation.

Of course all traditions in the Church cannot be accepted as binding on the conscience unless they can be shown to represent the mind of Christ and His apostles. They must be tested. Have they been handed on unintermittingly and uncorrupted from the beginning?[1] That

[1] A striking illustration of the force and value of tradition "from the beginning" is seen in the existence of the *Sursum Corda*, "Lift up your hearts," with its response, in every known liturgy in the world except two of no special note, namely, the Syro-Jacobite of S. Chrysostom, and of John of Antioch. (See Scudamore, *Notitia Eucharistica*, p. 523.) That such a very minor feature of the great Eucharistic Service should exist in practically every Church, no matter how widely apart in language, and character, and distance, can only be accounted for on one theory, namely, that the words formed part of the use of the Apostolic Church while still in its infancy in Jerusalem. It could not have been incorporated at any later period any more than the fly could have found its way into the amber at any stage later than the "beginning."

is the test that S. John in his old age applies to them. Living on into the twilight of the Apostolic age, all the companions of his early ministry dead and gone, the last writer of the New Testament harps continually on this one string. This old man eloquent, this "disciple whom Jesus loved," who lay on Jesus' breast and heard His heart beat, tells us that the one practical test of essential and fundamental truth and custom is its continuity, its existence in the Church "from the beginning." "Let that therefore abide in you," he writes, "which ye have heard from the beginning." And again, "This is the commandment, That as ye have heard from the beginning, ye should walk in it." "This is the message that ye have heard from the beginning."[1]

This then is the conclusive test which the Church still applies to many things besides the feast days of the Christian Year. It was on this that the motto of the earliest and greatest of the general councils of the Church, "Let the ancient customs prevail," was based. It is the reason which the Church, in her sixth Article of Religion, gives for claiming our acceptance of the Scriptures themselves. What she says is this: "In the name of the Holy Scripture we do understand those canonical books of the Old and New Testament, of whose authority was never any doubt in the Church." And again in the twentieth Article she declares that the Church is "a witness and a keeper of Holy Writ."

And as it is with the Bible so is it with the Ministry. That too, she asserts, is dependent on the tradition and continuous witness of the Church "from the beginning"; not apart from the witness which Holy Scripture, that other sacred tradition, gives it, but together with it;

[1] 1 John ii. 24; iii. 11; 2 John 6.

THE VALUE OF CUSTOM AND TRADITION 39

a double witness therefore. In the Preface to the Ordinal in the Prayer Book the Church says, " It is evident unto all men, diligently reading Holy Scripture and ancient Authors, that from the Apostles' time there have been these Orders of Ministers in Christ's Church,—Bishops, Priests, and Deacons." That is what tradition " from the beginning " gives us; the tradition concerning the Scriptures, and side by side with it the tradition concerning the Sacred Ministry by Apostolic Succession. The New Testament proves its right to our acceptance to-day because it has been accepted as the authentic teaching of Christ and His apostles and evangelists from very early days; and the Ministry has a still greater claim because it has been "from the beginning," even before a word of the New Testament was written. In fact the complete canon of the books of the New Testament was not formally determined by the Church until the third council of Carthage in A.D. 397; and the final form of the Creed not until the council of Nice in 325; while, by the common consent of all historical scholars, the three-fold Ministry was in existence everywhere in the Church before the martyrdom of S. Ignatius in A.D. 110. Thus the appeal of Holy Scripture to "tradition," "custom," and "ways" is simply what modern scholarship would call the appeal to history.

And what is true of the New Testament and the Ministry is true of many other things. It is for this reason for instance that the Church baptizes infants; admits women to the Holy Communion; requires "the laying on of hands" by a successor of the Apostles for the gift of the Holy Spirit in Confirmation; builds churches after the pattern of the Temple with an altar, and not after the pattern of a synagogue with a mere platform; employs a "form of sound words" for common prayer and confession of belief in public worship; celebrates the Holy Communion as the central act of all our worship on every Lord's Day; has the clergy wear appropriate vestments in divine service; and finally, observes a ritual year of festival and fast, setting forth before the eyes of the world the great foundation truths of the faith as manifested in the life and death of our Lord.

We are not to expect any of these things to be carefully recorded and commanded in the pages of the New Testament. They existed before the New Testament was written. They existed independently of the New Testament, and would have continued to exist if there never had been any New Testament. They are such customs and ways and traditions as those concerning which S. Paul writes to the Church in Corinth and Thessalonica. They are part of that "continuity in the Apostles' doctrine, and fellowship, and the breaking of the bread, and the prayers" which is noted by S. Luke as one of the essential characteristics of the Catholic and Apostolic Church as it came fresh from the hand of God. And the command comes to us equally as to them to "stand fast and hold" these customs and traditions as some of God's best gifts for our spiritual good. We thus see the absurdity of the motto, "The Bible, and the Bible only the religion of Protestants," when it is carried out to its logical limits in the rejection of all traditions. The Bible, itself a great tradition, is the supreme example of the value and the necessity of tradition in the Church "from the beginning."

It will be asked then very naturally, what is the purpose of Holy Scripture if traditions and customs and ways in the Church have such weight? It is well for us to understand very clearly the answer to this question.

THE VALUE OF CUSTOM AND TRADITION 41

"'I believe it to be an error," writes Archbishop Alexander, "to suppose that, as a matter of fact, our first or only knowledge of Christ and of His claim upon us is derived from that sacred volume. I cannot see the faintest indication in the New Testament itself that such a thing was ever contemplated by our Lord or by His apostles."[1] "The Church's earliest mind," writes Canon Scott Holland, "was strongly against writing. Writing was not its most natural method of preserving its story. It distrusted the accidents that beset it, the changes, the blunderings; it disliked the deadness of a dumb document. Our Lord had not written one word [except what He wrote on the dust of the Temple pavement, which the feet of the next passerby blotted out for ever].[2] He had definitely preferred to use living, human memories, written on the tablets of the heart; and the loyal impulses of the Church all set in the channels which He had marked down. Only very slowly, as the pressure of lengthening circumstances compelled her to face new possibilities, was she forced to see the necessity of depositing, in black and white, her witness to the Resurrection. And there can be no more convincing proof of her unwillingness to trust to writing than her own tradition that it was only when the death of the last apostle was ominously near, that S. John could be induced to write down his record."

Dean Hook has summed up this truth very forcibly when he says, "We receive our religion from the Church; we prove our religion from the Bible." Dr. Edward Hawkins, the Provost of Oriel College, says, "The Scriptures themselves presuppose tradition; the New Testament implies a previous acquaintance with the out-

---

[1] *Primary Convictions*, p. 172.   [2] S. John viii. 6.

line of its doctrines."[1] And all this is but another form of stating the fact enunciated by S. Luke when he gives the reason for writing the book which is called by his name, and which was at the first meant for the special use of his friend Theophilus. It is, he says, "That thou mightest know the certainty of those things wherein thou hast been instructed," literally "catechized," that is, taught by word of mouth.[2]

[1] *On the Use and Importance of Unauthoritative Tradition*, Oxford, 1819.
[2] S. Luke i. 3, 4.

CHAPTER VIII

THE CHURCH CALENDAR AND ITS USE

"My Prayer Book is a casket bright,
With gold and incense stored,
Which every day, and every night,
I open to the Lord:
Yet when I first unclasp its lids,
I find a bunch of myrrh
Embalming all our mortal life;
The Church's Calendar."
—*Bishop Coxe, Christian Ballads.*

WE are now in a position to understand the importance of the system which we name the Christian Year. A neglected part of the Prayer Book, yet one of great practical value and historical interest, is the Calendar with its accompanying tables. Before speaking of the feasts and fasts and other holy days into which the Calendar divided the year, I must speak first of the year itself as the early Christians found it in the Greek and Roman cities where they lived. The Greeks and Romans had their own calendars. Under the Greeks the computation of the years was by what were called Olympiads, that is, the intervals between two successive celebrations of the Olympic games. These were terms of four years beginning with what we call the year 776 B.C. (Before Christ). Under the Romans their years were dated from the foundation of their city, *Ab Urbe Condita*, or A.U.C.; which, according to our reckoning, would be 753 B.C.

The years of the Christian era, as we know, are dated from the birth of our Lord, or *Anno Domini*. But we must remember that this method was not adopted by Christians from the very beginning. A moment's thought will show us why. Such a method of reckoning the years would have clashed at once and uselessly with all the business, and social, and governmental life of their day. It is just as if Englishmen had adopted a new method of reckoning the years after the Norman Conquest, dating their time henceforth from A.D. 1066; or as if Americans after the war of the Revolution had made a new beginning of their calendar with the year of the Declaration of Independence, 1776; or, as the French revolutionists actually did when Year 1 was fixed to begin on September 22, 1792, the date of the proclamation of the Republic. It was not until after the year 313, when the empire became nominally Christian, that such a use was possible; and it was not until two centuries later, namely, in the year 541, that the custom was introduced of dating the time from the year of our Lord's birth. This was brought about by the work of a man named Dionysius Exiguus, or The Little, a learned and devout monk, a Scythian by birth, but residing in Rome.

This late date of the adoption of Anno Domini, or "the Year of the Lord," for universal reckoning accounts for an error which we now know crept into the computation. Modern astronomical and historical studies show us that our Lord was born four years earlier than Dionysius supposed, so that January 1, 541, as he numbered it, should have been January 1, 545. This error has never been corrected.

In considering the Church Calendar it is important to remember that a calendar is different from an almanac. An almanac has to be renewed every year. A calendar

THE CHURCH CALENDAR AND ITS USE 45

remains unchanged through all the centuries because it is "a permanent distribution of time on astronomical principles, adapted to civil and secular affairs as well as to religious."[1] It gets its name from a Greek word *kaleo*, signifying "to call." "The first day of the month was named by the ancient Romans the Calends, because on that day the people were called or summoned by the Pontifex into the Curia Calabra, and there informed of the holy days of the [coming] month."[2] The Greeks had no Calends, hence the saying "It will be paid on the Greek Calends," that is, never.

The civil calendar as we have it to-day we owe to the genius of Julius Cæsar. In his time the years were measured by the moon instead of by the sun, the months being literally *moonths*. By this imperfect method, which gave only 355 days to the year, with intercalary days added occasionally by way of correction, summer and winter would in time have changed places, and already the seasons were two months in arrears. With the advice of a learned man, Sosigenes, Cæsar fixed on 365 and a quarter days as the approximately true solar year; one day was added every fourth or "leap" year; the months were given the names and number of days as at present; two months, November and December, were skipped, and what would have been November 1, 45 B.C. was made January 1, 44 B.C., and the beginning of the new or Julian calendar.

But even this Julian year of 365 and a quarter days was only approximately correct, and after sixteen centuries had passed it was found by astronomers that the calendar was again slow by about ten days, so that what was March 11, 1582, was really the day of the vernal equinox, and should have been March 21. It was decreed therefore

[1] Seabury, p. 1.   [2] Ib. p. 2.

by Pope Gregory for the Churches in communion with Rome, after consultation with learned men, that October 5, 1582, should be reckoned as October 15. This " New Style" (N.S.), as it was called, was not accepted in England, probably through religious prejudice, until 1752, when the English Parliament abandoned the "Old Style" (O.S.) and adopted the New. By this time the error had increased to nearly twelve days instead of ten, which made Christmas Day of that year (O.S. 1752) to become the feast of the Epiphany (N.S. 1753), and caused the ignorant country folk to complain that they had been robbed of twelve days of their life. For this reason also the Epiphany came to be called by them " Old Christmas." The Greek and Russian Churches still retain the Old Style, but there is at present in Russia a movement to bring about the adoption of the New Style, and so bring the Oriental Churches into accord with the rest of the Christian world.

CHAPTER IX

TECHNICAL WORDS IN THE CALENDAR

> "God set the sun and moon for signs:
> The Church His signs doth know,
> And here, while sleeps the sluggish world,
> She marks them as they go.
> Here for His coming looks she forth
> As for her Spouse the bride;
> Here, at her lattice faithfully,
> She waits the morning-tide."
> —*Bishop Coxe, Christian Ballads.*

THERE are certain words found in the prefatory portion of the Prayer Book which demand explanation. The first of these is *Cycle*, more fully the *Lunar Cycle*. It is also called the *Metonic Cycle* after its Greek inventor, Meton, who flourished at Athens about the year 432 B.C. This is a term of nineteen years, during which time the sun and moon arrive at the same relative position in the heavens with which they began nineteen years before. "As reduced to more accurate dimensions by the Alexandrian Bishops,"[1] it is still used to find the correct time for the observance of Easter, which varies from year to year, being dependent, as we shall see later, on the age of the moon at the time of the vernal equinox (March 21st). Though the Metonic Cycle is not mathematically perfect it is so nearly so that, with the present provisions of the Gregorian Calendar, the error "will not amount to a day before the year 5200, when it will be only necessary, by an exception to the

[1] Seabury, *Theory and Use of the Church Calendar*, p. 105.

Gregorian rule, to take the year 5200 for a common year instead of a leap year to make our accounts as even as they were before."[1] The Jewish cycle was a period of eighty-four years, but after the Council of Nice, A.D. 325, when the Metonic Cycle was adopted by the Church, the Jews followed the example of Christians.

Another word is the *Golden Number*. This represents the number of the year (1st to 19th) since the beginning of the Lunar Cycle. It is used in the Calendar to designate the day of the full Paschal or Easter moon. These Golden Numbers are printed in the first column of the Calendar between March 21st and April 18th, being that portion of the year *after* which (March 22d to April 25th) Easter can alone fall. "In our Church Calendar the Golden Numbers are also called the *Primes;* probably because they serve to indicate the *prime*, a word which was formerly used to signify the *new moon*, but which in this sense is now obsolete."[2] The rule for finding the Golden Number is given under "Tables and Rules, etc.," in the Prayer Book. The origin of the term is said to be that the Athenians were so rejoiced over the discovery of Meton that they caused an account of the cycle to be engraved on tablets of brass with the numbers in gold letters.

The *Epact* is used to designate the age of the moon on the first day of January. Supposing a new moon to occur on January 1st, the new moon on the following January 1st would be eleven days old, because the lunar year of twelve lunar months contains only 355 days, whereas the solar year contains 365 and a quarter days. *Epact* is derived from a Greek word which means to *add*, because it designates the number of days (one to eleven) which must be added to the lunar year to make

[1] Seabury, p. 120.   [2] Ib. p. 90.

TECHNICAL WORDS IN THE CALENDAR 49

the time equal to the solar year. The word is still used in the English Church Calendar, but was dropped in the American.

Still another technical word of the Church Calendar is the *Dominical* or *Sunday Letter*. The purpose of this is to designate, as the word implies, the *Dominical* or Lord's Days (*Dies Domini*) in any particular year. It will be observed that, beginning with the first of January and continuing throughout the year, every day of every week has one letter of the alphabet from A to g, appended to it, the first day of the year being always A. When we know the Dominical or Sunday Letter for any particular year, then by means of the Calendar we can tell, without reference to an almanac, what day of the week is represented by any stated day of the year. (The rule for finding the Dominical Letter is given under "General Tables" in the Prayer Book.) Indeed, knowing the Dominical Letter for the year one can determine the day of the week for any stated day of the year without the use of the Calendar by remembering that the first day of each of the twelve months has an unchanging letter in the following order: A (Jan. 1st), $d, d, g, b, e, g, c, f, A, d, f$. "To assist him in doing so is the design of the following catch lines; which consist of twelve words answering in their order to the twelve months of the year, the first letter of each word being the proper letter for the first day of the corresponding month:

"At Dover Dwells George Brown Esquire,
Good Christopher Finch And David Fryar." [1]

An explanation of the term *Leap Year* is given in a rubric of the Prayer Book of Queen Elizabeth's reign as follows: " When the years of our Lord can be divided

[1] Seabury, p. 33.

into four equal parts [that is, when a given year can be divided by four without a remainder], then the Sunday letter *leapeth.*"[1] This means that when the *bissextus dies*, or intercalary day (29th), is added to February, the Sunday or Dominical Letter, which for the first two months may be *D*, is now changed to *C* for the remainder of the year. Another explanation is that the remaining days of the year *leap over* the 29th, that is, take no account of it, so as not to disarrange the letters for the rest of the year. For this reason February 29th has no letter given it in the English Calendar, and in the American it borrows the letter *d* of the day following.[2]

The word *Bissextile* (Latin for *twice sixth*), which is another name for Leap Year, is sometimes, though erroneously, supposed to be derived from the *two sixes* in the number of days in every Leap Year (366). The real origin of the word is this: The 24th of February in the old calendars was called, according to the ancient Roman use, the *sextus dies*, that is, the sixth day before the calends of March, with *f* for its proper letter, as it is to-day. In leap years, however, instead of inserting the intercalary day, as now, after the 28th, it was placed immediately after the 24th, and was also given the letter *f*, thus leaving the letters for the rest of the year unchanged. For this reason it was called the *bissextus dies*, or the *twice* sixth day, and so gave its name to the year.

An exception to the rule for finding the Leap Year is that all years exactly divisible by 100, but not by 400, are *not* leap years. For example, A.D. 1900 was not a Leap Year, but A.D. 2000 will be.

The word *Ferial*, though not used in the Prayer Books

---

[1] Seabury, p. 38.
[2] See "*A Table to find the Dominical or Sunday Letter*," in the Prayer Book.

TECHNICAL WORDS IN THE CALENDAR 51

of the Anglican Communion, in ecclesiastical language designates an ordinary week-day in contradistinction to a *festal* day. "The names most commonly given to the days of the week in the service-books and other ecclesiastical records are 'Dies Dominica' (rarely 'Dominicus') for the Lord's Day, or Sunday; 'Feria II' for Monday; 'Feria III' for Tuesday, and so on to Saturday which (with rare exceptions) is not Feria VII but 'Sabbatum.'"[1] "The astrological names for the days of the week, as of the Sun, of the Moon, of Mercury, etc., were generally avoided by Christians."[2] It is noteworthy that the Portuguese still retain the ancient numerical names for the days of the week, as *segunda feira* or second week-day, *terça feira* or third week-day, etc.

A *Vigil*, the Latin for *watchful*, is the eve or even of certain feast days, and is always a fast or day of abstinence. Only the following days have vigils in the Anglican Communion: Christmas, The Purification, The Annunciation, Easter-Day, Ascension-Day, Pentecost, S. Matthias, S. John Baptist, S. Peter, S. James, S. Bartholomew, S. Matthew, SS. Simon and Jude, S. Andrew, S. Thomas, All Saints. The vigils were omitted in the American revision of 1789, but were retained in the revision of the Church of Ireland in 1870.

Octave (literally *eighth*) signifies the eighth day after a festival. The intervening days are said to be " of " or " within " the octave. The octave had its origin among the Jews.[3] One purpose, doubtless, of prolonging the time in Israel was on account of the risk of error in the date of the great festivals, when most of the worshippers came to Jerusalem from a great distance.

---

[1] Bp. Dowden, p. 9. [2] Ib. p. 10.
[3] See Lev. xxiii. 36; Num. xxix. 35; 1 Kings. viii. 65, 66; 2 Chron. xxix. 17; xxx. 22; S. John. vii. 37.

The Immovable Feasts are those which, like Christmas, Circumcision, Epiphany, and the Saints' Days, have a fixed day in the Calendar. *The Movable Feasts* are those which are dependent on Easter, whose date follows the movements of the moon rather than of the sun.

CHAPTER X

THE BEGINNING OF THE YEAR—ADVENT AND CHRISTMAS

> "All time is hers, and, at its end,
> Her Lord shall come with more,
> As one for whom all time was made
> Thus guardeth she her store;
> And, doating o'er her letters old,
> As pores the wife bereft,
> Thus daily reads the Bride of Christ
> Each message He hath left."
> —*Bishop Coxe, Christian Ballads.*

WHEN we come to examine the calendars of the different national Churches throughout the world—Greek, Roman, Armenian, Russian, Coptic, English, etc.,—we find great variety in their details. Nevertheless, all have one central principle, namely the manifestation of the life of our Lord, from His Incarnation onward through His Passion, Resurrection, Ascension, and His sending of the Holy Ghost. These general features are common to all, and may be considered under three heads, namely, Christmas, Easter, and Pentecost or Whitsunday. Under a fourth head we may consider the Saints' Days as illustrating some of the ripe results and fruitage of the Incarnate Life.

Of the three great feasts which form the framework of the Christian Year in every calendar, we must remember that they correspond, in their historical character, and in their spiritual significance, to the three great feasts of the earlier Church which, in God's providence and purpose, was a shadow of, as well as a preparation for, the great realities that were to come after.[1] They correspond also in a general way in the time of their observance; Christmas to the feast of Tabernacles "in the end of the year"; Easter to the Passover in the spring; Whitsunday to Pentecost in the early summer.

1. "The Nativity of our Lord, or the Birthday of Christ, commonly called Christmas Day," is naturally the first subject of our thought. But before considering it we must notice the season of Advent, which means *coming*. This is but the period of preparation for Christmas, and therefore marks the beginning of the Church's Year. All the great feasts of the Church have these times of preparation on the natural principle that the mind must be fitted beforehand to grasp the marvellous mysteries which the great feasts commemorate. Advent, however, is not a fast like Lent, but is a time of solemn and penitential thought. "Advent Sunday is always the nearest Sunday to the Feast of S. Andrew, whether before or after."[2] The Scottish Prayer Book of 1637 adds the words, "or that Sunday which falleth upon any day from the 27th of November to the 3d of December inclusively," thus providing for the case of Advent Sunday falling on S. Andrew's Day itself (Nov. 30th).

Our record of the observance of Advent does not go back further than the fourth century. The Roman use under Gregory the Great at the end of the sixth century (A.D. 597), when Augustine landed in Kent to help convert the Anglo-Saxons, included four Sundays in Advent.

As regards the common name for the feast of the

[1] Col. ii. 17; Heb. x. 1.
[2] *Tables and Rules for the Movable and Immovable Feasts.*

BEGINNING OF THE CHURCH YEAR 55

Nativity our English-speaking Church seems to be peculiar. The Dutch name, *Kersmis*, is the only one that corresponds to it. Both mean of course the Mass of Christ, a word (in Latin *Missa*) which, whatever its origin, was applied to many services in the fourth century, and which came to be applied, though not exclusively, to the Holy Communion in the sixth and seventh centuries.[1] The word is analogous to such popular English terms as Michaelmas for the feast of S. Michael and All Angels; Lammas for the first of August, and Candlemas for the Purification. The names for the day among peoples of the Latin and Celtic races are corruptions of the Latin *Natale*, e.g., the French *Noel*, and the Welsh *Nadolig*. The German name *Weinachtsfest* has reference to the solemn vigils before the festival. The Scandinavian *Yule* is from the old heathen festival at that time of the year.[2]

The early observance of Christmas cannot be so distinctly traced as that of the other greatest festivals. "At Rome, however, Hippolytus (Bishop of Portus, near Rome), at the beginning of the third century, in his Commentary on Daniel [3] fixes the date as Wednesday the 25th of December, in the forty-second year of the Emperor Augustus."[4] S. Clemens of Alexandria, who died little more than a century after the death of S. John, speaks of its observance, while S. Chrysostom, the Bishop of Constantinople in the fourth century, describes it even then as of great antiquity.[5] In a letter he mentions that Julius I, Bishop of Rome from A.D. 337 to 352, had caused a strict examination of the Imperial records of the Roman census taken at the time

---

[1] See *Heortology*, p. 432.
[2] *Prayer Book Commentary*, S.P.C.K., p. 17.
[3] iv. 23.   [4] Duchesne, p. 258.   [5] *Hom. in Nat. I.*

of our Lord's birth,[1] and as a result confirmed its observance on December 25th.

Throughout the East, the 6th of January was the day when *three* events of our Lord's life were commemorated, namely, His birth, the adoration of the Magi, and His baptism. "It is thus clear," writes Duchesne, "that towards the end of the third century the custom of celebrating the birthday of Christ had spread throughout the whole Church, but it was not observed everywhere on the same day. In the West the 25th of December was chosen, in the East the 6th of January. The two customs, distinct at first, were finally both adopted, so that the two festivals were universally observed, or almost so."[2] The Armenian Church, alone in Christendom, has retained the old date (January 6th) to the present day.

Furthermore, there is a remarkable spiritual significance in the fact that, whether the exact date be correct or not, Christmas stands in the place of the ancient feast of Tabernacles, the great and joyous time of thanksgiving, when the people lived in booths or tents for eight days in remembrance of God's care of them during their journeyings forty years in the Wilderness.[3] So, too, S. John tells us, "The Word was made flesh and *tabernacled among us.*"[4]

It is sometimes asserted that the Roman Church was influenced in fixing on December 25th for the purpose of turning away the faithful from the excesses of the ancient pagan festival of the Saturnalia by diverting their thoughts to our Lord's Nativity. But as the Saturnalia began on December 17th and ended on the 23d this theory must

---

[1] S. Luke, ii. 1.   [2] Duchesne, p. 260.
[3] Lev. xxiii. 33 to end.
[4] S. John i, 14, Rev. Ver. margin. Compare 2 Peter i. 13, 14.

BEGINNING OF THE CHURCH YEAR   57

be discarded. "A better explanation," Duchesne says, "is that based on the [pagan] festival of the *Natalis Invicti*. . . . The Invictus is the Sun, whose birth coincides with the winter solstice, that is, with the 25th of December, according to the Roman Calendar."[1]

And if this be the true date (as there is great probability), it is very significant that it is the third day after the true winter solstice (December 22d) when the sun, after reaching the lowest point on the horizon, begins to ascend and to bring back light and life to a darkened and dying world. So also Christ, "the Light of the World," "the Sun of Righteousness, arises with healing in His wings."[2] There is surely in this nothing incredible, but rather the contrary, when we remember that the Child who was born in Bethlehem of the Blessed Virgin Mary, "in the winter wild," was He by whom this visible earth and sun and moon and stars were made, and "without whom was not anything made that was made."[3] All that we call "Nature" is His. It was "*His* star in the East,"[4] and under His guidance, that led the Wise Men to His cradle; it was His moon, "the faithful witness in heaven,"[5] that pointed to the day of His great sacrifice; and it was His sun that "hid as it were its face from Him,"[6] in sympathy with His dying agonies on the cross. Even in these ways "the heavens declare the glory of God and the firmament showeth His handiwork."[7]

[1] Duchesne, p. 261.   [2] S. John viii. 12; Mal. iv. 2.
[3] S. John i. 3.   [4] S. Matt. ii. 2.   [5] Psalm lxxxix. 36.
[6] Is. liii. 3.   [7] Ps. xix. 1.

CHAPTER XI

OTHER IMMOVABLE FEASTS OF OUR LORD

"This little index of thy life,
Thou, all thy life, shalt find
So teaching thee to tell thy days,
That wisdom thou mayst mind.
Oh live thou by the Calendar,
And when each morn you kneel,
Note how the numbered days go by,
Like spokes in Time's swift wheel."
Bishop Coxe, Christian Ballads.

OTHER Immovable Feasts of our Lord depending on Christmas as their centre are: the Circumcision, on January 1st; the Epiphany, on January 6th; the Presentation of Christ in the Temple, commonly called the Purification of Saint Mary the Virgin, on February 2d; and the Annunciation of the Blessed Virgin Mary on March 25th. The Transfiguration of Christ on August 6th, though a feast of our Lord, can scarcely be said to depend on the date of Christ's birth. Its selection is somewhat, if not wholly, arbitrary.

The **Circumcision** is observed by all Christendom one week after the Nativity (January 1st), except by the Armenian Church, which of course places it on January 13th, January 6th being their Christmas. Originally the day was observed only as the octave of the Nativity, and we learn from the sermons of S. Augustine [1] that in his time the Church kept it as a solemn fast, in protest against the "diabolical feast" of the pagans on that first

[1] *Ser.* 197, 198.

OTHER IMMOVABLE FEASTS OF OUR LORD 59

day of the year with its licentious revelry. When these heathen practices gradually ceased, its festal character as the octave of Christmas was restored to the day, and the admission of the Holy Child when eight days old to the privileges of membership in the Church of Israel became the central feature of its celebration.[1] Keble in the opening verse of his poem for the festival notes this combined tone of sadness and joy:

> "The year begins with Thee,
> And Thou beginn'st with woe,
> To let the world of sinners see
> That blood for sin must flow."
> —*The Christian Year.*

It should also be remembered concerning this feast that it is the day on which the Holy Child received the Name declared by the angel,[2] the "Name which is above every name," and to which "every knee should bow."[3] A "black-letter" day to commemorate this event occurs in the present English Calendar, called Name of Jesus, but in Saxon times it was observed on the Feast of the Circumcision, and later, on the Second Sunday after Epiphany.

In days when this holy Name is often treated so lightly and irreverently it should not be forgotten that, since the time of the Arian heresy in the fourth century, when our Lord's true nature as perfect God as well as perfect Man was so fiercely assailed, it has been a custom in the Church to show outward reverence for this Name by bowing at its utterance in the Creed and elsewhere. It is simply in recognition of this ancient custom that the Church of England ordains in her canons: "When in time of Divine Service the Lord Jesus shall be men-

---

[1] S. Luke ii. 21.
[2] S. Matt. i. 21. [3] Phil. ii. 9, 10.

tioned, due and lowly reverence shall be done by all persons present, *as it hath been accustomed.*" In this connection also S. Paul's custom is surely one to be followed. He never uses the Name casually. It is worthy of remembrance that out of 591 times that S. Paul refers to our Lord in his epistles (including Hebrews) "Jesus Christ" occurs 61 times; "Christ Jesus," 46 times; "The Lord Jesus," 18 times; "Jesus our Lord," 9 times; "Jesus Christ our Lord," 8 times; "Lord Jesus Christ," 68 times; "The Lord," 133 times; "Christ," 227 times, and only in 21 instances does he use the word "Jesus" alone, always with some special reason, as in Phil. ii. 10. In every other instance he adds or employs some word of honor as "Lord" or "Christ" either as prefix or affix.

Another name for the **Epiphany** (Jan. 6th) in the East is the *Theophany*. Epiphany is the Greek word for "Manifestation "; Theophany signifies the "Manifestation of God." This idea was chiefly connected with the first three occasions when "Jesus manifested forth His glory "; *to the Gentiles* when the Wise Men were led by "His star" to His cradle, and "worshipped Him "; *to the Jews* when He was baptized in Jordan, and the Voice came from heaven saying, "Thou art My beloved Son, in whom I am well pleased"; *to His own family and disciples* when He wrought His first miracle in Cana of Galilee.[1] The feast was universally observed in the fourth century, the East making the manifestation of Our Lord's Godhead at His Baptism the dominant thought, and the West laying the chief stress on the visit and adoration of the Magi, so that here the day was commonly designated the **Feast of the Three Kings**. In the East it is still known as the **Feast of Lights** on account

[1] S. Matt. ii. 1-13; S. Mark i. 11; S. John ii. 1-12.

OTHER IMMOVABLE FEASTS OF OUR LORD 61

of its connection with the Baptism of our Lord, baptism being called by the Greeks "the Illumination."

> "Did not the Gentile Church find grace,
> Our mother dear, this favored day?
> With gold and myrrh she sought Thy face,
> Nor didst Thou turn Thy face away."
> —*Keble, Christian Year.*

The number of Sundays after the Epiphany depends on the date of Easter. When Easter falls on one of the earliest days, March 22d, 23d, or 24th, there is only one Sunday after the Epiphany; when it falls on one of its latest days, April 22d, 23d, 24th, 25th, there are six Sundays.

"**The Presentation of Christ in the Temple,** commonly called the **Purification of Saint Mary the Virgin**" (Feb. 2d) was first known, both in the West and in the East, by the Greek name, "*Hypapante*" or "The Meeting," that is, the meeting of Simeon and Anna with Mary and her Child in the Temple.[1] This event, like that of the Circumcision, is another instance of the devout obedience of Mary and Joseph in fulfilling every ordinance of God in His Church.[2] The presentation was to be made when the Child was six weeks old, which fixes the day of the festival on February 2d. Though known better by its popular name of "**The Purification,**" the day is rather a feast of our Lord than of the Blessed Virgin. The Church of Rome, according to Duchesne, appears to have observed no festival of the Virgin, in fact, until the seventh century. **Candlemas,** the other popular English name for the day, had its origin in the early custom of carrying candles in procession as part of the ritual of the feast. This is supposed to have its

[1] S. Luke ii. 22-39.   [2] Lev. xii.

suggestion in the words of Simeon to the Holy Child, "A light to lighten the Gentiles."[1]

The Annunciation (March 25th) is really a feast of our Lord, and not merely of His Virgin Mother. It was already well established in the Church in the seventh century, according to Duchesne. As commemorating the actual Incarnation of Christ the date was placed just nine months before His Nativity. For this reason also it was reckoned in England and some other countries as the beginning of the civil year. This custom began to prevail in England in the twelfth century, and continued to be generally followed till the reformation of the Calendar by Parliament in 1752. The popular English name for the festival is Ladyday, regarding it as in honor of the Blessed Virgin, "Our Lady."

> " 'Twas on the day when England's Church of yore
> Hail'd the new year—a day to angels known,
> Since holy Gabriel to meek Mary bore
> The presence-token of the Incarnate Son." [1]
> —*Keble, Lyra Apostolica.*

Another feast of our Lord is the **Transfiguration** (August 6th). In the present English calendar by an unaccountable omission of the revisers, this has only a secondary place as a "black-letter" day. No special service was provided for it, though it had its own Epistle and Gospel in the Use of Sarum, or Salisbury. At the revision of the Prayer Book in 1892 the American Church, feeling that the great importance of this event in our Lord's life justified and demanded for it a higher position, made it a "red-letter" day, and provided it with proper Lessons, Collect, Epistle, and Gospel.

[1] S. Luke ii. 32.

"Lord, it is good for us to be
Entranced, enwrapt, alone with Thee;
And watch Thy glistering raiment glow
Whiter than Hermon's whitest snow,
The human lineaments that shine
Irradiant with a Light Divine:
Till we too change from grace to grace,
Gazing on that transfigured Face."
—*A. P. Stanley.*

CHAPTER XII

THE MOVABLE FEASTS—EASTER AND ASCENSION DAY

" ' Welcome, happy morning! ' age to age shall say,
Hell to-day is vanquish'd, heav'n is won to-day."
—*V. Fortunatus, Trans. J. Ellerton.*

THE purpose and origin of **Easter** have already been considered to some extent in Chapters IV and V.[1] Its connection with the Jewish Passover shows us why the day is not observed as an immovable feast, like Christmas, fixed to a particular month and day of the solar year. On the contrary it is dependent on the varying position of the moon at the time of the vernal equinox (March 21st). This historical association of 3400 years is the reason for the Church insisting on the retention of the ancient Jewish rule for its observance. For Easter, including of course the events of Good Friday, which is the real Passover, is not only the direct successor of the Jewish festival of Unleavened Bread, but represents its complete spiritual fulfilment. The Paschal Lamb slain and offered in sacrifice, then roasted and transfixed upon a wooden cross or spit, without the breaking of a bone; followed by the escape of the Israelites from the angel of destruction, and from the slavery of Egypt through the Red Sea water, all this was the shadow of the true " Lamb of God that taketh away the sins of the world," sacrificed on the wood of the Cross,

[1] For the Christian observance of the Lord's Day, or Sunday, see Chapter VI.

burnt up with His awful agony and feverish thirst, yet "not a bone of Him broken," and all followed by the mighty deliverance from the bondage of death in the sealed sepulchre of Joseph's garden.

The word *Easter* is peculiar to the Teutonic and Scandinavian nations. The Anglo-Saxon name for April was Eostur-monath, after the goddess Eostre. Hence the German *Ostera*. The Latin and Greek *Pascha* follows the Hebrew *Pesach* or Passover, and the French *Pâques* has the same origin.

The correct form of the English name, it should be observed, is *Easter-Day*, as in the Prayer Book, and not Easter-Sunday, inasmuch as the day is a Sunday necessarily. This recalls the great importance which the early Church attached to the day itself. A discussion arose in the Church about the year 136 as to whether the feast should be kept on the same day as the Jews kept it, namely the 14th day of the month Nisan, no matter on what day of the week it chanced to fall, or else on the Sunday following. Those who insisted on the 14th Nisan were called Quartodecimans, from the Latin word for fourteen. This rule was followed chiefly or solely by Eastern Christians, especially in the region of Ephesus, where it was claimed that it was the custom of S. John. The Western Churches, however, held that the better day was the Sunday following the full Paschal moon, that being the day of the week which our Lord Himself had sanctified by His rising from the dead.

The intense feeling which this controversy occasioned about a thing so apparently trifling, testifies to the vast practical importance which the early Church attached to the day as a witness to the historic reality of the Resurrection. On this single fact, they knew, rested all else of Christian faith, for if Christ's body never rose from the dead their faith in Him was all in vain.[1] It is owing to this fact also that the Eastern Church gave, and still gives, to the day the name "The Feast," as that which outranks all others, and that the Western Church regards it as "The Queen of Festivals."

This feeling in fact was so great that for a time a schism between the Eastern and the Western Churches seemed imminent. When Polycrates, Bishop of Ephesus at the close of the second century, in behalf of himself and the other Bishops of Asia, wrote to Victor, the then Bishop of Rome, defending the tradition of the East, Victor, writes Eusebius the historian, "forthwith endeavored to cut off the Churches of all Asia, together with the neighboring Churches, as heterodox, from the common unity." The Bishops of the West were not in sympathy with Victor in this extreme position, though agreeing with him that Easter should be kept on the Lord's Day, and Irenæus, the famous Bishop of Lyons, in the name of the Church of Gaul, wrote to him in expostulation. He reminds him that "when the blessed Polycarp went to Rome in the time of Anicetus [his predecessor] and they had a little difference among themselves likewise respecting other matters, they immediately were reconciled, not disputing much with one another on this head, . . . and they separated from each other in peace, all the Church being at peace; both those that observed [Easter on Sunday], and those that did not observe [it], maintaining peace."[2] These wise, broadminded words of Irenæus (whose Greek name signifies "Peaceful"), in opposition to the ill-judged zeal of Victor, are of value as applicable to other matters besides the proper day for celebrating our Lord's Resurrection. The

---
[1] See Rom. i. 4; 1 Cor. xv. 14-20.
[2] Eusebius, *H. E.*, chap. 23, 24.

THE MOVABLE FEASTS—EASTER, ETC. 67

result was that the Asiatic Churches were left undisturbed in their traditional usages, but it is evident that they fell into line with the West sometime before the meeting of the Council of Nice.

And the controversy as to the proper day of the week for observing the feast was not the only difficulty experienced regarding it in the first three centuries. Another was the lack of correct astronomical knowledge as to what was the true Paschal moon, that is, "the full moon which happens upon, or next after, the 21st day of March," which is the vernal equinox.[1]

This difficulty was occasioned by the various imperfect cycles of the moon in use in different countries, the most common being the old Jewish cycle of eighty-four years used by the Roman Church, and the Metonic cycle of nineteen years which the Egyptian Church employed. These questions were finally settled for all time by the great Ecumenical or General Council of Nice in A.D. 325. Then it was decided, among other things, not only that Easter should always be observed on the day of the week on which our Lord rose, namely, the Sunday after the Paschal moon, but also that the fixing of the proper day of the full moon should be left to the Bishop of Alexandria. The city was at this time the greatest seat of learning in the world. Here the Metonic cycle was regarded as that which was nearest perfection, and so it was agreed that, at each preceding Epiphany, the Bishop of that see should give notice of the day to the Bishop of Rome, and through him to all the other Bishops of the Church.[2]

It was this uncertainty as to what was the true cycle

[1] See "Tables and Rules for the Movable and Immovable Feasts."
[2] Seabury, pp. 77, 78.

of the moon that was one occasion of the refusal of the ancient British and Irish Churches to recognize and work with Augustine, whom, in the year 596, Pope Gregory I. had sent to England to help in the conversion of the heathen Anglo-Saxon invaders. On account of the barbarian invasions of the Roman empire in the fifth and sixth centuries, these native Churches had had no intercourse with Rome for a hundred years or more, and meanwhile many changes had taken place in that see. One of these changes was the adoption of the Metonic cycle of Alexandria which Rome had formerly opposed. But being far from the civilization of the Continent, the British and Irish Churches had continued to use the imperfect cycle of eighty-four years employed at first by Rome herself. They were not Quartodecimans, but after a century of lack of intercourse, their reckoning for Easter differed from that of the rest of the Church, and for a long time they stiffly asserted their independence as national Churches by refusing to accept what was really the better rule. This was at length adopted in the south of Ireland about 650; in the north of Ireland in 703; in Scotland in 716; and in South Wales in 802.[1]

All these facts, as I have said, testify to the vast importance which the Church everywhere attached to the right observance of the Easter festival. The whole truth of Christ's claims, and of the religion which He taught, rested on the fact of His actual bodily rising from the dead, and the perpetual and universal celebration of the day was one of the most powerful witnesses to its reality as a fact of history.[2]

Of the observance of **Ascension-Day,** the fortieth day after Easter,[3] we have no mention before the middle

[1] See Prof. Bury's *Life of S. Patrick*, pp. 371–374.
[2] Compare Acts. i. 22; iv. 2, 33; xvii. 18; xxiii. 6. [3] Acts. i. 3.

THE MOVABLE FEASTS—EASTER, ETC. 69

of the fourth century. However, in Augustine's time (A.D. 354-430) the observance of the day was universal, and the feast ranked with Easter and Pentecost. A manuscript of a very interesting character in connection with Church usages was discovered in Arezzo in Italy in the year 1884. It is entitled "The Pilgrimage of Silvia," and is dated by scholars at about A.D. 385. It describes a journey to the holy places in Palestine by a devout lady of Gaul "who could read the Fathers in Greek . . . knew the Bible well, and was a very accurate and quick observer."[1] Silvia tells us that in Jerusalem there was a solemn procession on Ascension-Day to the Mount of Olives, where the Empress Helena, who is said to have been born in England, in the city of York, had erected a church as a memorial of the event. Bede, the historian of the English Church in the eighth century, speaks of its celebration as almost as solemn as that of Easter.

Another name for the day in our Prayer Book is **Holy Thursday**.[2] Of the great importance attached by the Church to the bodily ascension of our Lord as witnessing to our own future entrance into Heaven, see the fourth Article of Religion, and the proper preface for Ascension-Day.

[1] Bp. John Wordsworth, *The Ministry of Grace*, p. 57.
[2] See "Other Days of Fasting."

CHAPTER XIII

OTHER MOVABLE FEASTS—WHITSUNDAY AND TRINITY

"When God of old came down from Heaven,
In power and wrath He came;
Before His feet the clouds were riven,
Half darkness and half flame.

"But when He came the second time,
He came in power and love,
Softer than gale at morning prime
Hovered His Holy Dove."
—*Keble, Christian Year.*

WE have already seen how natural it was that **Pentecost** or **Whitsunday** should be observed as a Christian festival from the very earliest day.[1] Its celebration is mentioned by Origen in the third century, and by Gregory Nazianzen and Chrysostom in the fourth. At first the entire fifty days between Easter and Pentecost were observed as a continuous festal season without fasting or kneeling. This early and universal observance of the day could not well have been otherwise considering the previous training of the Apostles and first Christians as devout members of God's ancient Church of Israel.

The coming of the Holy Ghost, the third Person in the Blessed Trinity, resembled the coming of the Eternal Son in that visible and audible signs, the "tongues like as of fire" and the "sound as of a rushing mighty wind," were vouchsafed as sacramental tokens of His presence.

[1] Chapter V.

OTHER MOVABLE FEASTS

Moreover, the day was the birthday of the Church. For just as Christmas had been the birthday of His natural body, so on Pentecost His mystical body, which like the body of Eve had been formed from the pierced side of the second Adam, had breathed into it "the breath of life, and it became a living soul."[1] The associations of the earlier Jewish feast would of course blend with the associations of the Christian festival, especially as "the Feast of Harvest," now fulfilled in the baptism of three thousand believers[2] as "the firstfruits" of the great harvest of risen souls that has been springing up all over the world ever since.[3] But the chief thought in the minds of the Apostles was of course the fulfilment of Christ's promise of "the Comforter" and of "power," without which all their best efforts would be in vain.[4]

Pentecost is the Greek word for *Fiftieth*. It was the name given to the feast by the Grecian Jews before Christ's coming. It is also used in our Prayer Book in "The Table of Fasts." The reference is to the day which closed the seven weeks which elapsed between the Exodus from Egypt and the arrival at Mount Sinai. For this reason it was also called the **Feast of Weeks.** Another name was the **Feast of Harvest** or **Firstfruits**,[5] being held in the early summer, which came naturally much earlier in Palestine than in northern climates.

The name **Whitsunday** (not Whitsun-Day) is peculiar to the English-speaking Church. The original word Pentecost is retained in all Latin countries. Whitsunday is held by some to be a corruption of the German Pfingstentag, but this is more than doubtful. About

---
[1] Gen. ii. 7.   [2] Acts. ii. 41.   [3] See Chapter **V.**
[4] S. John xiv. 16, 26; Acts i. 8; Rom. xv. 13.
[5] Ex. xxiii. 16; xxxiv. 22; Deut. xvii. 9.

the year 1200 the English spelling was Hwitesundei, and later Witesoneday, or Wittesonday. The reference may be either to the wearing of white robes by candidates for baptism on the feast, or else to the gift of "*wit*," an old Saxon word for wisdom (as in *witan*, wise man), by the outpouring of the "Spirit of wisdom,"[1] in fulfilment of Christ's promise.[2] The derivation from *white*, however, has strong confirmation in the Welsh, that is, the ancient British, word for the day, namely *Sulgwyn*, gwyn being the Welsh for white.

The name **Trinity Sunday** for the eighth day or octave after Whitsunday is derived from the fact that the revelation of God's nature as Father, Son, and Holy Ghost, which the Church has been unfolding since Advent, is now completed. The festival, therefore, marks the culmination and summing-up of the whole teaching of our Lord as expressed by Him in the formula for Holy Baptism, "the Name of the Father, and of the Son, and of the Holy Ghost"; and later in the Creed of the Church, "I believe in God the Father . . . I believe in His Son Jesus Christ . . . I believe in the Holy Ghost."

The festival is not of an early date. It makes its first appearance in the Low Countries in the tenth century, and makes its way slowly. According to Gervase of Canterbury, the day owes its origin to Thomas Becket, the famous Archbishop of that see from 1162 to 1170. "It was not until the fourteenth century, under the pontificate of John XXII, that the Roman Church received the feast of the Trinity and attached it to the first Sunday after Pentecost."[3] The Eastern Church has no Trinity Sunday, but calls the day "All Holy Martyrs."

[1] Eph. i. 17.   [2] S. John xvi. 13.
[3] Dowden, p. 46.

Both the Oriental and the Roman communions count the Sundays "after Pentecost" instead of "after Trinity." In fact the custom of calling the Sundays after Trinity is peculiar to the English-speaking Church, and to those German Churches which were founded by her missionaries. This is noteworthy as a token of the national independence of the British Churches, and also as a witness to their unbroken orthodoxy, inasmuch as the Arian heresy denying the perfect Godhead of our Lord, which so overspread all the rest of the Christian world, never obtained a foothold on British or Irish soil.

In accordance with the early or late date of Easter in any year, the Trinity season may consist of as many as twenty-seven Sundays, or of as few as twenty-two. As there are only twenty-five Collects, Epistles, and Gospels provided for the Sundays after Trinity, the additional Sundays in any year are to be supplied from those omitted in the Epiphany season; provided, however, that the twenty-fifth shall always be used for the Sunday next before Advent.[1]

As the Church Year from Advent to Trinity presents to us step by step the great drama of Redemption, from "the mystery of the Holy Incarnation, the Holy Nativity and Circumcision, the Baptism, Fasting, and Temptation, the Agony and Bloody Sweat, the Cross and Passion, the precious Death and Burial," on to "the glorious Resurrection and Ascension, and the Coming of the Holy Ghost," thus completing the fulness of the revelation of the love and mercy of God in the three sacred Persons of the Holy Trinity; so, for the remainder of the year, the Church presents to us the practical side of the Christian Life as the necessary fruit of such a glorious faith. The Collect, Epistle, and Gospel for the First

[1] See the rubric at the end of the Sunday next before Advent.

Sunday after Trinity, with their thought of "strength" and "weakness," "help" for the "keeping of God's commandments," and the love of God and our brother, or the absence of it, sound the keynote of all the Sundays till we reach Advent once more.

CHAPTER XIV

THE SAINTS' DAYS

"For all the Saints, who from their labors rest,
Who Thee by faith before the world confessed,
Thy name, O Jesu, be forever bless'd,
   Alleluia.
O may Thy soldiers, faithful, true, and bold,
Fight as the saints who nobly fought of old,
And win, with them, the victor's crown of gold.
   Alleluia.
—*W. W. How.*

HOOKER has these wise and weighty words concerning the observance of Saints' Days: "Forasmuch as we know that Christ hath not only been manifested great in Himself, but great in other His Saints also, the days of whose departure out of the world are to the Church of Christ as the birth and coronation days of kings or emperors, therefore especial choice being made of the very flower of all occasions in this kind, there are annual selected times to meditate of Christ glorified in them who had the honor to suffer for His sake before they had age and ability to know Him [the Holy Innocents]; glorified in them which knowing Him as Stephen, had the sight of that before death whereinto so acceptable death did lead; glorified in those sages of the East that came from far to adore Him and were conducted by strange light; glorified in the second Elias of the world sent before Him to prepare His way; glorified in every of those Apostles whom it pleased Him to use as founders of His kingdom here; glorified in the Angels as in Michael." [1]

There are two classes of Saints' Days in the English Calendar. The most important commemorate Saints of the New Testament, and, with certain other festivals, are called "red-letter days," because they were usually written or printed in red ink. The less important, commemorating Bishops, Martyrs, and Confessors of a later date and having no special services appointed for them, were called "black-letter days" for a similar reason. At the American revision in 1789, and the Irish in 1870, the black-letter days were all omitted. This in many respects was a distinct loss, inasmuch as most of the days commemorated holy men and women of the British, Irish, Scottish, and English Churches as well as of other branches of the Holy Catholic Church throughout the world, thus witnessing in a very definite way to the historic continuity of the English-speaking Church with the Church of all the ages. For this reason it is much to be desired that the Irish and American Churches should restore or provide commemorations for such notable names as S. Ignatius and S. Polycarp of Asia; S. Cyprian, S. Perpetua, S. Athanasius, and S. Augustine of Africa; S. Agnes, S. Ambrose, S. Jerome, and S. Gregory of Italy; S. Hilary of France; S. David of Wales; S. Patrick, and S. Columba of Ireland; S. Alban, S. Augustine of Canterbury, S. Hugh of Lincoln, and the Venerable Bede of England; and S. Boniface of England and Germany.

It was of Athanasius, "Keen-visioned Seer," the great defender of the Divinity of our Lord in the fourth century, that Newman wrote as an Anglican:

[1] *Ecc. Pol.* V. lxx. 8.

THE SAINTS' DAYS

> "When shall our northern Church her champion see,
> Raised by divine decree,
> To shield the ancient Truth at his own harm?
> Like him who stayed the arm
> Of tyrannous power, and learning sophist-tone,
> Keen-visioned Seer, alone."

And of others:

> "Cyprian is ours, since the high-souled primate laid
> Under the traitorous blade
> His silvered head. And Chrysostom we claim
> In that clear eloquent flame
> And deep-taught zeal in the same woe, which shone
> Bright round a Martyr's throne.
>
> "And Ambrose reared his crosier as of old,
> Less honored, but as bold,
> When in dark times our champion crossed a king."
> —*Lyra Apostolica.*

Among the red-letter days there are only sixteen devoted to the remembrance of New Testament Saints, most of them *Apostles;* one to **S. Stephen;** one to the **Holy Innocents** (in England popularly called **Childermas**); one to **S. Michael and All Angels,** and one to **All Saints.** The **Annunciation of the Blessed Virgin Mary** (the true feast of the Incarnation), and **The Presentation of Christ in the Temple,** commonly called **The Purification of Saint Mary the Virgin,** may be regarded in a double capacity as the commemorations of her who was declared to be "blessed among women,"[1] and also as festivals of our Lord. There is much lost in the true balance and "proportion of faith"[2] when these festivals are ignored or forgotten.

The day chosen for the commemoration of Saints is

---

[1] S. Luke i. 28.   [2] Rom. xii. 6.

usually the day of their death, that being their birthday, *dies natalis*, into the higher life of Paradise. But there are two exceptions to this rule, namely, **The Nativity of S. John Baptist,** and **The Conversion of S. Paul.** Of the former S. Augustine wrote, "The Church celebrates two birthdays only, John's and Christ's." Assuming that December 25th and June 24th ("the sixth month"[1] before), are the correct dates, it is curious to note how the days correspond to the two solstices.[2] Even Augustine could see in the dates the fulfilment of the Baptist's own self-effacing confession, "He must increase, but I must decrease,"[3] since the days lengthen from the Nativity of Christ, while they shorten from the Nativity of S. John.

> "How didst thou start, thou holy Baptist, bid
> To pour repentance on the Sinless Brow!
> Then all thy meekness, from thy hearers hid,
> Beneath the ascetic's port and preacher's fire,
> Flowed forth, and with a pang thou didst desire
> He might be chief, not thou."
>
> —*Newman, Lyra Apostolica.*

In this connection also some have seen in the date of S. Thomas's festival (December 21st), when the sun seems to hesitate at the winter solstice, a certain fitness to the doubting character of that Apostle. "S. Andrew's Day," Bishop John Wordsworth says, "is perhaps the only festival of an Apostle claiming to be really on the

---

[1] S. Luke i. 36.

[2] The reason why the 24th was chosen instead of the 25th, which would be exactly six months before Christmas Day, is this: the dates were fixed when the old notation of the days was in use. As December had 31 days and June had only 30, the 8th before the calends of January would be December 25, whereas the 8th before the calends of July would be June 24.

[3] S. John iii. 30.

anniversary of his death." [1] All the more striking therefore is the significance of the date (November 30th) at the beginning of Advent, as S. Andrew was the first of the Twelve Disciples chosen by our Lord, and as he was the first to lead his brother Peter and others to Christ.

The practice of commemorating the lives of Christian saints seems to have originated in the holding of services beside the grave of martyrs on the anniversary of their deaths. We have accounts of these in the martyrdom of Ignatius, Bishop of Antioch (d. A.D. 115), Polycarp, Bishop of Smyrna (d. A.D. 166), and the martyrs of Lyons and Vienne (d. A.D. 177). S. Peter and S. Paul were commemorated very early, and on the same day, June 29th, and it is to be regretted that the English revisers of the Calendar omitted S. Paul on that day, leaving his conversion on January 25th as his only memorial, a feast which dates only from the ninth century.

It is worthy of note that the three holy days following Christmas, December 26th, 27th, and 28th, may have been placed there close to our Lord's Nativity to illustrate the three kinds of martyrdom; S. Stephen nearest as a martyr both in will and deed; S. John next as a martyr in will though not in deed; the Holy Innocents as martyrs in deed though not in will.

"The commemoration of Saints," writes Bishop Westcott, "is one of the provisions that has been wisely made by our Church to bring home to us our connection with the invisible life; to help us to confess that they who once lived to God live still; to know that we are heirs not of a dead past, but of a past fresh with new lessons; to learn that consecrated gifts become an eternal blessing; to understand—most touching mystery—that Christ

[1] *Ministry of Grace*, p. 419.

is pleased to reveal Himself little by little, 'in many parts and in many fashions,' in the persons of His servants. Thus it is that each saint received and shows some trait of the perfect Manhood of His Master. And 'we that are but parts' can recognize in a scale suited to our weakness, now this grace and now that, according to our needs."[1]

"Let us live," writes Bishop Ellicott, "as if they were still with us in the flesh; let us make ourselves meet to enjoy the fulness of communion with them hereafter. Oh, let us bless God for their examples; let us pray to Him for strength to emulate their self-denial, for grace to follow after their meek wisdom, for courage patiently and hopefully to labor in the service of God, even as they labored—to live as they lived, and to die as they died."[2] Or again, as Newman expresses this thought of the great Saints: "They animate us by their example; they cheer us by their company; they are on our right hand and on our left, Martyrs, Confessors, and the like, high and low, who used the same creeds, and celebrated the same mysteries, and preached the same Gospel as we do. And to them were joined, as ages went on, even in fallen times, nay, even now in times of division, fresh and fresh witnesses from the Church below. In the world of spirits there is no difference of parties. . . . Greece and Rome, England and France, give no color to those souls which have been cleansed in the one Baptism, nourished by the One Body, and moulded by the One Faith. . . . Therefore it is good to throw ourselves into the unseen world, it is 'good to be there,' and to build tabernacles for those who speak 'a pure language' and 'serve the Lord with one consent'; not indeed to draw them forth from their

[1] *Social Aspects of Christianity.* [2] *The Destiny of the Creature.*

secure dwelling-places, not superstitiously to honor them, or wilfully to rely on them, lest they be a snare to us, but silently to contemplate them for our edification." [1]

[1] *Parochial and Plain Sermons*, vol. iii.

CHAPTER XV

THE FEAST OF S. MICHAEL AND ALL ANGELS

"Therefore with Angels and Archangels, and with all the company of heaven, we laud and magnify Thy glorious Name; evermore praising Thee and saying, HOLY, HOLY, HOLY, Lord God of Hosts, Heaven and earth are full of Thy glory; Glory be to Thee, O Lord Most High."—*Order for the Holy Communion.*

Two of the most beautiful and most helpful festivals of the year come as "the sere and yellow leaf" begins to remind us of the end of all things, and of our own brief life on earth, namely, the feasts of **S. Michael and All Angels,** or **Michaelmas,** and **All Saints.** One tells us of that "innumerable company"[1] "ordained and constituted" by God, not only to "do Him service in heaven," but "that they may succor and defend us on earth".[2] The other speaks of the "great cloud of witnesses"[3] watching and waiting for us in Paradise; "the glorious company of the Apostles, the goodly fellowship of the Prophets, the noble army of Martyrs"; but especially on this day, those "whom we have loved, and lost awhile." Both days are important to recall us from our forgetfulness of "the things which are unseen" and yet alone are "eternal." "Persons," says Newman, "commonly speak as if the other world did not exist now, but would after death. No, it exists now, though we see it not. It is among us and around us. Jacob was shown this in his dream. Angels were all about him though he knew it not. And what Jacob saw in his sleep, that

[1] Heb. xii. 22.   [2] *Collect for All Angels.*   [3] Heb. xii. 1

S. MICHAEL AND ALL ANGELS 83

Elisha's servant saw as if with his eyes; and the shepherds at the time of the Nativity not only saw but heard."[1]

There are only two angels mentioned by name in the canonical Scriptures, namely Gabriel[2] and Michael.[3] The special commemoration of S. Michael is due doubtless to the fact that he is named in Scripture as a "prince" or "archangel" among the holy inhabitants of heaven. It is a reminder to us that in heaven, as in the Church on earth, there must be many gradations as well as "many mansions." Even there also "all members have not the same office."[4] The angelic host, or "Sabaoth," has its unequal, vastly diverse personal intelligences. "It has its ranks, its degrees, its various celestial nationalities, so to speak. Daniel tells of 'princes' in the heavenly host, and Holy Scripture elsewhere gives us at least nine orders of the celestial hierarchy, angels, archangels, cherubim, seraphim, thrones, dominions, virtues, principalities, powers."[5] In "the books called Apocrypha" two other "princes" among the angels are mentioned by name; Raphael in Tobit viii. 2, and xii. 15, and Uriel in II. Esdras v. 20. The feast of S. Michael the Archangel has been observed in the Eastern Church for 1500 years at least. In the Western Church the day has been September 29th; in the East, November 8th.

Practical Christians of to-day are apt to look upon such a commemoration as a pious sentiment fitted rather for imaginative women or childish men. But plainly

[1] *Parochial and Plain Sermons*, vol. iv.
[2] Dan. viii. 16; ix. 21; S. Luke i. 19, 26.
[3] Dan. x. 13, 21; xii. 1; S. Jude 9; Rev. xii. 7.   [4] Rom. xii. 4.
[5] Col. i. 16; Eph. i. 21; W. Gwynne, *Some Purposes of Paradise*, p. 55.

our Lord did not so judge. In the prayer which He framed for all lips and for our daily use, He deliberately inserted one petition which directs our thought continually to those holy beings, and bids us pray, "Thy will be done on earth as it is done in heaven," that is, by the Angels. As a direct result of His own entrance into this world as Man, there is, He tells us, a great influx, not only of spiritual *power*, but of spiritual *persons*, as helpers in that mighty work which He came to do for men. "Ye shall see heaven open," He said to Nathanael, "and the angels of God ascending and descending upon the Son of Man."[1] What the ladder was to Jacob in his night vision, Christ would have us know, the Son of Man who was also the Son of God is to us, a ladder connecting heaven and earth, a channel for the tender care and ministrations of angels. Before His coming such ministries were but fitful and infrequent. Not until Christ was born, and angels sang their *Gloria in Excelsis* over the fields of Bethlehem, not until they waited on Him in His Temptation, and comforted Him in His Agony, and watched at His Sepulchre, and worshipped Him at His Ascension, was that Way fully opened, and that Ladder set up in all its fulness from earth to heaven. No one can read the later books of the New Testament without seeing that all their writers considered the presence and ministration of angels, not as a devout poetical imagination, but as a sober actual fact in the every-day experience of every Christian. "We are come," exclaims one of these writers, "to an innumerable company of angels."[2] "Are they not all ministering spirits," he asks, "sent forth to minister to them who shall be heirs of salvation?"[3] "Angels came and ministered unto him" is doubtless the simple description of

[1] S. John i. 51.   [2] Heb. xii. 21.   [3] Heb. i. 14.

S. MICHAEL AND ALL ANGELS

many an event, an assuaged sorrow or a conquered temptation, in our own lives, as it was in that of our Lord.[1]

The human heart left to its own devices, its sorrows or its struggles, would say "Give me back the spirits of my friends, my loved ones, my children, to be near me and to comfort me." It cries with Tennyson,

> "Be near me when my light is low,
>   When the blood creeps, and the nerves prick
> And tingle; and the heart is sick,
> And all the wheels of being slow."
>
> —*In Memoriam.*

That is the heart's unreasoning wish. It is the way of fanaticisms in every age, necromancy, and so-called spiritualism, and it is just that which Scripture frowns on and forbids. On the other hand, the promise of angelic messengers in the Bible is full and unreserved. No petition for that loving guardianship is too great for God's fulfilment. Other ages may have been in danger of thinking too much of these heavenly helpers; our danger is that of thinking too little, and therefore slighting and despising them. "He shall give His angels charge over thee to keep thee in all thy ways" is a promise of which we are all too forgetful, and for which All Angels' Day is the wholesome and most necessary reminder. It is of their ministry to us on earth that Edmund Spenser writes:

> "How oft do they their silver bowers leave,
> To come to succor us that succor want,
> How oft do they with golden pinions cleave
> The flitting skies like flying pursuivant,
> Against foul fiends to aid us militant!

[1] S. Matt. iv. 11

They for us fight, they watch and duly ward,
And their bright squadrons round about us plant;
And all for love, and nothing for reward—
O why should heavenly God to men have such regard?"
—*Fairy Queen*, II. viii. 2.

It is related of Richard Hooker, the great defender of the Church's "polity," that his friend Dr. Saravia, finding him "deep in contemplation" during his last day on earth, asked him concerning his thoughts, to which Hooker replied, "That he was meditating the number and nature of angels, and their blessed obedience and order, without which, peace could not be in heaven; and oh that it might be so on earth." [1]

[1] *Life*, by Isaac Walton.

CHAPTER XVI

THE FEAST OF ALL SAINTS

" 'Tis sweet, as year by year we lose
Friends out of sight, in faith to muse
How grows in Paradise our store."
—*Keble, Burial of the Dead.*

"Give them rest, O Lord, there in the land of the living, in Thy Kingdom, in the delight of Paradise, in the bosom of Abraham, Isaac, and Jacob, our holy fathers, whence pain, sorrow, and groaning is exiled, where the light of Thy countenance looks down and always shines."—*Liturgy of S. James.*

A FESTIVAL in honor of **All Saints** was observed by the Greeks as early as the fourth century on what we call Trinity Sunday. It was not, however, until the middle of the ninth century that the festival became generally observed throughout the West, and then the day chosen was November 1st. The early English name for the day was **All Hallows,** that is, *All Holies.* It is from this we derive the popular name for the preceding day, **Hallowe'en,** or the Even of All Hallows, October 31st.

It is evident that the adoption of this festival was a natural instinct of the human heart and its needs; a day which would not be confined to the remembrance of the *great* Saints and Martyrs of the whole Catholic Church, or of national or local Churches, but of all those devout and unnamed or unknown servants of God who "have departed this life in His faith and fear." The purpose was plainly to give to every individual Christian opportunity to remember their own holy dead as still "living unto God" in Paradise, still members of the One Holy Catholic and Apostolic Church, the Communion of Saints, "no longer trammelled and fettered, compelled to fight for very life in an enemy's country, but free to love, free to will and to obey, free to worship and to work, as they never were in the days of their earthly existence."[1] And not only to remember them, but to pray for their peace and progress that "we, with all those who are departed in the true faith of God's holy Name, may have our perfect consummation and bliss, both in body and soul, in His eternal and everlasting glory" at the Resurrection of the Dead[2] (*Burial Office*).

For such a day in remembrance of the faithful departed, and especially our own, there is and always will be great need. As with the Holy Angels, so with the disembodied spirits of the faithful, there is always great danger of our forgetfulness. They have passed out of sight indeed, but they are not separated from us. "The gates of Hades," or the unseen world of spirits, can "not prevail against" the Church to separate them from it. They are no more beyond our love, or the influence of our prayers than when they were on earth, though doubtless they have less need of them. "The souls of the righteous are in the hand of God, and there shall no torment touch them."[3] They are "in Paradise," but Paradise is not Heaven. "I am not yet ascended," our Lord said to Mary Magdalene on Easter morning, though He had been in Paradise ever since He gave up the

---

[1] *Some Purposes of Paradise*, p. 49.

[2] That prayer of the faithful departed is scriptural, primitive, natural, Christian, see *Some Purposes of Paradise*, Chapters XI and XII.

[3] Wisdom, iii. 1.

THE FEAST OF ALL SAINTS 89

ghost on the cross on Good Friday.[1] Paradise, Scripture plainly tells us, is only the place of preparation for the Resurrection and for Heaven. To quote some words which I have used elsewhere: "Paradise was the word in common use throughout the East, among Persians and Greeks as well as Hebrews, for a royal park. It was not the king's palace, but the royal garden surrounding the palace, with its cool delights and shady walks; not Heaven, but the ante-chamber of Heaven, where souls might pause a while before the king came out to bring them in to His secret presence-chamber, His supreme delights."[2]

In an age when this truth of the Intermediate State between death and the Resurrection, so plainly revealed in the New Testament, has passed largely out of the thought of multitudes of Christian people, All Saints' Day is of more practical importance than ever. Other great days in the Christian Year bring to our remembrance events of a distant past. This recalls us to the immediate present. It is a constant witness and reminder to us of that holy place and that "great multitude which no man can number,"[3] the vast majority indeed of Christ's Holy Church, who are even now advancing in knowledge and grace, and preparing with longing expectation for the fulness of Christ's victory at His second coming.

It is such thoughts as these that All Saints' Day brings home to us, as no other day in the Christian Year can do so fully. To the Christian the death line seems to have vanished. "The death of the body is indeed rarely mentioned in the New Testament, and in no place is it represented either as the end or the beginning

[1] S. John xx. 17.
[2] *Some Purposes of Paradise*, p. 21.   [3] Rev. vii. 9.

of life. To all it is but a stage in life's journey, and not the attainment of its goal. To the Christian it is but the striking of a tent,[1] the 'unloosing' of sails and rudder-bands, as S. Paul twice calls it.[2] It is merely the preparation for another and a sunnier stretch of sea, but one whose true haven is not reached until the Resurrection and the Judgment. It is said even of the elder saints who 'died in faith, not having received the promises,' that 'they *now* [that is, in Paradise] desire a better country, that is, an heavenly . . . for God hath prepared for them a city.' "[3]

> "Sweet is the calm of Paradise the blest.
> But lo! there breaks a yet more glorious day;
> The saints triumphant rise in bright array;
> The King of Glory passes on His way.
> Alleluia."
> —*Bishop W. W. How.*

A Day of National Thanksgiving

Thanksgiving Day is peculiar to the American Church in having a special Collect, Epistle, and Gospel provided for it. It is to be "observed as a day of Thanksgiving to Almighty God, for the Fruits of the Earth, and all other Blessings of His merciful Providence" (*Rubric*). The observance probably had its origin in the Harvest Home festivals which were, and are still, common in the English Church. The first settlers in New England seem to have brought the custom with them to America. When the revision of the Prayer Book was adopted by the General Convention in 1789, the date was fixed for "the first Thursday in November, or such other day as shall be appointed by the Civil Authority." The Civil

---

[1] 2 Cor. v. 1.   [2] Phil. i. 23; 2 Tim. iv. 6.
[3] Heb. xi. 13, 16. *Some Purposes of Paradise*, pp. 27, 28.

Authority, that is, the Governors of the different States of the Union, and the President of the United States, are now accustomed to appoint the *last* Thursday in that month. The observance, outside the Church, was largely confined to New England and her people until after the Civil War (1861 to 1865), when it became a Day of National Thanksgiving.

CHAPTER XVII

THE BLACK-LETTER DAYS

> "Oh live ye by the Calendar,
> And with the good ye dwell;
> The Spirit that comes down on them
> Shall lighten you as well."
> —*Coxe, Christian Ballads.*

A Black-Letter Day is a minor festival for which no "liturgical proper," that is, Collect, Epistle, and Gospel, with "Proper Lessons," "Proper Psalms," etc., is provided. The basis of the present Calendar of the Church of England, as finally revised in 1661, is that of the Use of Sarum, both in its Missal, or Service for the Holy Communion, and its Breviary, or choir offices. Many of the Sarum commemorations, which had grown altogether too numerous, were at this time omitted, and a few names such as the Venerable Bede and S. Alban, which were strangely absent from the Sarum Use, were added. The revision of this part of the Book of Common Prayer, in the matter of the minor festivals, is generally regarded as most unsatisfactory both in what might well have been added and what was omitted.

The reasons which actuated the Bishops at this revision may best be gathered from their answer to the Puritans, who desired the omission of all but four of the black-letter days. They said, "The other names are left in the Calendar, not that they should be so kept as holy days, but they are useful for the preservation of their memories, and for other reasons, as for leases, law-days, etc."

THE BLACK-LETTER DAYS

In the present English Calendar as given below, the red-letter days are printed in heavy type. The notes which I have added in italics are intended to give a few facts in regard to the persons or events commemorated, together with the date of death or of occurrence. A Confessor is one who has suffered persecution for the faith.

January

1. **Circumcision of our Lord.**
6. **Epiphany of our Lord.**
8. Lucian, Priest and Martyr. *Of France*, A.D. 290.
13. Hilary, Bishop and Confessor. *Of Poictiers*, A.D. 368. *This festival gives its name to the Hilary term in the law courts, which begins January 11th and ends January 31st.*
18. Prisca, Roman Virgin and Martyr. A.D. 275.
20. Fabian, Bishop of Rome and Martyr. A.D. 250.
21. Agnes, Roman Virgin and Martyr. A.D. 304.
22. Vincent, Spanish Deacon and Martyr. A.D. 304.
25. **Conversion of S. Paul.**

February

2. **Purification of the Blessed Virgin Mary.**
3. Blasius, an Armenian Bishop and Martyr. A.D. 316.
5. Agatha, a Sicilian Virgin and Martyr. A.D. 251.
14. Valentine, Bishop and Martyr. *Of Rome.* A.D. 270.
24. **S. Matthias, Apostle and Martyr.**

March

1. David, Archbishop of Menevia. *Also named Dewi, national Saint of Wales.* A.D. 544.
2. Cedde, or Chad, Bishop of Lichfield. A.D. 673.

7. Perpetua, Mauritanian Martyr. A.D. 203.
12. Gregory M., Bishop of Rome and Confessor. *M. in this case does not stand for Martyr, but for Magnus, or the Great. It was this Bishop who sent Augustine to England in 596 to convert the Anglo-Saxons. Died* A.D. 604.
18. Edward, King of the West Saxons. A.D. 978.
21. Benedict, Abbot. *Founder of the Benedictine order of Monks, of Mount Cassino, Italy.* A.D. 543.
25. **Annunciation of the Blessed Virgin Mary.**

April

3. Richard, Bishop of Chichester. A.D. 1253.
4. S. Ambrose, Bishop of Milan. A.D. 397.
19. Alphege, Archbishop of Canterbury. *Martyred by the Danes.* A.D. 1012.
23. S. George, Martyr. *Native of Cappadocia, a soldier in the Roman army in the time of Diocletian, early in the fourth century. The Patron Saint of England since* A.D. 1220.
25. **S. Mark, Evangelist and Martyr.**

May

1. **S. Philip and S. James, Apostles and Martyrs.**
3. Invention of the Cross. *Commemorates the Invention that is, the Finding, of the cross on which our Lord suffered, by the Empress Helena, the mother of Constantine, the first Christian Emperor; about* A.D. 326.
6. S. John Evangelist, ante Portam Latinam. *Commemorates his miraculous deliverance when cast into a cauldron of boiling oil "before the Latin Gate" of Rome in the time of Domitian.*

THE BLACK-LETTER DAYS 95

19. Dunstan, Archbishop of Canterbury. A.D. 988.
26. Augustine, first Archbishop of Canterbury. A.D. 604.
27. Venerable Bede, Priest. *Abbott of Jarrow, the most distinguished scholar of his age, and the first historian of the English Church.* A.D. 735.

June

1. Nicomede, Roman Priest and Martyr. A.D. 90.
5. Boniface, Bishop of Mentz and Martyr. *Called the Apostle of Germany; native of England, and originally named Winfrid.* A.D. 755.
11. S. Barnabas, Apostle and Martyr.
17. S. Alban, Martyr. *The first recorded British Martyr,* A.D. 303. *The Sarum Calendar gave the 22d as the day.*
20. Translation of Edward, King of the West Saxons. *Murdered* A.D. 978; *body reinterred* A.D. 981. *See March,* 18*th.*
24. Nativity of S. John Baptist.
29. S. Peter, Apostle and Martyr.

July

2. Visitation of the Blessed Virgin Mary. *That is, to her cousin Elizabeth.*[1]
4. Translation of S. Martin, Bishop and Confessor. *Reinterment of his body in a new church dedicated to his honor near Tours, his see city.* A.D. 397. *See Nov.* 11.
15. Swithun, Bishop of Winchester, Translation. *Also spelled Swithin. Celebrated for his humility, as well as his deeds of charity. "He died July* 2 A.D. 862, *and was buried at his own request outside the*

[1] S. Luke i. 39, etc.

THE CHRISTIAN YEAR

church, where men might walk over him, and the rain water his grave. In A.D. 971 the relics were translated to a rich shrine within the cathedral; but it is recorded that a most violent rain fell on the destined day, and continued for thirty-nine days, whence arose the popular notion that if it rain on S. Swithin's Day, it will for thirty-nine following." [1]

20. Margaret, Virgin and Martyr at Antioch (*in Pisidia*). A.D. 278.
22. S. Mary Magdalen.
25. **S. James, Apostle and Martyr.**
26. S. Anne, Mother of the Blessed Virgin Mary. *Not named in Holy Scripture, but early tradition speaks of her and her husband Joachim as the parents of the Blessed Virgin.*

August

1. Lammas Day. "*The observation of this day as a feast of thanksgiving for the firstfruits of the corn dates from Saxon times, in which it was called Hlaf-maesse, or Loaf-mass, from the offering, at the Mass, of bread made of the new corn. . . . This is one of the four Cross-quarter days, at which rents were formerly due.*" [2]
6. Transfiguration of our Lord. See pp. 62, 63.
7. Name of Jesus. See p. 59.
10. S. Laurence, Archdeacon of Rome and Martyr, A.D. 258.
24. **S. Bartholomew, Apostle and Martyr.**
28. S. Augustine, Bishop of Hippo, Confessor and Doctor. A.D. 430.
29. Beheading of S. John Baptist. *S. Matt. xiv.* 1-13.

[1] Blunt's *Annotated Prayer Book*, p. [51].   [2] Ib., p. [53].

THE BLACK-LETTER DAYS

September

1. Giles, Abbot and Confessor. *Diocese of Nismes, France.* A.D. 725.
7. Eunurchus, Bishop of Orleans. *Also named Evortius.* A.D. 340.
8. Nativity of the Blessed Virgin Mary. *See* p. 127.
14. Holy Cross Day. *Commemorates the public exhibition of the "true cross," which took place on September 14th,* A.D. 335, *in the church erected in Jerusalem by the Empress Helena in honor of its " invention," or finding. See May* 3d.
17. Lambert, Bishop and Martyr. *Of Maestricht in the Netherlands.* A.D. 709.
21. **S. Matthew, Apostle, Evangelist, and Martyr.**
26. S. Cyprian, Archbishop of Carthage, and Martyr. A.D. 258.
29. **S. Michael and All Angels.**
30. S. Jerome, Priest, Confessor, and Doctor. A.D. 420.

October

1. Remigius, Bishop of Rhemes. *Also called Remi.* A.D. 535.
6. Faith, Virgin, and Martyr. *Of France; Latin name Fides.* A.D. 290.
9. S. Denys Areopagite, Bishop and Martyr. *Abbreviated from Dionysius. Not the Bishop of Paris, who was also a Martyr in* A.D. 272, *and the patron saint of France; but Dionysius the Areopagite, the first Bishop of Athens, who died* A.D. 96. *Acts xvii.* 34.
13. Translation of King Edward Confessor. *Died* A.D. 1066; *the body removed in* 1163 *to the new shrine in Westminster Abbey (which he had refounded).*

THE CHRISTIAN YEAR

17. Etheldreda, Virgin. *Daughter of the King of the East Angles. Died June 23d,* A.D. *679; body translated to new tomb, October 17,* A.D. *695.*
18. S. Luke, Evangelist.
25. Crispin, Martyr. *In the Salisbury Calendar he was commemorated with his twin brother Crispinian. Shakespeare makes Henry V. exclaim at the battle of Agincourt, "Crispin Crispian shall ne'er go by, . . . But we in it shall be remembered." (IV. sc. iii). The brothers were companions of S. Denys, the first Bishop of Paris, and worked as shoemakers in order to support themselves as missionaries. They were beheaded in* A.D. *288, and became the Patron Saints of shoemakers.*
28. **S. Simon and S. Jude, Apostles and Martyrs.**

November

1. **All Saints' Day.**
6. Leonard, Confessor. *Deacon and nobleman of France.* A.D. *599.*
11. S. Martin, Bishop and Confessor. *Born in Hungary, military tribune in Constantine's army; became Bishop of Tours in France. Died* A.D. *397. "Martinmas" is still one of the four Cross-quarter days in England.*
13. Britius, Bishop. *Also called Brice. Friend and successor of S. Martin as Bishop of Tours. Died* A.D. *444.*
15. Machutus, Bishop. *Known also as S. Malo. Born in Wales; became Bishop of Aleth in Brittany. Died* A.D. *564.*
17. Hugh, Bishop of Lincoln. *Born in Burgundy. Died* A.D. *1200.*

THE BLACK-LETTER DAYS

20. Edmund, King and Martyr. *East Anglia, killed by the Danes*, A.D. 870.
22. Cecilia, Virgin and Martyr. *Of Rome, Patron Saint of music.* A.D. 230.
23. S. Clement I., Bishop of Rome and Martyr. A.D. 100. *See Phil. iv. 3.*
25. Catherine, Virgin and Martyr. A.D. 307, *at Alexandria.*
30. S. Andrew, Apostle and Martyr.

December

6. Nicolas, Bishop of Myra in Lycia. A.D. 342.
8. Conception of the Blessed Virgin Mary. *See* pp. 127, 128.
13. Lucy, Virgin and Martyr. *Of Syracuse in Sicily.* A.D. 304.
16. O Sapientia. *This is merely a liturgical note to show that here begin the eight Advent antiphons to the Magnificat, the last coming on December 23d. The first words of the first antiphon are "O Sapientia," or "O Wisdom."*
21. S. Thomas, Apostle and Martyr.
25. Christmas Day.
26. S. Stephen, the first Martyr.
27. S. John, Apostle and Evangelist.
28. Innocents' Day.
31. Silvester, Bishop of Rome. A.D. 335.

The three following red-letter days were omitted from the Calendar of the Church of England in 1859: January 30th, King Charles the Martyr; May 29th, Charles II., Nativity and Return; November 5th, Papists' Conspiracy.

Much information concerning the black-letter Saints

and Days is to be found in Blunt, *Annotated Prayer Book*, pp. [36] to [61]. Writing of the Calendar as a whole, Mr. Blunt says: "It will be seen that the whole number of individual Saints commemorated is seventy-three. Of these, twenty-one are especially connected with our Blessed Lord; twenty are Martyrs in the age of persecutions; twenty-one are specially connected with our own Church; and eleven are either great and learned defenders of the Faith, like S. Hilary and S. Augustine, or Saints of France, whose names were probably retained as a memorial of the ancient close connection between the Churches of France and England."

Bishop Dowden writes: "It must be confessed that the black-letter saints of the modern English Calendar form by no means an ideal presentation of the worthies and heroes of the Church Catholic. The Bishop of Salisbury [J. Wordsworth] has some admirable remarks on the future reform of our English Calendar in his *Ministry of Grace*, pp. 421-425."[1]

> "O God of Saints, to Thee we cry;
> O Saviour, plead for us on high;
> O Holy Ghost, our Guide and Friend,
> Grant us Thy grace till life shall end;
> That with all Saints our rest may be
> In that bright Paradise with Thee."
>
> —*Bishop Maclagan.*

[1] *The Church Year*, p. 152.

CHAPTER XVIII

THE FASTS OF THE CHRISTIAN YEAR

> "'Lord, I have fasted, I have prayed,
> And sackcloth has my girdle been,
> To purge my soul I have assayed
> With hunger blank and vigil keen.
> O God of mercy! why am I
> Still haunted by the self I fly?'
>
> "Sackcloth is a girdle good,
> O bind it round thee still;
> Fasting, it is Angels' food,
> And Jesus loved the night air chill;
> Yet think not prayer and fast were given
> To make one step 'twixt earth and heaven."
> —*R. Hurrell Froude, Lyra Apostolica.*

FASTS equally with feasts are particularly open to abuse. Christians as well as ancient Jews can keep fast in such a way as to cause men merely to ridicule the custom. One reads to-day of "Lenten outings," "Lenten excursions," and "Lenten entertainments," where the thin disguise of religion is scarcely intended to hide the worldliness. And yet, no matter how much the practice may be perverted or ridiculed, the duty of keeping fast must remain as long as Christ's words remain. As George Herbert puts it:

> "Neither ought other men's abuse of Lent
> Spoil the good use; lest by that argument
> We forfeit all our creed."

When the ancient Jews made not only their fasts, but also their feasts, and sacrifices, and prayers "an abomination" in God's sight, He did not abrogate one or other. He merely set His erring people right by telling them what *kind* of feast and fast and prayer was alone acceptable to Him.[1]

And when we come to the teaching of our Lord and His Apostles, we find no different rule. The New Testament as well as the Old is full of directions as to fasting. The caricature and abuse of fasting in our Lord's day may seem to flippant and shallow Christians a convenient excuse for ridiculing and rejecting the whole idea of asceticism as a necessary part of the Christian life. Yet it cannot be too distinctly remembered that it was in face of the most utter abuse of fasting that the Lord Jesus insisted upon the duty as strongly as any Jewish prophet or rabbi ever did. In fact His own ministry begins with a fast, and that, the most rigorous that was ever kept by mortal man. So, too, in His teaching of the multitude in the Sermon on the Mount, intended, we know, as the foundation law of His coming Church, we find Him placing bodily abstinence on the same high level as prayer and almsgiving, not commanding them as duties, but assuming them as already such, and only laying down rules as to how to practise them. He does not say "Ye shall fast," but "*When* ye fast," and then, after laying down rules for the observance of the duty, He adds the assurance of His Father's most certain reward for all true and faithful fasting.[2]

On another occasion our Lord defends His disciples for their present omission of fasting, not by declaring the uselessness of the practice, as a thing affecting only the body, but by telling His critics that it was simply

[1] Is. i. 11-16; lviii. 1-8.   [2] S. Matt. vi. 16, 17, 18.

THE FASTS OF THE CHRISTIAN YEAR 103

a question of proper times and seasons. The time of His disciples had not yet come. "The Bridegroom," as He calls Himself, was still with them. But the day would come when the Bridegroom would be taken away from them, and "then shall they fast." [1]

When, therefore, their Lord had ascended into heaven, we find great Apostles and humble believers alike practising that which our Lord practised. It was while the Church in Antioch was keeping some penitential season, "as they ministered to the Lord and fasted," that the message came to them by the Holy Ghost to ordain and send out Barnabas and Paul on their great mission.[2] It was to laymen in the Church of Corinth S. Paul, a few years later, gave the special advice that they should "give themselves to fasting and prayer."[3] S. Paul began his own life as a Christian layman with a three-days' fast;[4] in ordaining clergy as an Apostle, it is done by him with "prayer and fasting";[5] and he declares it to be one of the signs of his own faithfulness as a minister of Christ that he had "approved himself in fastings" as well as "in patience and in afflictions."[6]

It is plain then that the religion that drops fasts and fasting out of the list of its duties, or rather from the list of its spiritual "armor,"[7] is not, and cannot be, the religion of Jesus Christ, or of His Apostles, or of His Scriptures. It is "the Scriptures," George Herbert reminds us, that "bid us fast." All that the Church does in Lent and other times is to add the word "now" to our Lord's word "when." Just as she does for His other precepts concerning prayer and almsgiving, so here,

[1] S. Matt. ix. 15.   [2] Acts xiii. 1, 2, 3.
[3] 1 Cor. vii. 5.   [4] Acts ix. 9.
[5] Acts xiv. 23.   [6] 2 Cor. vi. 5; also xi. 27.
[7] Eph. vi. 13.

she simply appoints the times and seasons when they may be most wisely exercised.

But though the authority for fasting is so unquestionable, and its claim upon our obedience so plain, the purpose of it all must be kept distinctly in view if we are to escape grievous errors in regard to it. This purpose is not to be found in any theory that the pain of His creatures is pleasing to God. As a wholesome preparation for the Baptism of adults,[1] and for the Holy Communion, it is primarily an act of reverence in approaching more worthily those holy sacraments. Its chief purpose, however, is for deepening the sense of sin within us, and as an instrument of self-discipline. "The sacrifices of God are a broken spirit,"[2] and we cannot conceive of a truly repentant or broken spirit in one who is perpetually engrossed in the pleasures of the world and the flesh. Christ came to save the body as well as the soul, and that He may do so the body must be brought into subjection to the higher nature. What, therefore, the gymnasium is to the athlete, what the severity of the study is to the scholar, and the drill of camp life is to the soldier, the discipline of fasting and abstinence is to the Christian. The real Lent, writes Bishop Phillips Brooks, "is the putting forth of a man's hand to quiet his own passions and to push them aside, that the higher voices may speak to him and the higher touches fall upon him; it is the making of an emptiness about the soul that the higher fulness may fill it."

It is the peculiarity of our branch of the Church that, while she appoints days and seasons for fasting, she leaves her children free as to the method of their fast. Only two days in the whole year, namely Ash Wednesday and Good Friday, does she name as absolute fasts, when,

[1] See first rubric in service.   [2] Ps. li. 17.

THE FASTS OF THE CHRISTIAN YEAR 105

so far as our health allows, she expects us to abstain from food until the afternoon, "the ninth hour" (three o'clock) according to the ancient custom. All other days the Church speaks of as "days on which she requires such a measure of abstinence as is more especially suited to extraordinary acts and exercises of devotion."[1] This "measure of abstinence" she does not define. It does not necessarily consist in the substitution of one kind of food for another, but rather in the voluntary giving up for a time of luxuries and pleasures, not only in food and clothing, but also in amusements and entertainments. The final purpose of all such efforts at self-discipline is not to narrow our lives or diminish our joys, for He "giveth us richly all things to enjoy,"[2] but the very opposite. It is to secure for our higher nature a freedom to develop its powers which the world and the flesh are ever tending to contract and cramp. As Wordsworth says:

"The world is too much with us; late and soon,
Getting and spending, we lay waste our powers."

[1] "Table of Fasts."   [2] 1 Tim. vi. 17.

CHAPTER XIX

LENT AND PRE-LENT

"Welcome, dear feast of Lent: who loves not thee,
He loves not temperance, or authority,
But is composed of passion.
The Scriptures bid us fast; the Church says, now:
Give to thy mother what thou wouldst allow
To every corporation.

. . . . . .

" 'Tis true, we cannot reach Christ's fortieth day;
Yet to go part of that religious way
Is better than to rest:
We cannot reach our Saviour's purity;
Yet we are bid, 'Be holy e'en as He.'
In both let's do our best.

"Who goeth in the way which Christ hath gone,
Is much more sure to meet with Him, than one
That travelleth by-ways.
Perhaps my God, though He be far before,
May turn, and take me by the hand, and more
May strengthen my decays."
—*George Herbert, The Temple.*

THE word **Lent** is derived from the Anglo-Saxon *Lencten,* which means Spring. The Latin name is *Quadragesima,* which signifies *fortieth,* in reference to the number of fast days in the season, omitting the six Sundays, which are always feasts. The word Quadragesima is also used once in the Prayer Book for the First Sunday in Lent.[1] *Carême,* the modern French word for Lent, in old French *Quaresme,* is simply an abbreviation and corruption of Quadragesima.

[1] See "Rules for Movable Feasts."

We have here doubtless the origin of the names given to the three Pre-Lenten Sundays which act as a kind of warning of the approaching fast. As the first Sunday in Lent is **Quadragesima** or the fortieth day before Easter, so, in round numbers, **Quinquagesima** is fiftieth, **Sexagesima** sixtieth, and **Septuagesima** seventieth. It is worthy of note in this connection that in the services for all these three Sundays before Lent the Apostle S. Paul is held up as a noble example of zeal, and self-denial, and suffering for Christ. On *Quinquagesima* his great words about the worthlessness of all such self-sacrifice and zeal without love give the true Christian watchword for a right Lent-keeping.

The custom of keeping a fast in preparation for Easter is of very early origin. It is mentioned by Irenæus, the Bishop of Lyons who died in A.D. 202, and by Tertullian, a priest and a native of Carthage, who died in 220. There was at first, however, great variation in the length of the season. Irenæus speaks of it variously as one day, or forty hours, or two days or more. Socrates, the Church historian, who was born in 380, speaks of the fast as three weeks, while Sozomen, who continued Socrates' history down to 440, refers to it as six weeks. "The observance of the forty days of Lent is first distinctly mentioned in the fifth canon of Nicæa, A.D. 325."[1] It was not, however, till the end of the sixth century that the present arrangement of the forty days was established. It was Gregory the Great, the Bishop of Rome who sent Augustine the monk to England in 596, who fixed the beginning of the season on Ash-Wednesday, forty-six days before Easter, thus giving forty days of abstinence by leaving out the Sundays, which are called "in" and not "of" Lent.

[1] Duchesne, p. 365.

"The primary object of the institution of a fast before Easter," writes Mr. Blunt, "was doubtless that of perpetuating in the hearts of every generation of Christians the sorrow and mourning which the Apostles and Disciples felt during the time that the Bridegroom was taken away from them.[1] This sorrow had, indeed, been turned into joy by the Resurrection, but no Easter joys could ever erase from the mind of the Church the memory of those awful forty hours of blank and desolation which followed the last sufferings of her Lord; and she lives over year by year the time from the morning of [the first] Good Friday to the morning of [the first] Easter-Day by a re-presentation of Christ 'evidently set forth crucified among us'.[2] This probably was the earliest idea of a fast before Easter. But it almost necessarily followed that sorrow concerning the death of Christ should be accompanied by sorrow concerning the cause of that death; and hence the Lenten fast became a period of self-discipline; and was so probably from its first institution in Apostolic times. And, according to the literal habit which the early Church had of looking up to the pattern of her Divine Master, the forty days of His fasting in the wilderness, while He was undergoing temptation, became the gauge of the servants' Lent, deriving still more force as an example from the typical prophecy of it which was so evident in the case of Moses and Elijah."[3]

The popular name of **Ash-Wednesday,** the first day of Lent, has been acquired "from the custom of blessing ashes made from the palms distributed on the Palm Sunday of the preceding year, and signing the cross with them on the heads of those who knelt before the officia-

---
[1] S. Matt. ix. 15.   [2] Gal. iii. 1.
[3] Deut. x. 10; 1 Kings xix. 9. *The Annotated Prayer Book,* p. 90.

ting minister for the purpose, while he said, 'Remember, man, that thou art dust, and unto dust shalt thou return'."[1] The day before Ash-Wednesday is popularly known as **Shrove Tuesday** because, in mediæval days penitents were accustomed to go to private confession on that day, and to be *shriven*, that is, absolved, in preparation for a good Lent. In Shakespeare's time it had become the equivalent of the Italian *carnival*, which signifies "farewell to flesh," in reference to the giving up of flesh-meat during Lent; both words thus acquiring a meaning the reverse of their original one.

Though the Sundays in Lent are not fast days, it may be best to note here the popular name given to the Fourth Sunday. Besides being known as **Mid-Lent Sunday** (in French, *Mi-Carême*), it is commonly called **Refreshment Sunday** on account of the Gospel for the day, which contains the story of the Miraculous Feeding of the Five Thousand in the wilderness.

[1] *Ann. Pr. Bk.*, p. 91.

CHAPTER XX

HOLY WEEK

"We are drawing nearer and nearer to the Cross; and do not our hearts burn within us in the way? To those who really know the love of Christ, which passeth knowledge, what a season is this!"—*Bp. Coxe, Thoughts on the Services.*

> "The royal banners forward go,
> The Cross shines forth in mystic glow,
> Where He in flesh, our flesh who made,
> Our sentence bore, our ransom paid."
> —*V. Fortunatus.*

It is a common mistake to speak of the last week in Lent as **Passion Week**. That name belongs properly to the week preceding. The Fifth Sunday is **Passion Sunday**, when the Epistle for the day begins to tell the story of the great Sacrifice. The correct name for the last week is **Holy Week**. The Germans give it the significant name of *Still*, or *Silent Week*. The Orientals call it the *Great Week*. The first day of the week, the Sixth Sunday or the Sunday next before Easter, is popularly known as **Palm Sunday**, that being the day of our Lord's solemn entry into Jerusalem proclaiming His Messiahship.[1] In "The Pilgrimage of Silvia" she gives us an account of the ceremonies of Holy week in Jerusalem in the fourth century, and of the procession of palm-bearers on Palm Sunday.[2]

As denoting the vast importance of these last days of

[1] S. John xii. 13.   [2] Duchesne, p. 484.

HOLY WEEK

our Lord's brief life on earth, it is very significant that more than one-fourth of the four gospels is taken up with the record of the events of Holy Week, beginning with Palm Sunday. Though no attempt is made in the Prayer Book to follow chronologically the scenes leading to and around the Cross which form the one absorbing subject of the Gospels for every day, nevertheless it is well for us to take due note of the events of the three days following Palm Sunday.

On *Monday*, on His way to Jerusalem, our Lord pronounces His judgment on the barren fig-tree as a type of the Jewish Church. He cleanses the Temple for the second time, driving the buyers and sellers from its courts. The chief priests and scribes take counsel to put Him to death.[1]

On *Tuesday* Christ teaches in the Temple; answers the questions of His enemies; speaks many parables; denounces woe on the scribes and Pharisees; sits with His disciples on the Mount of Olives overlooking the city, and foretells its destruction.[2] The last day of His public ministry.

On *Wednesday* He foretells His betrayal. The chief priests agree with Judas for thirty pieces of silver.[3]

Maundy Thursday is the popular name given to the Thursday before Easter, the day on which our Lord made preparation to eat the Passover with His disciples. It was on the evening of this day according to our reckoning, but on the commencement of Good Friday according to the Jewish reckoning, that He ate the Passover, and afterwards instituted the Holy Eucharist at the table, and out of the very elements of the ancient feast, which was but the shadow of the new and infinitely

---

[1] S. Mark xi. 12-20.
[2] S. Mark xi. 20-end; xii., xiii.   [3] S. Luke xxii. 1-7.

greater feast. Here were given the "new commandments" to "do this in remembrance" of Him, and to "love one another" as He had loved them, and it is from one or other of these "commandments" or "*mandates*" that the day receives its name of *Maundy Thursday*, or *Dies Mandati*.

In mediæval times the particular mandate of our Lord was taken to be the symbolical washing of one another's feet in token of love and humility, for which He had Himself just given them an example.[1] In England two clergy of the highest rank present washed the feet of all in the choir, and of each other. This custom, which is still retained in some portions of the Church, was continued in England by the Sovereigns until the latter part of the seventeenth century (James II was the last to perform the office), and by the Archbishops of York on their behalf until the middle of the eighteenth century.[2]

In the ancient offices of the English Church the commemoration of the Institution of the Holy Eucharist was observed on this day (called *Natalis Calicis*, or the Birthday of the Cup), by a celebration of the Holy Communion at Vespers.[3] This was the custom of the Church in Carthage as early as the year 397, when, "in view of the original institution of the Eucharist having been 'after supper,' it made an express synodical declaration that the rule of fasting communion was binding 'excepto uno die anniversario, quo cœna Domini celebratur,'" that is, except on this single anniversary.[4] S. Augustine in the same century agrees with this view "that it is lawful for the Body and Blood of the Lord to be offered and received after other food has been par-

[1] S. John xiii. 14. [2] See Blunt, *Ann. Pr. Bk.*, pp. 98, 99.
[3] Blunt, p. 99.
[4] Bingham, *Antiq.*, XXI., c. i. 30; Dowden, p. 41.

taken of, on one fixed day of the year, the day on which the Lord instituted the Supper, in order to give special solemnity to the service on that anniversary." He adds, however, "I think that, in this case, it would be more seemly to have it celebrated at such an hour as would leave it in the power of any who have fasted to attend the service before the repast which is customary at the ninth hour. Wherefore we neither compel, nor do we dare to forbid, any one to break his fast before the Lord's Supper on that day." [1]

In this connection Bishop Coxe has a very thoughtful remark. "Two Thursdays," he writes, "aid us in gaining the full idea of the Eucharist, Maundy Thursday, and 'Holy Thursday,' or Ascension Day. On the first, the bread and wine were taken and received as Christ's Body and Blood, while the unchanged Christ stood before them. On the second, the Body of our Lord became invisible to human eyes; but it is required of faith to behold that Body at the right hand of the Father, and at the same time to 'discern the Lord's Body' in the Lord's Supper. And this is just what the Lord prepared us for [2] when He said, 'Doth this offend you? what and if ye shall see the Son of Man ascend up where He was before?'"

[1] *Ep.* LIV *to Januarius,* c. vii. 9. [2] S. John vi. 62.

CHAPTER XXI

GOOD FRIDAY AND EASTER-EVEN

"Is it not strange, the darkest hour
   That ever dawned on sinful earth
Should touch the heart with softer power
   For comfort, than an angel's mirth?
That to the Cross the mourner's eye should turn
Sooner than where the stars of Christmas burn?

"Sooner than where the Easter sun
   Shines glorious on yon open grave,
And to and fro the tidings run,
   'Who died to heal, is risen to save'?
Sooner than where upon the Saviour's friends
The very Comforter in light and love descends?"
—*Keble, Christian Year.*

IT would seem as if this thought of Mr. Keble concerning **Good Friday** was the first thought in the mind and heart of the Church in her earliest days. For "strange" indeed as it may appear, the anniversary of our Lord's great Sacrifice upon the Cross was kept at first, not as a fast day, but as a feast. It is in fact strictly speaking of the events of Good Friday, and not of Easter, that S. Paul is thinking when he writes: "Christ our Passover is *sacrificed* for us, therefore let us *keep the feast.*"[1] Foreign as it may seem to our thought to-day, Christians, whose whole early life had been spent as Jews in the atmosphere of the Temple, and the Old Testament

---

[1] 1 Cor. v. 7; "keep festival," R. V. margin.

would naturally think of the anniversary of their Lord's Crucifixion on the great fourteenth day of the month Nisan, as the fulfilment and the successor of their ancient Pascha or Passover, the glorious festal day on which the true Lamb of God offered Himself for their redemption. They would not, and could not, indeed, separate this awful yet most blessed event from that which followed as its necessary complement on Easter Day. For, unlike the lamb of the typical sacrifice, which had no resurrection, their Lord had risen from the dead, and had thus proved Himself to be "the Son of God with power."[1]

It is this double thought also which forms the theme of the old Latin hymn for Easter:

> "At the Lamb's high feast we sing
> Praise to our victorious King,
> Who hath washed us in the tide
> Flowing from His pierced side;
> Praise we Him whose love divine
> Gives His sacred blood for wine,
> Gives His body for the feast,
> Christ the Victim, Christ the Priest."

In endeavoring to account for this fact of Good Friday as at the first a feast day, Bishop Dowden says: "We must suppose that the realization of the blessings of the redemption purchased by the Saviour's blood *overtoned* (to borrow a term from the art of music) the imaginative presentment of the historical sufferings of the Cross. Our own English term, 'Good Friday,'" he adds, "seems to have originated with a similar way of regarding the facts."[2] This method of celebrating the Pascha, or Passover, that is, the day of the Crucifixion, in close union with the two following days, as one feast, lingered on in the

[1] Rom. i. 4.   [2] *The Church Year*, pp. 106, 107.

Church until the Council of Nice in 325. Even at this date we find the Emperor Constantine, in a letter addressed to the Church, stating that the Lord has left us "only one *festal* day of our deliverance, that is to say, of *His holy Passion.*" From which it is plain that "the dominant thought connected with the word Pascha was still that of the Crucifixion." [1]

It was not until the Council of Nice that it was definitely settled that the anniversary of the Resurrection should always be held on the Sunday after the day of the Crucifixion, and not on a week-day. Consequently, when this division of the commemoration was made, it was most natural that the previous Friday should acquire much of its present character as a day of profound meditation on our Lord's sufferings, and as a penitential preparation for the joy of Easter.

It is evident from this primitive custom of regarding the Day of the Crucifixion, in conjunction with the two following days, as a festival, that the Holy Eucharist would of course be celebrated on that day. When, however, the separation of the days took place, it was natural that the day of the Crucifixion should be observed in a different way. It is about this time we find the custom of omitting the Consecration growing up in the Church, on the ground of its being inconsistent with the sad memories of that day.[2] This did not, however, prevent the *receiving* of the Holy Communion on Good Friday, as the Sacrament was reserved from the celebration on Maundy Thursday, according to a canon of the Church of England in the tenth century, for the priest, "and whosoever else pleases." [3] "In fact, Martene

---

[1] Dowden, p. 119.
[2] See Scudamore, *Not. Euch.*, Chapter XVII, sec. 3.
[3] Johnson, *Canons*, i. 404.

GOOD FRIDAY AND EASTER-EVEN 117

proves that Communion of the laity as well as of the priest on this day was the prevailing custom of the Church until the tenth century at least, and there are strong grounds for believing that the practice continued down to the time of the Reformation."[1]

"The appointment of an Epistle and Gospel," Mr. Blunt adds, "is a *prima facie* evidence that Consecration on Good Friday was intended to supersede the Mass of the Pre-sanctified [the reserved Sacrament] which had been hitherto used, and Communion was of course intended to follow. . . . The practice of the Church of England since the Reformation certainly seems to have been to celebrate the Holy Communion on this day. . . . The conclusions that may be drawn are, (1) that the Church of England never intended so far to depart from ancient habits as to be without the Sacramental Presence of Christ on the Day when His Sacrifice is more vividly brought to mind than on any other day of the year; (2) that from the introduction of the un-Catholic custom of Communion by the priest alone, or for some other reason, it was thought best to disuse the Mass of the Pre-sanctified and substitute Consecration; (3) that it is a less evil to depart from ancient usage by consecrating on this day than to be without the Sacramental Presence of our Lord."[2]

It is worthy of note that Bishop King had an early celebration during Holy Week, Good Friday not excepted (1889), in his Cathedral of Lincoln, and that this was also the custom in S. Paul's, London, under Dean Church, Canon Gregory (afterwards Dean), and Dr. Liddon.[3]

It should be observed that **Easter Even** is not an Eve in the usual sense of that word. The term applies to

[1] Blunt, *Ann. Pr. Bk.*, p. 101.
[2] Ib., pp. 101-2.   [3] See Liddon's *Life*, by Johnston, pp. 331-2.

the whole day during which our Lord's Body lay in the sepulchre. Though the Disciples did not yet know it, the battle was fought, and the victory already won, for while the sacred Body rests peacefully in the tomb in Joseph's fragrant garden, in the sunshine, or under the full beams of the Paschal moon, His soul, as the Epistle reminds us, is "preaching," that is, telling the glad tidings of His victory to the departed in Paradise. It is only His friends on earth who see Him not who are sad, because "the Bridegroom is taken away from them."[1]

"At length the worst is o'er, and Thou art laid
  Deep in Thy darksome bed;
All still and cold beneath yon dreary stone
  Thy sacred form is gone;
Around those sacred lips where power and mercy hung,
  The dews of death have clung;
The dull earth o'er Thee, and Thy foes around,
Thou sleep'st a silent corse, in funeral fetters wound.

"Sleep'st Thou indeed? or is Thy spirit fled
  At large among the dead?
Whether in Eden bowers Thy welcome voice
  Wake Abraham to rejoice,
Or in some drearier scene Thine eye controls
  The thronging band of souls;
That, as Thy blood won earth, Thine agony
Might set the shadowy realm from sin and sorrow free."
—*Keble, Christian Year.*

The Collect with its reference to the fact of our being "buried with Christ in Baptism,"[2] recalls to us the custom of the primitive Church to receive on this day, and early on Easter morning, those catechumens who have been preparing for Holy Baptism during Lent.

"The holy women," writes Bishop Coxe, "have pre-

[1] S. Matt. ix. 15.   [2] Col. ii. 12.

GOOD FRIDAY AND EASTER-EVEN 119

pared their spices, and are unconsciously giving a new meaning to the language of the Canticles: 'I charge you, O ye daughters of Jerusalem, that ye stir not up, nor awake my love, till He please. . . . I will get me to the mountain of myrrh, and the hill of frankincense, until the day break, and the shadows flee away.' " [1]

[1] Song of Solomon, ii. 7; iv. 6; *Thoughts on the Services*, Easter Even.

CHAPTER XXII

" OTHER DAYS OF FASTING "

"Its wisdom is forever old and perpetually new; its calendar celebrates all seasons of the rolling year; its narrative is the simplest, the most pathetic, the most rapturous, and the most ennobling the world has ever known."—*Edmund C. Stedman on The Book of Common Prayer.*

THE other fasts of the Church are:

1. "**The Ember Days** at the Four Seasons, being the Wednesday, Friday, and Saturday after the First Sunday in Lent, the Feast of Pentecost, September 14th, and December 13th. The last two seasons are placed just before the autumnal equinox, and the winter solstice. The word *Ember* is an abbreviation of the German *Quatember*, which in its turn is a corruption of the Latin *Quatuor Tempora*, or Four Seasons. Similarly the French name is *Quatre Temps*.[1]

The Ember Days are the times set apart for special intercession in preparation for the ordination of the Clergy. They have their primary authority in the example of our Lord, whose fast in the Wilderness was the preparation for His own entrance on the Ministry to which, at His Baptism, He had just been "called of God

[1] The word, however, may have a double origin in English. According to Professor Skeat its primary root is the Anglo-Saxon "ymbren" from "ymb," round, and "ren," to run, and so equivalent to "circuit," that is, the circuit of the four seasons of the year.—*Etymological Dictionary*, p. 188.

"OTHER DAYS OF FASTING" 121

as was Aaron."[1] Before He ordained His Apostles also, He passed the whole night in prayer.[2] Compare the example of the Apostles themselves in Acts xiii. 2, 3; xiv. 23. "He who faithfully keeps the Ember Seasons," writes Bishop Coxe, "will have done more for the Church in his lifetime than a thousand satirists of the Clergy, or an army of censorious declaimers setting forth their own ideas of what the ministry should be. Indeed he has no right to find fault with his spiritual pastors, who has never helped them with the offices which the Church, knowing their peculiar dangers, has provided and enjoined for their assistance and support. How often does the Apostle Paul crave the like benefit from those to whom he ministered! And surely the 'earthen vessels' which bear the treasure of the Gospel now are as much in need of the prayers of the faithful as he was."[3]

2. **The Rogation Days** are "the Monday, Tuesday, and Wednesday before Holy Thursday or the Ascension of our Lord" (Table of Fasts). Rogation means *Asking*, with special reference to the time of His withdrawal from the sight of His Disciples. The Fifth Sunday after Easter, which is the first day of Rogation Week, is usually called *Rogation Sunday*. The Epistle and Gospel for the day have been in use since the fourth century. The fast was probably instituted as early as the fifth century for the purpose of asking God's blessing on the rising produce of the fields. With this view the Irish and American Prayer Books have provided prayers for "Fruitful Seasons" on these days. Mamertus, the Bishop of Vienne in France, is said to have instituted the fast in A.D. 452, when storms and pestilence, coupled with the ravages of the barbarians then threatening

[1] S. Matt. iii. 13 to end; Heb. v. 4, 5.
[2] S. Luke vi. 12, 13.   [3] *Thoughts on the Services.*

the very existence of the Church, had laid waste his diocese and city. As a part of the observances solemn processions with litanies were made in deprecation of God's chastisement.

In view of this origin, the petitions in our own Litany for "the kindly fruits of the earth," against "plague, pestilence, and famine," against "battle and murder, and sudden [that is, violent] death," acquire a profound meaning. With this thought in mind, how impressive too is the appeal, "O God, we have heard with our ears, and our fathers have declared unto us, the noble works that Thou didst in their days and in the old time before them," with its response, "O Lord, arise, help us, and deliver us for Thine honor." And again, "From our enemies defend us, O Christ," with the response, "Graciously look upon our afflictions": "With pity behold the sorrows of our hearts," and its answer, "Mercifully forgive the sins of Thy people." George Herbert tells us in his "Country Parson" that the use of the Litany in procession, with priest and people, around the bounds of the parish, with prayer for a blessing on the fruits of the field, was a custom in his day, and it is still practised in some of the rural parishes of England.

3. "All the Fridays in the Year" are fast days, the Church tells us in her Prayer Book, though the great majority of her children seem wholly to forget it. Just as every Sunday is a little Easter, so every Friday should be a little Good-Friday, reminding us continually of the sufferings of our Lord for our redemption. It should at least be a day of quietness, and abstinence from the more exciting pleasures of life. The Fridays have been regarded as fast days from the very earliest times. There is but one exception noted in our Prayer Book, namely, Christmas Day, which is always a feast.

"OTHER DAYS OF FASTING" 123

4. Other days of fasting or abstinence appointed by the English Church are the **Vigils** or **Eves** of certain festivals, namely, The Nativity of our Lord, The Purification, The Annunciation, Easter-Day, Ascension-Day, Pentecost, S. Matthias, S. John Baptist, S. Peter, S. James, S. Bartholomew, S. Matthew, S. Simon and S. Jude, S. Andrew, S. Thomas, and All Saints. And the rule is added, "That if any of these Feast-days fall upon a Monday, then the Vigil or Fast-day shall be kept upon the Saturday, and not upon the Sunday next before it." The American Church omitted these vigils in the revision of 1789. The Irish Church retained them in its revision of 1870.

CHAPTER XXIII

VARIATIONS AND REVISIONS OF NATIONAL CALENDARS

"Every scribe which is instructed unto the Kingdom of Heaven is like unto a man that is an householder, which bringeth forth out of his treasure things new and old.—*S. Matt.* xiii. 52.

FROM the earliest age no national branch of the Holy Catholic Church has been without its own Liturgy or Liturgies, that is, an office for the celebration of the Holy Communion. Every Liturgy had also its own Calendar. Dr. John Mason Neale in his English version of the five Primitive Liturgies [1] gives a list of no less than eighty extant national or diocesan variations of these five principal families. Dr. Littledale, who edited the second edition of Dr. Neale's book, gives excerpts from twenty-four other Liturgies "either unknown to Dr. Neale, or beyond his reach at the time when the first edition of his book was published."

All of these hundred and more extant liturgies, in many tongues and of many lands, from India in the East to Spain and Ireland in the West, have certain clearly defined features, such as, among others, (1) the Preparation or Pro-anaphora, down to the *Sursum Corda;* (2) Epistles and Gospels; (3) the Creed; (4) the Offertory; (5) the great Eucharistic Prayer, including the Ter-Sanctus, or Triumphal Hymn, "Holy, Holy, Holy,"

[1] *Translations of the Principal Liturgies.* 1, Of S. James, or Jerusalem; 2, of S. Mark, or Alexandria; 3, of S. Thaddeus, or the East; 4, of S. Peter, or Rome; 5, of S. John, or Ephesus.

the words of Institution, the Oblation, the Invocation of the Holy Ghost (omitted in the Roman); (6) the great Intercession, including the Lord's Prayer; (7) the Prayer of Humble Access, Confession, Communion, and Thanksgiving.

But along with these features which they have in common, there are as many variations in detail as there are "Uses," that is, liturgical forms of the particular country or diocese. Moreover, these various "Uses" have always been subject to revision from age to age according to the special or supposed needs of the time or country. For instance, the Roman Liturgy, which was originally in Greek, and confined to use in the local Greek-speaking Church of Rome, was at some unknown date turned into Latin, which had then become the vernacular of the majority of the Roman Christians. This was revised by Pope Leo I. (440–461); by Pope Gelasius (492–496); by Gregory I. (590–604), and has had many additions made to it in later times. The original Liturgy of the ancient British, Irish, and Scottish Churches had its source in the Ephesine and the Gallican or French Liturgy, but when Augustine came to Canterbury from Rome in 596, he brought the revised Roman service. After these Celtic Churches of the north and west had united with the Italian missions among the Angles and Saxons in the south, a new revision came gradually into use which incorporated many features of the older Churches. After the Norman Conquest Bishop Osmund of Sarum or Salisbury (1078–1099) undertook a new revision of the English service books, and his work was considered so favorably that the "*Missal according to the Use of Sarum*" became practically the Liturgy of the whole English Church, though various other diocesan Uses, such as Hereford, York, Bangor, and Lincoln, and even of S. Paul's Cathedral, London, continued to be employed more or less in the worship of the Church.[1] "It was adopted also in Ireland in the twelfth century, and in various Scottish dioceses in the twelfth and thirteenth centuries."[2]

The next revision of the English Liturgy was that in the sixteenth and seventeenth centuries (1549, 1552, 1561, 1604, 1661), when, as in Rome in the early days, the services were restored to "the tongue understanded of the people,"[3] and other corrections in practice and doctrine were made.

Together with all these various forms of the Liturgy by nations and dioceses, there were also many and various forms of the Calendar, or order for observing the fasts and festivals of the Christian Year. Here, too, while all branches of the Catholic Church the world over observed the same great outlines of the year based upon the Incarnation, Death, Resurrection, and Ascension of our Lord, and the Coming of the Holy Ghost, each national Church, and often each diocese, had its own particular Use. Originally every Bishop, subject to certain limitations, had power to regulate the Calendar as well as the services of his own diocese. This naturally led to great diversity and multiplicity of festivals, especially of local saints, and in the method of conducting the worship of the Church. In course of time it became a source of serious practical evil which needed correction. "The abuses," writes Kellner, "resulting from the excessive multiplication of holy days [which reduced the number of working days for the poor, and encouraged others in laziness and pleasure-seeking] was remarked on

---

[1] See *Preface to the English Book of Common Prayer.*
[2] F. E. Warren in *Art. Liturgy in Ency. Brit.*
[3] *Articles of Religion*, XXIV.

by John Gerson," the great chancellor of the University of Paris, as early as the year 1408.[1]

In the matter of diversity in national calendars, one of the most striking features of the modern Roman Calendar is the peculiar emphasis which, in the course of the centuries, it has given to the festivals in honor of the mother of our Lord. While the present English Calendar has only two feast days of the first rank in her honor, namely, the Annunciation on March 25th (concerning which even Kellner says that it was "formerly regarded more as a festival of our Lord than of our Lady");[2] and the Purification on February 2d; and one black-letter day, the Nativity of the Virgin Mary, on September 8th; the Roman Calendar has five others, none of them of early origin. These are as follows:

1. **The Death and Assumption** (that is, her bodily taking-up into heaven), on August 15th, was instituted in the seventh century to celebrate her death only. The *Assumption* was a later addition, founded on a mere local legend. Kellner says, "Among the Latins the festival did not at first bear the name of *Assumption*, but was called *Domitio* or *Pausatio*," that is, *Sleep* or *Repose*.[3]

2. **The Immaculate Conception** on December 8th was "originally only a *festum Conceptionis B.V.M.* . . . If we consult the service-books printed before 1854," writes Kellner, "we find in them indeed on the 8th of December the *festum Conceptionis*, but the word *Immaculata* is nowhere found in the office for the feast."[4] Even when *Conception*, without *Immaculate*, was introduced into England in the twelfth century, Kellner adds, "two Bishops, Roger of Salisbury, and Bernard of S. Davids,

[1] Kellner, *Heortology*, p. 30.   [2] Ib., p. 231.
[3] Ib., p. 238.   [4] Ib., p. 241.

128 THE CHRISTIAN YEAR

held a synod, and forbade the feast as an absurd novelty."[1] So also, "the greatest doctor of the thirteenth century, Thomas Aquinas," states that the Roman Church did not celebrate even the feast of the *Conception,* though she tolerated the practice of other Churches which did celebrate it.[2] Moreover, it was not until Dec. 8, 1854, that the word *Immaculate* was added, by an ordinance of Pope Pius IX.

3. **The Name of Mary,** celebrated on the Sunday after the **Nativity of our Lady,** was "first authorized by the Apostolic See [Rome] for the diocese of Cuença, in Spain, in 1513."[3]

4. **The Presentation of our Lady in the Temple,** November 21st, was "introduced into the West" in the fourteenth century.[4]

5. **The Visitation,** July 2d. "The earliest traces of the feast are found in the thirteenth century."[5]

To these may be added the minor festivals of S. Mary of the Snows, The Espousals, The Seven Sorrows, The Rosary, Blessed Mary of Mount Carmel, The Expectation of Delivery, and still others.[6]

The extraordinary growth of the *cultus* of the Blessed Virgin is seen in the fact that *no festival of the Virgin* was celebrated in the Church of Rome before the seventh century.[7]

The commemoration of **All Souls** on November 2d does not appear until the ninth century, and "it was not until the close of the tenth century, under the special impetus supplied by the reported vision of a pilgrim from Jerusalem, who declared that he had seen the tortures of the souls suffering purgatorial fire, that

---

[1] Kellner, p. 250.   [2] Dowden, p. 55.   [3] Kellner, p. 264.
[4] Ib., p. 266.   [5] Ib., p. 267.
[6] See the *Catholic Dictionary.*   [7] Dowden, xv.

VARIATIONS OF NATIONAL CALENDARS 129

the observance made headway."[1] The **Feast of Corpus Christi** (Body of Christ), which now ranks as one of the highest festivals in the Roman Calendar ("a double of the first class"), was not officially adopted till the fourteenth century.

The Orthodox Church of the East has thirteen festivals of the first rank, with their corresponding English names as follows: Christmas, Epiphany, the Purification, the Annunciation, Palm Sunday, Easter, the Ascension, Pentecost, the Transfiguration, August 6th; the Repose of the Blessed Virgin, or Theotokos, August 15th; the Nativity of the Blessed Virgin, or Theotokos, September 8th; the Exaltation of the Cross, September 14th; the Entrance of the Blessed Virgin, or Theotokos, into the Temple, November 21st. Next in dignity to these are four festivals of high rank: the Circumcision, January 1st; the Nativity of S. John Baptist, June 24th; S. Peter and S. Paul, June 29th; the Beheading of S. John Baptist, Aug. 29th.[2] Four other days are observed in honor of the Blessed Virgin, July 2d, August 31st, December 9th (the Conception), and December 26th (the Flight into Egypt, supposed to be one year and a day after the birth).[3]

The Russian Calendar corresponds largely to the Greek or Byzantine, but there are of course in all calendars, besides these and the Roman, many commemorations of persons and events peculiar to each Church. "The Eastern Calendars contrast in a striking way with the Western in the prominence given to commemoration of the saints and heroes of the Old Testament. All the prophets and many of the righteous men of Hebrew history have their days."[4]

[1] Dowden, xiv.   [2] Ib., p. 135.
[3] Ib., p. 57.   [4] Ib., 137.

APPENDIX

THE LITURGICAL COLORS

DIFFERENT colors in altar hangings, vestments, stoles, etc., have been in use in the Church for many centuries, in order to mark to the eye the different character of the seasons and days of the Christian Year. This custom does not seem, however, to have been employed before the ninth century. Kellner says, "For many centuries the liturgical vestments were exclusively white. The writers of the Carolingian period were the first to remember that different colors were used in the vestments of the Jewish High Priest." [1]

The following account of the use of colors in the worship of the Church is taken in substance from "The Ritual Reason Why," by Charles Walker.[2]

The usual colors employed in modern times are white, red, violet, green, and black. According to the old English use, blue, brown, gray, and yellow were also employed. *White* is used on all the great festivals of our Lord, of the Blessed Virgin, and of all Saints who did not suffer martyrdom; white being the color appropriate to joy, and signifying purity. *Red* is used on the feasts of martyrs, typifying that they shed their blood for the testimony of Jesus, and at Whitsuntide, when the Holy Ghost

---
[1] *Heortology*, p. 428.
[2] J. T. Hayes, London, 1868.

descended in the likeness of fire. *Violet* is the penitential color, and is used in Advent, Lent, Vigils, etc. *Green* is the ordinary color for days that are neither feasts nor fasts, as being the pervading color of nature, or as typifying the Resurrection. *Black* is made use of at funerals, and on Good Friday. (Many, however, prefer to use violet at funerals.)

In the old English use, *red* was employed on all Sundays throughout the year, except from Easter to Whitsunday, unless a festival superseded the Sunday services. The same color served for Ash Wednesday, Good Friday, Maundy Thursday, and Easter and Whitsun Eves. *White* was employed throughout Eastertide, whether a Sunday or a Saint's Day. *Yellow* was employed for the feasts of Confessors. *Blue* was used indifferently with green; and *brown* or *gray* with *violet* for penitential times.

LEADING QUESTIONS FOR REVIEW OR EXAMINATION

1. What are some of the practical purposes of the observance of the Christian Year?

2. Give some reasons for such a system being in accord with human needs.

3. State some of the objections of the Puritans, and the answers of the "Judicious" Hooker.

4. In what relation does the Church of Christ, in its ministry and sacraments, stand to the Church of Israel, as described by Isaiah?

5. Give some account of the Ritual Year of the Church of Israel.

6. In what way did the Jewish customs of fast and festival affect the Church of Christ?

7. Give some examples of our Lord's loyalty to the Church of His forefathers.

8. What is there remarkable in this connection as to the traditional date of His Birth?

9. What is there still more remarkable in the exact day of His Crucifixion, and of His sending of the Holy Ghost?

10. Besides His thus honoring these ancient sacred days, what practical reason did our Lord have in deliberately choosing them for certain events in His own life?

---

11. What hints do we find in the New Testament of the beginnings of a Christian Year in the days of the Apostles?

12. In view of ancient Jewish custom what was there remarkable in the adoption of Sunday, or the first day of the week, instead of Saturday, or the seventh day according to the Jewish reckoning?

13. Show that the change was nevertheless not contrary to either the spirit or the letter of the Fourth Commandment.

14. What clue have we to those unwritten instructions which, S. Luke (Acts i. 4) tells us, our Lord gave to His Apostles during the great forty days between His Resurrection and His Ascension?

15. What evident reasons did our Lord have for not writing, or commanding others to write, a record of His teaching?

16. What great value does this give to "acts" of Apostles, and to "traditions," "customs," and "ways" of the Church while the Apostles were still living?

17. What test does S. John, in his epistles, apply to such traditions, customs, and ways?

18. Give some examples of traditions and customs freely practised by modern denominations of Christians, yet without any written command for them in the New Testament.

19. What then is the purpose of the New Testament as declared by S. Luke in Acts i. 4?

---

20. When was the term *Anno Domini* (Year of our Lord) by which we date our years adopted, and why was it not adopted earlier?

21. Explain the terms "Old Style" and "New Style," and give the reason for the error in the Calendar which occasioned them.

22. Explain the words Cycle, Golden Number, Paschal Moon, Dominical Letter, Bissextile, Ferial and Festal, Vigil and Eve, Octave, Movable and Immovable Feasts.

23. Name the chief seasons of the Christian Year, and the Immovable Feasts of our Lord, in their order.

24. While the Calendars of national Churches differ in details, in what main features are they all agreed, thus testifying to a common origin?

25. In what way is Christmas the fulfilment of the ancient feast of Tabernacles?

26. If, as is probable, December 25 and June 24 are the actual days of the only two Nativities observed, both of them miraculous, what striking fitness is there in their occurrence just after the winter and the summer solstice?

27. To what must we attribute the immense importance attached universally by the early Church to the proper observance of Easter?

28. What is the Church's rule, in the Preface to the Book of Common Prayer, as to the proper day for Easter?

29. Give the historical reasons why all the Movable Feasts are dependent on the position of the moon in the heavens, while the Immovable Feasts are dependent on the sun.

QUESTIONS FOR REVIEW OR EXAMINATION

30. On what grounds, and by what great Council of the Church, were the controversies concerning the keeping of Easter always on a Sunday, instead of on any other day of the week, finally settled?

31. How did it happen that the British and Irish rule for the day on which to observe Easter differed from that of Italy, and of the Eastern Churches?

32. Why has the Church always attached so much importance to the observance of Ascension-day, and in what special ways does she do so?

33. Why did the Grecian Jews give the name of Pentecost to what the Hebrew-speaking Jews called the Feast of Weeks, and of Harvest?

34. In what ways was the first Christian Whitsunday the fulfilment of, and a contrast to, the first Jewish Pentecost? (See Keble's *Christian Year*, Whitsunday.)

35. Why is Trinity Sunday a fitting close to the great doctrinal division of the Christian Year?

---

36. Give Hooker's reasons for the observance of Saints' Days, and some account of their origin.

37. What is meant by "Red-letter" and "Black-letter" days?

38. Why is a Saint's Day called *Dies Natalis*, or Birthday?

39. Explain the appropriateness of the dates for the only two Nativities in the Calendar, and for some of the Saints' Days.

40. What prominence is given, in both the New and the Old Testament, to the ministration of Angels to men, and what great practical purpose is meant to be served by this clear revelation?

41. What important truth concerning the condition of the departed does All Saints' Day help us to bear in mind?

42. Give some of the Scripture reasons for the practice of fasting, and for the observance of fast days.

43. Explain the words Septuagesima, Sexagesima, Quinquagesima, and Quadragesima.

44. Give some account of the origin of Lent.

45. Explain the words Passion Week, Holy Week, Palm Sunday, and Maundy Thursday.

46. Explain why Good Friday was originally kept as a feast day, and how the change in its observance came about.

47. What is the evident intention of the Anglican Communion in regard to celebrating the Holy Communion on Good Friday?

48. Give some account of the other days of fasting and abstinence appointed in our Calendar.

49. What is the strict meaning of the word Liturgy, and the word Use when employed in connection with a Liturgy?

50. To what does the identity of the leading features of all ancient Liturgies, in spite of many local "uses" and revisions, distinctly testify?

INDEX

A

Ab, 19
Abib, 16, 17, 19
Adar, 19
Advent, 54
Agnes, S., 76, 93
Alban, S., 76, 92, 95
Alexander, Archbishop, 41
Alexander, Mrs., vii
Alexandria, 47, 67
Almanac, 44
All Hallows, 87
All Saints, 82, 87-90
All Souls, 128
Ambrose, S., 33, 76
American Prayer Book, 62, 76, 90, 121
American Revolution, 44
Andrew, S., 78, 79
Angels, 55, 82-86
Anglo-Saxons, 68
Anicetus, Bp., 66
Anne, S., 96
Anno Domini, 44
Annotated Prayer Book, see Blunt.
Annunciation, 62
Antioch, 79
Antiochus Epiphanes, 19
Antiquities of the Christian Church, see Bingham.
Apostles as Jews, 22-27

Apostolic Constitutions, 33
Aquinas, 128
Arezzo, 69
Arian Heresy, 59, 73
Armenian Church, 53, 56, 58
Articles of Religion, 38, 69, 126
Ascension-day, 68
Ash-Wednesday, 104, 107-109
Assumption, 127
Assyrians, 3
Athanasius, S., 76, 77
Atonement, Day of, 19, 21
A. U. C., 43
Augustine of Canterbury, 68, 76, 107
Augustine of Hippo, 7, 12, 33, 58, 69, 76, 78, 112
Augustus, Emperor, 55

B

Bacon, Lord, 5
Baptism of Infants, 39
B. C., 43
Becket, 72
Bede, Venerable, 69, 76, 92, 95
Benedict, S., 94
"Beginning, From the," 38, 40
"Bible only," 40
Bingham, vi, 112
Bissextile, 50
Black-letter days, 76, 92-100

138   INDEX

Blunt, J. H., 96, 100, 108, 109, 112, 117
Boniface, S., 76, 95
British Church, see English Church.
Brooks, Phillips, 104
Butler, Archer, 1
Byzantine Calendar, 129

C

Cæsar, Julius, 45
Calendar, 43-46, 93-100, 124-129. See also Seabury.
Calends, 45
Candlemas, 55, 61
Canon of New Testament, 39
Canterbury, 125
Carême, 106
Carthage, 39, 112
Caswall, E., vii
Ceremonies, Value of, 35
Charles I., 99
Chisleu, 19
Christ a loyal Jew, 22-27
Christian Ballads, see Coxe.
Christian Year in New Testament, 11, 12
Christmas, 8, 9, 46, 54-56, 78
Chrysostom, S., 37, 55, 70
Church, Dean, 117
"Church, The," 30, 31
Circumcision, 58, 59
Civil festivals, 3
Clemens of Alexandria, 55
Colors, Liturgical, 131, 132
Columba, S., 36, 76
Communion, Holy, 32, 39, 55, 111-113, 116, 117
Conception, Feast of, 127, 128
Confirmation, 39
Confessors, 93-98, 132
Constantine, Emperor, 34

Conversion of S. Paul, 78
Coptic Church, 53
Corpus Christi, 129
Coxe, Bp., vi, 4, 43, 47, 53, 58, 92, 110, 113, 118, 121
Creed, Nicene, 39
Crispin, S., 98
Cross-quarter, 96, 98
Customs, 35-40
Cycle, 47, 67
Cyprian, S., 76, 77, 97

D

David, S., 76, 93
Dedication, Feast of, 18-20, 24
Denys, S., 97
Dies Domini, 49
Dies Mandati, 112
Dies Natalis, 78
Dionysius Exiguus, 44
Dominical Letters, 49
Domitio of B. V., 127
Dowden, Bp., v, 33, 51, 72, 100, 112, 115, 116, 128, 129
Duchesne, vi, 55-57, 62, 107, 110

E

Easter, 29, 32, 61, 64, 65-68
Easter Even, 117-119
Eastern Church, 72, 129
Ecclesiastical Polity, see Hooker.
Edersheim, 17, 20
Egypt, 3, 67
Ellicott, Bp., 80
Elul, 19
Ember Days, 120, 121
English Calendar, 93-100
English Church, 7, 62, 68, 76, 92, 107, 125, 126
English Parliament, 8, 46, 62
Epact, 48

INDEX 139

Epiphany, 46, 60, 61, 67
Esther, 19, 20
Eucharist, see Communion, Holy.
Eusebius, 34, 66
Eutychus, 34
Eves, 51, 123

F
Fasting, 101–105, 120–123
Fasts, Jewish, 19
Ferial and Festal, 50, 51
"First day of the week," 32
First Fruits, 71
"Form of sound words," 39
Fortunatus, 64, 110
Fourth Commandment, 32
French Church, see Gallican.
French Revolution, 3, 44
Fridays, 122
Froude, R. H., 101

G
Gabriel, 83
Gallican Church, 69, 125
Gelasius, 125
Gentile Christians, 32, 61
George, S., 94
German Church, 73, 95
Gerson, 127
Gervase, 72
Golden Number, 48
Good Friday, 64, 104, 114–119
Greek Calendar, 129
Greek Church, 46
Greeks, 3, 43
Gregorian Calendar, 47
Gregory, Dean, 117
Gregory Nazianzen, 70
Gregory I, or the Great, 68, 76, 94, 107, 125
Gwyn, 72
Gwynne, W., see Paradise.

H
Hallowe'en, 87
Haman, 18
Harvest, Feast of, 18, 71
Hawkins, Dr. E., 41
Helena, Empress, 69
Heortology, see Kellner.
Herbert, George, 101, 103, 106, 122
Hilary, 76, 93
Hippolytus, 55
Holland, Scott, 41
Holy Communion, see Communion.
Holy Cross Day, 97
Holy Thursday, 69
Holy Week, 110–119
Hook, Dean, 41
Hooker, v, 5–8, 75, 86
How, Bp. W. W., 75, 90
Hugh, S., 76, 98
Huntington, Bp. F. D., 8
Hypapante, 61

I
Ignatius, S., 39, 76, 79
Immaculate Conception, 127
Immovable Feasts, 52, 58
Ingathering, Feast of, 18
Invention of the Cross, 94
Irenæus, 66, 107
Irish Church, 36, 51, 68, 73, 76, 121, 123–126
Isaiah, 13
Israel, Church of, 11–21
Iyyar, 19

J
James, Liturgy of S., 87, 124
Jerome, S., 76, 97
Jesus, Name of, 59, 60

INDEX

Jewish Cycle, 48, 67
Jewish Hours of the Day, 34
John Baptist, S., 78, 95
John the Evangelist, 38, 94
John XXII, 72
Johnson, J., 116
Julius I., 55

K
Keble, J., vii, 59, 61, 62, 70, 87, 114, 118
Kellner, v, vii, 1, 55, 127, 128, 131
Ken, Bp., vii
Kersmis, 55
King, Bp., 117
Kingdom of God, and Heaven, 30, 31

L
Ladyday, 62, 127
Lammas, 55, 96
Leap Year, 49, 50
Lent, 101, 104, 106–119
Leo I, 125
Liddon, Dr. H. P., 7
Lights, Feast of, 18, 19
Littledale, Dr. R. F., 124
"Liturgical Proper," 92
Liturgies, 124–126
Lord's Day, 32, 33
Lunar Cycle, 47, 48
Lyons, 79
Lyra Apostolica, vii

M
Maccabees, 17, 19, 20, 24
Maclagan, Bp., 100
Malo, or Machutus, S., 98
Mamertus, Bp., 121
Marchesvan, 19
Martene, 116

Martinmas, 98
Martyr, Justin, 17
Mary, Virgin, 127–129
Mass, 55
Maundy Thursday, 111–113
Meton, 47, 48
Metonic Cycle, 47, 48, 67
Mi-Carême, 109
Michaelmas, 55, 82–86
Mid-Lent Sunday, 109
Milan, 33
Ministry of Grace, see J. Wordsworth.
Ministry, Holy, 38, 39
Missal, 125
Monica, 33
Months, 45
Moon, New and Full, 9, 18, 47, 67
Movable Feasts, 52, 64–74

N
Nadolig, 55
Name of JESUS, 59, 60
Natale, 55
Natalis Calicis, 112
Natalis Invicti, 57
Nativity, of S. John Baptist, 78
Nativity, The, 55
Neale, Dr. J. M., 124
Newman, Dr. J. H., 76, 77, 80, 82
New Moon, 18, 67
New Style, 46
New Year, 18, 21
Nice, or Nicæa, Council of, 39, 48, 67, 107, 116
Nisan, 16, 19
Noel, 55
Norman Conquest, 44, 125
Notitia Eucharistica, see Scudamore.

INDEX 141

O
Octave, 51, 72
"Old Style," 46
Olympiads, 43
Ordinal, 39
Oriental Churches, 46
Origen, 70
Origines du Culte Chrétien, see Duchesne.
Orthodox Church, 46, 129
Osmund, Bp., 125
Ostera, 65

P
Palgrave, vii
Palm Sunday, 108, 110
Papists' Conspiracy, 99
Pâques, 65
Paradise, 88–90
Parliament, English, 8, 46, 62
Pascha, 29, 65, 115
Paschal Lamb, 64
Paschal Moon, see Moon.
Passion Sunday, 110
Passover, 16, 20, 24, 29, 64, 115
Patrick, S., 68
Paul, Cathedral of S., 117, 126
Paul, Conversion of S., 78, 93
Pausatio, 127
Pentecost, 17, 25, 28, 29, 71
Perpetua, S., 76
Persecutions, 33
Pesach, 16, 65
Pfingstentag, 71
Picts, 36
Pius IX., 128
Poetry of the Christian Year, vii
Polycarp, 76, 79
Polycrates, 66
Prayer Book Commentary, 55

Pre-Lent, 106, 107
Presentation of Christ, 61
Primes, 48
Primitive Liturgies, 124
Pro-anaphora, 124
"Protestants, Religion of," 40
Purification, Feast of, 55, 61
Purim, 18, 20
Puritans, 7–9

Q
Quadragesima, 106, 107
Quaresme, 106
Quartodeciman, 65, 68
Quatember, 120
Quatre Temps, *Quatuor Tempora*, 120

R
Raphael, 83
Red-letter Days, 76, 77
Refreshment Sunday, 109
Religio Illicita, 33
Revision of Calendars, 124–126
Ritual Year, 1–6, 40
Rogation Days, 121
Roman Calendar, 127, 128
Roman Liturgy, 125
Romans, 3, 33
Russian Church, 46, 129

S
Sabaoth, 83
Sabbath, 9, 10, 15, 16
Saints' Days, 75–90
Salisbury, and Sarum, 62, 92, 125
Sapientia, O, 99
Saravia, Dr., 86
Saturnalia, 56
Scottish Church, 36, 54, 68, 125, 126

INDEX

Scripture, Holy, 39, 40, 41
Scudamore, 37, 116
Seabury, vi, 8, 45, 47–49, 67
Septuagesima, 107
Seventh Day Baptists, 31
Sexagesima, 107
Shakespeare, 5, 98, 109
Shebat, 19
Shipley, Orby, vii
Shrove Tuesday, 109
Silvia, Pilgrimage of, 69, 110
Sinai, 26, 29
Sivan, 19
Skeat, Prof., 120
Smyrna, 79
Socrates, 107
Some Purposes of Paradise, 83, 88, 89, 90
Sosigenes, 45
South, Dr., 8
Sozomen, 34, 107
Spenser, Edmund, 85, 86
Staley, v
Stanley, Dean, 63
Stedman, E. C., 120
Stephen, S., 79, 99
"Still Week," 110
Sulgwyn, 72
Sunday, 30, 31
Sunday Letter, 49
Sundays after Epiphany, 61
Sursum Corda, 37, 124
Swithin, S., 95, 96
Synagogue, 39

T

Tabernacles, Feast of, 18, 56
Tammuz, 19
Tebeth, 19
Temple, Destruction of, 19, 24
Temple, Worship of, 22, 39
Tennyson, vii, 85

Ter-Sanctus, 124
Tertullian, 17, 107
Thanksgiving Day, 90, 91
Theophany, 60
Theory and Use of the Church Calendar, see Seabury.
Theotokos, 129
Thomas, S., 78, 99
Thoughts on the Services, see Coxe.
Three Kings, Feast of the, 60, 61
Thursday, Holy, 69, 113
Tishri, 17, 19
Tobit, 17, 83
Torch-race, 37
Traditions, 35–42
Transfiguration, 58, 62, 63, **96**
Translation (Reinterment), **95–98**
Trinity Sunday, 72
Troas, 32, 34
Trumpets, Feast of, 18, 21

U

Unleavened Bread, Feast of, 17
Uriel, 83
"Uses," 125

V

Vernal Equinox, 67
Vestments, 40
Victor, Bp., 66
Vienne, 79
Vigil, 51, 123
Virgin Mary, see Mary.

W

Walker, Charles, 131
Walton, Isaac, 86
"Way, The," 35
Ways, 35–40

Weeks, Feast of, 18, 71
Weinachsfest, 55
Welsh Church, 68, 72
Westcott, Bp., 79
Whitsunday, 70–72
Williams, Isaac, vii

Wordsworth, Bp. John, vi, 78, 100
Wordsworth, William, vii, 1, 105

Y

Yule, 55

www.ingramcontent.com/pod-product-compliance
Lightning Source LLC
Chambersburg PA
CBHW072144160426
43197CB00012B/2239

FIJI FACTIONS

Brij V Lal

E PRESS

Published by ANU E Press
The Australian National University
Canberra ACT 0200, Australia
Email: anuepress@anu.edu.au
This title is also available online at http://epress.anu.edu.au

National Library of Australia Cataloguing-in-Publication entry

Author: Lal, Brij V., author.

Title: Turnings : Fiji factions / Brij V. Lal.

ISBN: 9781922144904 (paperback) 9781922144911 (eBook)

Subjects: East Indians--Fiji.
          East Indians--Fiji--Social life and customs

Dewey Number: 305.89141109611

All rights reserved. No part of this publication may be reproduced, stored in a retrieval syst
or transmitted in any form or by any means, electronic, mechanical, photocopying or otherw
without the prior permission of the publisher.

First published by the Fiji Institute of Applied Studies, 2008

This edition © 2013 ANU E Press

For
Rani (1990–2007)
Beloved of us all
from all her grateful staff

Turnings

Why do you come to tease and touch
unknown places in my heart
singing with love's sharp knife.

Enticing me to abandon respect and reputation
to exchange strange caresses
savour an explorer's taste.

Your words tempt my years
dismantle the careful structures
the house built of staid scholarship.

Yet I am drawn to you
you open different doors
leaving me disoriented, unsure which way to go.

As is the life of the leaves so is that of men.
The wind scatters the leaves
to the ground: the vigorous forest puts forth others,
and they grow in
the spring-season. So one generation of men
comes and another ceases.

Norma Davis, *Bush Pageant*
quoted in Margaret Kiddle, *Men of Yesterday*

Table of Contents

1	The Road to Mr Tulsi's Store	1
2	The Dux of Nasinu	13
3	Marriage	35
4	Masterji	53
5	Across the Fence	71
6	A Gap in the Hedge	95
7	In Mr Tom's Country	123
8	A Change of Seasons	151
9	An Australian Fusion	173
10	One Life, Three Worlds	197
	Acknowledgements	223

1

The Road to Mr Tulsi's Store

> Things past belong to memory alone
> Things future are the property of hope.

For a child growing up in postwar Fiji, an ambition to become a scholar or writer of any kind was certain to invite ridicule, derision, sarcasm, pity, disbelief, enough to be told to have your head examined. Everything — culture, history, politics, a raw, uncertain life on the outer fringes of poverty — everything pointed to the utter futility of pursuing that pointless ambition. Colonial Fiji had no place for thinkers and writers and dreamers. The country needed useful, pliant cogs for the colonial bureaucratic wheel, not half-baked babus who might ask tricky questions and create mischief. We were also taught from an early age that the humanities were for no-hopers. Bright children did law, medicine, pharmacy, accountancy and the hard sciences. That was the path to wealth and status and powerful connections, professions which brought fame and fortune to families, secured good marriages. And yet, despite that brutal perception, many of us managed to break out and do the unthinkable.

The ambition to be somebody other than a poor farmer's son, inheriting his father's world of debt and degradation in the large looming shadow of indenture came to us early. Like most Indo-Fijians of the time, we were struggling cane growers making a measly living on ten acre plots of leased land. The ten-acre plot was the handiwork of the CSR Company which dominated our life for nearly a century. The Company was the reason why we were in Fiji in the first place. With careful husbandry, the limited acreage could be big enough to make the farm economically viable, but certainly not big enough to make us too big for our boots. The CSR was no fool. We were encouraged to seek alternatives, to get some education and to look for a career. If we were lucky enough, we could end up as a junior bank clerk, a subaltern in the civil service, as a primary school teacher. Anything else was beyond our collective imaginative horizon.

We were lucky. The timing was right. By the late 1960s, Fiji was on its way to independence which came in 1970, the year I finished my high school. The new nation needed teachers, public servants, economists, accountants. Employment prospects looked promising. We were fortunate, too, that the University of the South Pacific opened in 1968, giving us an opportunity for higher education denied the earlier generations of whom only a few — perhaps ten or so a year, the cream of the crop — were sent overseas on government scholarships. The rest disappeared into the lower bowels of the burgeoning bureaucracy, to remain there obscure and hidden for the rest of their lives. The opening of the local university in Suva must constitute one of the turning points in modern Pacific Islands history.

The university was for me an enormously enlarging experience. We encountered new and strange people from other parts of the Pacific, at first an unnerving experience for a boy from a traditional Indo-Fijian family from an isolated rural community. We thought more about the world around us. We glimpsed the uncharted contours of our own local history. For the first time in our studies, we came across names of local people and places and events in printed text, which made everything real, authentic, and so enthralling. As I read more and matured, I realised that this is the life I wanted for myself, a life of reading and writing, causing consternation among some relatives and village people who somehow thought it strange for grown up men to spend all their time with their heads buried in books, engaged in 'waste time' activity. I was determined to become an academic, and an academic I have been all my life.

History was, and remains, my discipline. The emphasis at school and university was on acquiring information, not on learning how history was actually done. That basic knowledge, so necessary, was acquired late, privately, haphazardly. And gaps remain. History, we were taught, was contained in written documents. Facts spoke for themselves. A heavily footnoted text, closely argued, close to the facts, was the ideal we aspired for. Oral evidence could be used to spice the story, but it had to be chutney, not the main dish. It is not the kind of history I read or write now. I am comfortable with the notion that knowledge is tentative and partial, in both senses of the term. And I accept that those binary oppositions, which once seemed so sacrosanct, taken as given, are porous and problematic. I still profess my discipline, but I find writing about unwritten pasts creatively and imaginatively more intellectually challenging and emotionally rewarding.

It is not easy. Whatever their particular idiosyncrasies and predilections, historians have their basic rules of engagement. We may embroider, speculate, and generalize, but we should never invent. That is a cardinal sin. Our imagination is disciplined. We work with what has already existed. How we shape that into an argument, a thesis, a narrative, will depend on the values, assumptions and understandings we bring to bear on our work. The process of reasoning and argumentation must be transparent and referenced. But conventional historical approaches fail when dealing with unwritten pasts where memory is not properly archived and written documents do not exist.

The idea of writing history creatively came to me when I spent a year in India in the late 1970s gathering material for my doctoral dissertation on the background of Fiji's indentured migrants. For nearly six months, I lived in the rural, impoverished region in northeast India from which most of the indentured labourers, including my grandfather had come. I soon discovered that for me, India was not just another site for fieldwork, not just another country. It was the land of my forebears. We grew up in Fiji with its myths and legends, its popular sacred texts, with sweet, syrupy Hindi songs and films. Our thatched, bamboo-walled huts were plastered with pictures of film stars and various multi-coloured gods and goddesses. In short, India was an important cultural reference point for us. But I also discovered, while in India, how un-Indian I was in my values and outlook, how much I valued my own individuality and freedom, how Fijian I actually was. The Indian obsession with your 'good name' and status, the routine acceptance of ritually-sanctioned hierarchy, the addiction to horoscope, was beyond my comprehension. Out of that intense, emotionally wrenching experience came my first effort at quasi-creative writing as I sought to understand the confluence of forces which had formed and deformed me.

Encouraged, I began re-visiting in my spare time my unwritten village past. I began keeping a record of my conversation with people in the village, notes on things that seemed strange and curious. To give a concrete example. As a child, I was always intrigued by the presence of certain plants and other items at the prayer mound on auspicious occasions. Why bamboos, banana stems, rice and coconut? The village priest answered my queries squarely. Bamboo bends; it never breaks. So it was hoped would the family line. A banana plant is strong, prolific, difficult to kill off. Rice symbolises fertility. And coconut milk-water is offered to the gods because it is pure, uncontaminated by human hands. Why do we fast on certain days and not others? Why do Hindus worship the Tulsi plant? Why do we apply ash to our foreheads after prayer? Why did the pandit blow the conch a certain number of times while doing puja? Questions like that. An archive of anecdotes and information was slowly building up.

'Mr Tulsi's Store: A Fijian Journey' is the result of that private investigation over many years. My main aim was not factual accuracy in the conventional sense of footnoted facts to support a conclusion. Rather, it was to discover the inner truths of a community's life, its fears, hopes and aspirations, its rituals and ceremonies that gave it purpose and cohesion, the way it celebrated life and mourned its passing, the way it educated its young and taught them about their place in the world. In such an exercise, the historian's traditional concern for truth and understanding must mingle in some way with the approach of an imaginative writer to create a work of art. Non-fiction and fiction fuse to produce what I call 'faction,' that is, lived, factual experience rendered through a quasi-fictional approach. In this endeavour, the writer gives his solemn word to tell the truth as he sees it. He is on oath. The rules of engagement here are more flexible; there is space for imaginative reconstruction and rumination. But all within limits. The material is given to the writer, and preserving its essential truth (as opposed to its factual accuracy) is his primary concern. His 'characters' are not the inventions of the writer's imagination; they represent real people whom he has seen and observed or whose stories he has been told. The stories have their own inner logic and destination beyond the control of the writer; he is merely the vehicle for their expression. The narrative is not 'sexed up' for literary effect in the way it is in works of fiction. Its singular purpose is to tell the story as truthfully as possible, without hype or hyperbole.

The book is largely a conversation about the Indo-Fijian village life of my childhood. Tabia is an Indo-Fijian settlement like most others in the sugar cane belts of Fiji. It was where I was born, but now it is a labyrinth of evanescent memories. I would not have considered it in any serious way but for two things. The first was the effect of the coups in 1987 of which the Indo-Fijians were the main target. I had written generally about the coups as an involved, scholarly observer, but an opportunity to serve on a commission to recommend a new constitution for Fiji brought me close to the coalface of raw life they lived on the raw fringes, on the sufferance of others. The world which was once intimately familiar to me was vanishing. As the leases expired and Fijian landowners took their land back, people were leaving, uprooted and unwanted, to look for alternative employment. And modernity had touched life in numerous ways. There was greater contact with the larger world through radio, newspapers and television. People had migrated. The self-contained, struggling, isolated village of my childhood was gone. I wanted to record its old ways before it was too late.

    I wanted to do that partly for its own sake. But there was another motivation as well. Since the coups of 1987, more than 120,000 Fiji citizens, mostly Indo-Fijians have migrated, with about 40 percent of them coming to Australia. A new migrant, or shall I say transmigrant, community is forming. Children are growing up uncertain of their cultural identity, unsure of their way in the world. They are from Fiji but they are not Fijian; they look Indian but they are not Indian. My own children are no exception. Confused about who they are themselves, they are disbelieving of my own background. The world that formed me is alien to them. They find it hard to believe that I was born in a thatched hut on my father's farm, delivered by an illiterate Indo-Fijian midwife, that I grew up without electricity, running water or paved roads, that our generation's motto, a painful reminder of our unpredictable and uncertain condition was 'one step at a time.' They think their old man is hallucinating. 'Mr Tulsi's Store' is my attempt to connect today's disconnected and dispersed generation of Indo-Fijians with their historical and cultural roots.

    And what a story there is to tell. Here was a community, struggling to escape the shadow of servitude, cut off from its cultural roots and cooped up in a hostile environment, making do with what it could, starting all over again, all on its own. And yet managing in time to build up a cohesive and coherent community. Within a generation, a people who had begun with nothing, had achieved so much. How did that happen? What was their inner world like? What kept the community together? How did people cope with sorrow and grief? What brought joy to the community? How were disputes settled? How did people comprehend the forces of change which lapped the boundaries of the village? Things like that. A whole unwritten world waiting for exploration.

We were from the village, but immensely knowledgeable about the wider world, probably more than most children today. That was a legacy of our colonial education. In geography classes, children had lessons on Burma, Central China, Malaya, Singapore, Manchuria, East Anglia, the Midland Valley of Scotland, about Brittany, Denmark and the Mediterranean coastlands of France, about California, the Canadian maritime provinces, the corn belt of the United States, Florida and the St. Lawrence Valley, about the Snowy River Scheme, irrigation farming in Renmark, South Australia, the transport problems of the Cook Islands — they had transport problems there? — the relief maps and the sheep industry in New Zealand and Australia. I did not do well in geography because, among other things, I did not know the name of the highest mountain in Australia. It knew it began with a 'K', but wasn't sure whether it was Kosciusko or Kilimanjaro! Coolgardie and Kalgoorlie confused me. And try as I might, I just could not spell Murrumbidgee. What kind of name was that?

In history in the lower grades, we studied the rise of the Liberal Party in New Zealand, the importance of the refrigeration industry to New Zealand Agriculture, the Wakefield scheme, the Maori Wars, about John Macarthur, the merino sheep and squatters, the effects of the Victorian gold rushes and the rapidly expanding wool industry, topics like that. In higher grades, we left the antipodes to focus on the grand themes of modern history. So we studied the unification of Germany and Italy, the Crimean crisis and the First World War, the Bolshevik Revolution, the rise of Adolph Hitler and Mussolini, the emergence of the trade union movement in the United Kingdom and, briefly, the rise of new nations in Asia. Pupils ahead of us by a few years had studied the causes of the 1929 Depression, the Partition of Africa, the social reform policies of Gladstone and Disraeli, the significance of the 'Import Duties Act of 1931,' the Gold Standard, the Abdication crisis, the Irish Free State. Important and highly relevant topics like that. I am not sure we understood all that we read. But that was not the point. The history books opened up a window to a past — even if that past was remote to all of us — that connected us to a wider world and to other human experiences in history. The process of learning, I suppose, was more important than the content. The hunger to know more about the world has remained with me.

In our English classes at secondary school, we studied both literature and language. I did not take much to grammar, could not get passionate about infinite and intransitive verbs or about predicates and prepositions. The knowledge was necessary, I suppose, but very dry. Literature, though, was something else, good, solid, untrendy stuff, that would be dismissed today as hugely Eurocentric and elitist: novels, short stories, poems and plays by John Steinbeck (*The Pearl*), William Golding (*Lord of the Flies*), Emily Bronte (*Wuthering Heights*), Joseph Conrad (*Lord Jim*), William Wordsworth (*Daffodils*), Samuel Taylor Coleridge (*Ancient Mariner*), Edgar Alan Poe (*Raven*), DH Lawrence (*The Snake*), William Shakespeare (*Hamlet* and *Merchant of Venice*), TS Eliot (*Love Song of J. Alfred Prufrock* and *The Wasteland*). The list could go on endlessly.

Reading, broadening our imaginative horizon, was fun, but writing short composition pieces could be tricky. Try as we might, we found it hard to write a long meaningful paragraph on modern art, the astronauts, western films, the bottle drive or collecting for Corso, about the main stand at a flower show, the case for or against television in the home (we had no idea what this creature was), a climbing adventure, baby sitting or, of all things, a winter morning. In hot, humid Tabia! A few years ago, an old timer from Fiji living in Brisbane told me that in Senior Cambridge English exam, he was asked to write an essay on the 'Phenomenon of the Beatles.' Not paying heed to the spelling of the word and completely unaware of the existence of the musical group, he proceeded to write a long and meaningful essay on rhinoceros beetles which had recently ravaged Fiji's coconut industry! Coming from that kind of background, it was a miracle that we passed our external exams, and with good marks, too.

The metaphors of our own culture and allusions to our own past had no place in higher colonial learning, although in primary school we learnt Hindi and read about our ancestral culture and history, about various gods and goddesses and the heroes of Indian history. We had enough of the language to read the *Ramayana* and Hindi newspapers to our unlettered parents. The Hindi films, the Hindi music, the religious texts, the ceremonies and rituals we performed with mundane regularity, kept us intact as a community, connected us to our cultural roots, our inner selves. Thankfully, Hindi has remained with me as a hobby. I read and write it whenever I can.

But there was no Hindi in secondary school and beyond. I regret that now, but it did not seem to matter then. We were taught to learn and not question the value of colonial education. Still, for all their cultural biases, the western texts opened up new worlds for us, levelled hierarchies based on economic wealth and social status, and connected us to other worlds and other pasts. They awakened our imagination, emphasized our common humanity across boundaries of culture and race, and sowed the seeds of future possibilities. The idea of the fundamental oneness of humanity has remained with me. For me still, knowledge comes from reading. Words I read in primary and secondary schools about the importance of books lodged deep into my consciousness. 'Books are the storehouses of all the knowledge in the world.' The printed word still retains its magic. Reading and all that it entails — discovery, exploration, adventure — is my life. For that, I am grateful to my 'colonial' heritage.

As I saw the world of my childhood fragment before my own eyes, I knew that I had to write down what I knew, both as a record as well as a reminder. Easier said than done. 'Mr Tulsi's Store' is the most difficult book I have ever written. And, therefore, more rewarding. I am not sure that after this book, I will be able to enjoy the kind of history I was used to. I don't regret the rupture, although there is, of course, a certain sadness in parting company with someone who has been with you a long time, been good to and for you. That feeling of loss, though, is compensated by the thrill and challenge of setting sail in unfamiliar winds. Time will tell, as it always does, whether I took the right turn at the right moment. But it has been a bountiful journey so far.

Turnings is not a sequel to *Mr Tulsi's Store*, but it attempts the same task of capturing the lived experiences of unwritten lives. It too is about margins and movements, a record and a reminder of a time, a place and a people. It is intended for the reader interested in the stories of fragile lives half hidden from view, just beneath the surface, simmering, stories of ordinary folk — teachers, farmers, workers, children, rural shopkeepers, housewives — caught in the grip of turning times, forced to change, adapt and move on. The book is not for the smugly self-referential, endlessly self-indulgent and aggressively self-promoting literary critics who drain the humanities of their true significance through obscurantist prose without saying much at all. If *Turnings* fosters a deeper and more sympathetic awareness of the predicaments facing a people caught in circumstances beyond their control, my purpose in writing it will have been amply achieved.

Mr Tulsi's Store: A Fijian Journey was published by Pandanus Books (Canberra) in 2001. It was judged one of ten 'Notable Books' for the Asia-Pacific for 2002 by the committee of the San Francisco-based Kiriyama Prize and was 'Highly Commended' 2002 ACT 'Book of the Year'.

2

The Dux of Nasinu

> I am not a teacher: only a fellow traveller
> of whom you asked the way. I pointed
> ahead of myself as well as of you.

The death notice in the local daily read: 'Mr Kali Charan, 1935–1995. Teacher, Brother, Uncle to Many. Passed Away Peacefully. Sadly Missed By All. Cremation will take place at the Vatuwaqa Crematorium at 2 pm on Saturday.' The name rang a bell; the studio photograph in the notice confirmed it. A tall, fine-featured man, dark, bald, steady, penetrating eyes, in suit and tie. He was briefly the head master of Tabia Sanatan Dharam School in the mid-1960s but had reportedly left under a cloud.

About a hundred people turned up at the crematorium amidst warm drizzling Suva rain. Most were retired teachers, Mr Charan's ex-pupils and former education officers. Mr Shiu Prasad, Education Officer (Primary) in Labasa in the mid-1960s, spoke briefly. 'Kali did us proud,' he said. 'He was a stubborn man, but a man of courage and honour whose 'victims' are some of the leading citizens of our country. We are not likely to see the likes of Kali again soon.' His former students nodded silently in approval.

The priest in white dhoti and flowing kurta intoned some mantras from a book covered in red cloth before the flames claimed the body. Mr Prasad then walked towards me. 'Very good of you to come, doc,' he said. 'Did you know him?' he asked gently. 'Slightly,' I replied. 'I was in the early grades. Mr Charan taught the higher classes.' 'What a fine teacher, what a fine record,' Mr Prasad remarked. 'He could have gone places, but he chose to spend his whole career in the classroom.'

There was something about the old-timers like Mr Charan that demanded admiration and respect. Many like him in the early days would have come from poor farming backgrounds, the first ones in their families to complete primary school, carrying on their shoulders the hopes of everyone. Teachers were the pillars of the community, exemplars of moral behaviour and window to the outside world. After a couple of years of training at the Nasinu Teachers College, they would be posted to places far away from home, often among strangers, without the basic amenities in the living quarters, but never complaining, imbued with the spirit of public service. They saw teaching as both a profession as well as an honoured way of life. Mr Charan belonged to that pioneering generation.

I knew little about Mr Charan except that he had always remained a mysterious, forgotten figure in Tabia, his name erased from local memory. Mr Shiu Prasad was the person to ask. From Tabia, Mr Charan had been posted to Natabua Primary and subsequently to other major schools in the cane belt of Western Viti Levu, ending up, at the special invitation of the Education Department, as the headmaster of the perennially plagued Dabuti Primary, a Fijian school in Suva. 'We sent him wherever they needed a good teacher and wherever standards had to be raised.' Mr Charan preferred it that way. I was interested in Mr Charan's Tabia sojourn.

Mr Kali Charan would have been in his mid-thirties when he was appointed to Tabia, initially over the quiet objection of the School Committee. They wanted some one from Labasa. The village 'owned' the School and they wanted a headmaster of their own choice, some one who understood their needs and concerns and would heed their advice. Normally, the Education Department would have obliged, but good head teachers were in short supply. Mr Kali Charan had a rising reputation as being among the best and with an unblemished record. The Committee accepted the decision reluctantly. They had no choice.

Nausori-born, Mr Charan was respected by his peers for his probity and progressive views, stubborn but fair-minded, not a man to mince words or evade argument, ready to take the 'path less trodden,' as he liked to say. Admirable qualities, but in retrospect they seemed ill-suited to a place like Tabia. At the outer edges of Labasa's sugar belt, Tabia was a rolling cane-growing settlement of loosely-connected villages, predominantly Indian and Sanatani (orthodox) Hindu, conservative and acutely self conscious, wary of the outside world. The School was the struggling community's proud symbol of achievement, its marker of progress. They wanted it to mirror the cultural values of the community as well.

Mr Charan set the example at the school. He would arrive punctually at seven thirty, inspect the teachers' teaching schedule for the day, prepare notes for staff meetings, and make contingency plans for absentee teachers. At morning tea, he encouraged teachers to talk to him and among themselves, read the weeklies he had in his office. He would enquire about impending events in the community to acquaint himself with its affairs and to introduce himself. Teaching was his true vocation. There was no greater or better gift that teachers could give to the country than the instruction of the children, he would tell everyone. His philosophy of teaching was summed up in three words: 'Respect the Child.' Some teachers used to wielding the ruler or the belt demurred, but most welcomed Mr Charan's humane approach.

It was not with his colleagues at school but with the community that Mr Charan experienced friction when his liberal views clashed with their rustic conservatism. At an early general meeting, the village resolved that Hindu prayers should be made compulsory in every class before teaching began. All the usual arguments were advanced: imparting the right moral values to the children, preparing up-standing citizens, preserving tradition and culture. But there were objections. Arya Samajis, the reformist Hindus, wanted to know what kind of Hindu prayers would be said. And the Muslims were upset as well. 'We pay the building and school fees like everyone else. Why should our children be forced to recite Hindu prayers?' Some in protest threatened to withdraw their children from the school and send them to Vunimoli Muslim Primary some fifteen miles away.

The Sanatanis refused to budge. 'Muslims have Muslim prayers in their schools. Why shouldn't we have Hindu payers in ours?' they argued. 'And how many Samajis are there in the village? Two, three families? And they tell us what to do? Why should the tail wag the dog? That's the problem with us: slight push and we bend over.' It was a tense meeting full of erupting anger and heated words.

Mr Charan suggested a compromise. They couldn't insist on a daily Hindu classroom prayer. 'Education Department will not allow it. Public money is involved. Yes, our Sanatan people started this school, but it now belongs to everybody. It *should* belong to everybody.' That went down poorly with many: their *own* teacher telling them this! 'We should have one weekly prayer at assembly time. It will not be compulsory. The Muslim children can pray at the mosque across the road before coming to school.' It was a sensible suggestion grudgingly accepted by the Sanatanis. 'Okay,' they said, 'but the prayers should be on Tuesdays,' the Sanatan day of prayer. Mr Charan had no problem with that.

Soon afterwards, another crisis engulfed the school. A Hindu boy, sharing lunch with his Muslim friend, had surreptitiously stolen a few pieces of curried meat from his friend's lunch box (*sispaan*) while his friend had gone to get water from the tap. When his friend told him apologetically it was beef (*bull gos*), the boy got violently ill and told his father. The Sanatanis erupted and went straight to Nanka Boss, the village *agua*, leader and chairman of the School Committee. 'This is their revenge,' some people said, meaning the Muslims. 'They will not rest until they have destroyed us. First they did it in India, and now they are trying to do it here.' 'I thought beef was banned from the school compound. If it wasn't it should have been. This school is like our mandir,' Nanka told Mr Charan. Meat was not banned, at least not through formal notice. 'We must straight away expel the boy who brought beef. Teach them a lesson. They must know who runs this school. Whose place this is.'

'Kaka, it was a mistake, an accident,' Mr Charan explained. 'There is no conspiracy. Children bring goat, chicken, pork, everything to school.' 'Yes, but beef is beef,' Nanka replied adamantly. 'In case you Suva people don't know.' Mr Charan himself was a vegetarian. 'Expelling the boy will achieve nothing,' Mr Charan pleaded. 'You will ruin his future and there will be more friction among our people.' This was Mr Charan's first encounter with religious controversy. It had to be stopped immediately before things went too far. 'This is not the time for division among ourselves, Kaka,' he told Nanka politely but firmly. 'Don't bring religion into this. The partition of India has nothing to do with this. We have far more important things to worry about.'

'Beef will not be allowed, Master, whatever happens,' Nanka said defiantly, with an air of finality characteristic of community leaders. 'Otherwise you will have blood on your hands. Please tread carefully. I am telling you.' Being even handed, Mr Charan suggested that both beef and pork should be banned from the school compound. He rejected the call by some to have all meat banned. Cutting our nose to spite our face was how he put it. Once again, the committee reluctantly accepted Mr Charan's advice. Nanka was frustrated, as were many others in the village. They 'owned' the school but could not control what went inside it.

Nanka's relationship with Mr Charan, never warm, slowly began its downward slide. He had opposed Mr Charan's appointment in the first place. Suva always sent out the second best, the rejects and the misfits to Labasa, he suspected. The best remained in Viti Levu. Besides, he had a Labasa-born candidate, distantly related, in mind. Mr Charan, new and independent, was a potential threat. Before he had arrived,

Nanka had been the village's eyes and ears, their main contact with the world outside. Visiting dignitaries and aspiring politicians visited him whenever they passed through the settlement. He wielded considerable influence as the chairman of the local advisory council. He was the unofficial interpreter of local public opinion. He was Mr Tabia.

Barely literate, Nanka was proud of his home grown wisdom. Tabia was his world; he was possessive about it; he cared for none other. It gave him a sense of place and identity and purpose. He had seen it evolve from a small collection of rudimentary thatched huts scattered haphazardly over rough land, damaged by poverty and despair, a place where no father in his right mind would marry his daughter, into a slowly flourishing place beginning to be noticed and commanding respect. And he wanted that enclosed, culturally self-sufficient world shielded from undesirable outside influences. And that included teachers from Viti Levu.

Mr Charan was a complete contrast. He was, in his way, an intellectual, moved by a passion for ideas rather than by attachment to place. A private man, he read widely. He was aware of political changes taking place in the country. The talk of independence was intensifying. The colonialists were dragging their feet, raising objections, playing the race card, but he knew in his heart that Fiji would become independent in his lifetime. Mr Charan did not hide his political views. He subscribed to *Pacific Review* and *Jagriti*, the two main anti-colonial papers aligned to the Federation Party. He saw politics as an essential part of education. 'Today's children will be tomorrow's leaders,' he used to tell the teachers. 'Child Our Hope.'

Informal debates — *bahas* — were common in Tabia in the 1960s, at the local shop, during wedding celebrations and other social gatherings. Many Muslims, some Arya Samajis and a handful of Sanatanis supported the Alliance, some from fear of Sanatani domination and others from genuine conviction and commitment to the party's proclaimed multiracial platform. But this was solid cane country and proud Federation heartland, solid in support of immediate independence. The Alliance supporters were often derided as opportunists and turncoats and sometimes even excluded from social gatherings. Politics was peoples' passion in Tabia. Mr Charan said little about the Indian and Fijian supporters of the party, reserving his wrath for the *machars*, mosquitoes, the European colonial masters, blood-suckers who had kept the country divided for so long. The Federation Party's motto, 'One Country, One Nation, One People,' was his as well.

Nanka never directly confronted Mr Charan in the debates. 'I am with the people,' he would say when asked for his views, 'but some of us should be on the other side as well. That is good for us. Then, I will know all their secrets, *poll*.' To clinch the argument, he would cite passages from the Ramayan. 'Lanka was destroyed only because Vibhishan [Ravana's brother] revealed the secrets from the inside. *Ghar ke bhedi lanka dhaawe.* 'Blood will always be thicker than water.'

To the district administration officials, he presented himself as a true and trusted friend, spreading the good word on their behalf, slowly gaining ground in their favour – as long as they kept him as chairman of the advisory council. He was a master at playing the two sides against each other. Piped water here, a culvert there, and a bridge somewhere else meant a lot to Nanka and to his standing in the community. Mr Charan had the full measure of the man, knew all his plans in advance, his contacts. Mr Shiu Prasad's deputy was his eyes and ears in the civil service. And they thought only Europeans could play this game, Mr Charan chuckled to himself. Trumped constantly in front of people who looked up to him, Nanka grew ever more irritated with Mr Charan.

When the general elections were announced, Mr Charan went into a different gear. He was a Federation man, but more than promoting the interests of his political party, he wanted people in the village to get engaged with the wider debate about the future of the country. He invited the candidates, both Fijian and Indian, and local party leaders to speak at the school. He once even organised a debate on 'Should Fiji Become Independent?' at the school and got the teachers to take sides. School children carried notices of meetings and rallies to their parents.

Nanka objected. 'Master, the school should not get involved in politics,' he told him. 'I am hearing things from people. Not good things. People want education, not politics. Stick to teaching.' 'It is not politics, Kaka, it's the future of the country, the future of our children. If we don't talk about it, who will? The freedom to have the right to live as we wish: what could be more important than that?' School facilities were open to all parties and independent candidates. But that was precisely the problem for Nanka. Federation rallies were packed, complete with food and music and rousing, long-remembered speeches full of fire and pretended fury, but only a paltry few turned up to Alliance meetings and then, too, somewhat apologetically. The villagers welcomed the opportunity to listen to the leaders, and there was little Nanka could do about it. Mr Charan was becoming a bit of hero for bringing distant debates and national political leaders to them. Tabia had not experienced anything like this before.

But just when Mr Charan's star was on the rise, the world collapsed on his head. An insidious rumour spread that Mr Charan was having an affair with the head girl, Jaswanti. Embroidered with lurid details and salacious gossip, it became the talk of the village.'A head master doing this: *kaisan zamaana aye gaye hai: Pura Kalyug*, people said. What has the world come to! Having caught the village's attention, Nanka quietly stoked the fire. People believed him. He was their leader. The matter was reported to the District Education Office. Mr Shiu Prasad was asked to investigate.

'So, what did you find, Master?' I asked. 'It was the Committee's word against Kali's. Kali denied everything. I believed him. I know the man. But by then matters had gone beyond control. Some rascals were threatening to burn down his quarters and beat him up, even kill him. That was Tabia in those days. Wild place full of fanatical men willing do anything to defend the honour of their women. *Izzat* was big with those fellows,' honour. 'Probably still is.' A report was sent to the head office. 'They knew my position, but they were worried about the escalating tension, about Kali's safety. No doubt there were some of the old crusty types who disapproved of Kali's politics and were eager to get him removed. Frankly, I was glad to have Kali out of there myself.'

Tabia was never what it appeared to be. Calm, friendly and laid back to outsiders, its residents knew it as a place full of intrigue and machination and double-dealing. Feuds and intra-village rivalries had long racked the community. People were always seeking advantage for themselves at every opportunity. Arguments and disputes abounded about everything. 'We can have an argument with an empty house,' one of them had said, although when need arose and circumstances demanded, people put their personal differences aside for the greater collective good. The world saw that side of Tabia.

At Tali's shop one day, drinking kava with the usual gang — Mohan, Badri, Bhima and Piyare, I said, 'Mr Kali Charan died about a month ago, did you know?' I asked. 'Yes, we heard the news on the radio,' the group chorused. 'He taught me in class eight,' Piyare said, 'the best teacher I ever had. Arithmetic: he could add and subtract in his head, just like that. *Jaise machine*,' like a machine. 'And he was single,' Bhima added. 'His house was always open to senior students. We actually camped in his house when we were preparing for the Entrance exam.' 'Cent per cent pass that year,' Badri remembered. 'The proudest moment of my life.'

'He wasn't here long?' I asked. 'About two years,' Mohan replied. 'That's short.' 'Yes. He was forced to resign.' I remembered Mr Shiu Prasad's account. 'So what happened?' I asked pretending ignorance. Everyone looked at Piyare. 'Well, we all knew that Mr Charan was single and he seemed to be fond of Jaswanti.' 'Who wouldn't have been,' Bhima interjected. 'Yes, she was tall, very fair, very beautiful and very smart. *Poora Rani*,' like a queen. 'We couldn't touch her. We thought she would marry a lawyer or a doctor.' Piyare continued, 'She was snooty, ate her lunch by herself, didn't talk to anyone at recess. Sometimes, she would go to Mr Charan's quarters at lunch time.'

Word spread and gossip began. Whether Mr Charan or Jaswanti were aware, no one knew, but they were the talk of the senior class and, in time, of the village wags. 'One day, Jaswanti left class early mid-morning to go to Mr Charan's quarters,' Piyare remembered. 'Girl problem. We all saw a red patch on the back of her dress as she was leaving school that day. That was when it all exploded.' 'But Mr Charan was teaching,' I said. 'Yes, but he went home for lunch,' Badri replied. 'Anything could have happened. We didn't know about women's problem in those days.'

'Santu was the culprit,' Piyare said. Santu was Bhagwandin's son who had since left the village to go to Savu Savu with his entire family. Santu had a crush on Jaswanti. He told all his friends that he would marry her one day, come what may. Jaswanti was indifferent. She was cold towards him, never returning his gaze or smiles, always ignoring him at recess and in the classroom. Rumour about Mr Charan devastated Santu. 'What happened, *yaar*,' his friends teased him. 'Not good enough, eh.' 'Or not old, enough,' Piyare recalled the cruel teasing. *U to maange murga, tum to chota unda*. She wants a real man, and you are just a kid. All this got Santu.

'I will show them who a real man is,' Santu resolved. He confided his plan to his closest friend, Kamla. They would swear that they had both looked through the window of the quarters and seen Mr Charan and Jaswanti kissing and cuddling. No one would dare contradict them. How could they? *Aankho dekha haal*. Eye witness account. Everyone had seen the red blotch on Jaswanti's pink dress. And they all knew that Jaswanti went to the quarters for lunch by herself. Rehearsing the details to perfection, Santu and Kamla approached Nanka. They told him their concocted story. Nanka nodded. 'Don't mention this to anyone, or you might get into trouble. Police trouble. I will take care of it myself.' 'We had no idea of what was happening until it was all over,' Mohan recalled.

A hastily convened meeting of the School Committee sat at Nanka's house one evening, Sadhu, Harpal and Kasi.

'Very bad news, *bhai, samaj ke barbaadi*' they all agreed, bad for the community. 'What to do?' 'We must get rid of the master before he does more damage,' Nanka advised. 'But we must be very careful,' Kasi added. 'One wrong step, and we could lose government funds.' '*E to sub khaali sunaa huwa baat hai, bhai*, all this is hearsay,' Harpal said. He was the most independent-minded of them. 'We have to get to the bottom of this.' 'We will, we will,' Nanka promised.

The next day after school, Nanka got hold of Mr Ram Prasad, the senior teacher, as he was walking home to Laqere. 'What's the story, master?' he asked. And, then, winking at him, he said, 'It will be good to have someone from Labasa, one of our own, to head the school. Why should they always dump Suva people on us?' Ram had been bypassed the last time in favour of Mr Charan. 'Yes, Boss, we are all disturbed by what we hear. What can we do? *Hum log ka kar sakit hai?* The morale is down among us. One thing is sure, we have lost respect and confidence in the headmaster.' 'Good, good, you must tell this to the Committee.' Nanka encouraged him. 'They must hear this from the horse's mouth. You tell them, master, tell them good and proper.'

The School Committee met the following week. The first to be interviewed were select members of the senior class, among them Piayre and Badri. 'What did you hear and see,' Nanka asked from behind a huge desk, his large hairy hands clasped together. 'Nothing,' Piayre replied. 'Nothing? What? Who told you to lie? *Moor kaun bharis haye*, who has filled your head [with lies]. Did she go to the master's quarters or not?' 'Yes, sir.' 'How many times?' 'Two or three times a week.' Badri concurred. 'Did you see anything in class, boy?' Sadhu asked without Nanka's belligerence. 'No sir.' 'Did he favour the girl over you boys?' 'No Sir.' 'Then why does she come first all the time? 'Don't know sir.'

Santu and Kamla repeated their story to the Committee. 'Can you place your right hand on the Ramayan and swear that what you are telling is the truth?' Harpal asked. 'Yes, sir.' '*Court ke maamla hoye sake haye,*' Kasi reminded him, this could lead to a court case. The boys looked at Nanka, who nodded gently. 'Yes, sir.' 'Those two boys are from good families. *Accha gharana ke ladkan haye.* They will never lie to us. I know them,' Nanka reassured the other members. Master Ram Prasad told the Committee what he had told Nanka. 'The other teachers are very upset. All our reputations will be ruined,' he added. 'No good teacher would want to come here.' The Committee took Mr Ram Prasad at his word. None of the other teachers were interviewed. Nor was Jaswanti. 'The poor girl has had enough as it is,' Nanka told the Committee. 'We must spare her further pain.'

Then it was Mr Charan's turn. 'Master, what do you have to say?' Harpal asked. 'It's all lies,' he replied calmly. 'So everyone else is telling lies and you are the only one telling the truth?' Nanka asked, looking straight at him. 'Yes.' 'Why is it that the girl gets the highest marks and always comes first in class?' Kasi asked. 'Because she is the brightest of them all,' Mr Charan replied directly. 'She is the brightest student I have ever taught.' 'Is it true that she often goes to your quarters at lunch hour?' Kasi asked. 'Yes.' 'Why can't she study in the classroom, like the other children? And why is she the only girl who goes to your quarters?'

Mr Charan answered the question calmly. 'Kaka, this school prides itself on its good pass rate in the Entrance exam. It is among the best in Vanua Levu. You want good results.

You want the grant-in-aid increased. You want the classrooms upgraded, piped water improved.' The committee nodded uncertainly, not knowing what Mr Charan had in mind. 'All that depends on how well we do in the exams. Every mid-year, we do a selection test. Only those who pass are allowed to sit the Entrance exam. That way, we improve our pass rate. This year, Jaswanti was the only girl who passed, with six other boys. She needs all the quiet study time she can get. I have a spare desk at the quarters. She goes there during lunch time to study and complete her assignments. This is nothing new. I have done this for years, wherever I have taught.'

'What about the boys, or don't they matter?' Nanka asked. 'Yes. All the boys have been camping in the school for the last two months. I myself open the classroom at night and supervise them. They cook at my place. Good pass does not come easy, Kaka. *Khelwaar nahin haye*. We have to work doubly hard to make sure we do well. Jaswanti can't camp, she can't come to school in the weekends. That is why I have made a private arrangement for her to study at my quarters.' 'You know what people are saying, Master?' Harpal asked. He had been listening to Mr Charan's words intently. 'I don't know, Kaka. And I don't care. If I listened to all the rumours, I won't get anything done. These children and their success are my first priority, as they are yours. Or should be.'

'Don't mind, Master,' Sadhu asked apologetically, 'but why a man of your age and income never married?' 'I will tell you,' Mr Charan replied, pulling out his wallet and fetching a passport size photograph of his dead wife. 'This is Shanti. We were married many years ago, over fifteen. She and our little boy died in a car accident near Navua. See this?' Mr Charan said, pointing to a healed gash on the right side of his head.

'Since then, marriage and family have never entered my mind. I could have married if I wanted to, but no. I have other things to do.' 'I am very sorry to hear that, Master, very sorry,' Harpal and Kasi said. '*Kaka, Ishwar ki mahima haye*, it's God will.'

'Very smooth, like oil on water' Nanka remarked after the interview. 'I believe him,' Harpal replied. 'I think the man is telling the truth. Poor fellow.' 'We must not rush to judgement,' Kasi advised. 'Yes, yes,' Nanka interjected. Sadhu as usual had not said much during the entire proceeding. 'If we let Master go, who will replace him?' he asked. *Kaun aur haye*: who else is there? 'Master Ram Prasad is qualified,' Nanka replied instantly. 'I have spoken with him. He is ready to take over.'

Baat bahut duur tak phail gaye haye, Nanka said as they sat mulling, word has spread widely. *Ab hum log ke izzat ke sawaal haye*. It's the question of honour now. 'Master can always find another school somewhere, but this will be the end of everything for us.' And then he reminded the others of all the hard work and sacrifice the people of the village had made to get the school started. *E samaj ke amaanat haye*. It should not be allowed to come to nothing. People have chosen us to uphold the *izzat* not only of the school but of the entire community. Let us not forget that. We are the custodians of their trust.'

A week later, the School Committee went to the District Education Office and told Mr Shiu Prasad about Mr Charan. 'We haven't taken this decision lightly,' Mr Nanka assured him earnestly. 'It is our unanimous decision. The whole community is behind us.' Mr Prasad went to the school and talked to the teachers. Apart from Ram Prasad, others were not forthcoming. They all seemed distressed by the whole affair though no one spoke in Mr Charan's support either. It was too risky to go against the tide in a place like Tabia.

Mr Charan himself denied an impropriety. 'What a silly thing to do, Kali,' Mr Shiu Prasad told the headmaster, like the old friend that he had long been, 'letting a girl come alone to your private quarters at odd hours. This is not Suva, yaar, this is Tabia, just out of the jungle. I thought you had more sense than this, the Dux of Nasinu. No, as always, blind to everything but to your principles. Pig-headed. Your own worst enemy.'

Mr Charan was unrepentant and unapologetic but appreciated Mr Shiu Prasad's candour. 'I have done nothing wrong. We have got to break these ancient attitudes. I mean, here's the brightest student I have had in years. Given the opportunity, she will go places. Probably the first doctor or lawyer from this village. And all I did was to give her a little helping hand. Why won't they believe me? May be I should have asked her parents or something, but I never thought of that. I never thought this was a big deal. '

'These people are just beginning to walk, yaar, and you want to make them run?' Mr Shiu Prasad reminded him. 'Education is for boys, Kali. Girls are sent to school to learn the alphabets to become good wives and mothers. Remember Nasinu? The first priority for girls was to find a good husband.' 'Yes, and all that talent lost to mindless domestic, *gharana-grahsthi*, duties.' 'This is not the place for your kind of values and ideals, Kali,' Mr Shiu Prasad said. 'This is a grant-in-aid school, and there is little we can do. The Committee's views will have to prevail.'

'So what happens now? I leave, and this place goes on about its rotten ways?' Mr Charan asked. 'Pretty much,' Mr Shiu Prasad replied. 'Ram Prasad will be appointed acting headmaster next week. There's an opening for a senior master at Natabua Primary. It's yours for the asking.' 'I have no choice, have I?' Mr Shiu Prasad shook his head. 'Kali, this place does not deserve you. You have far great things ahead of you.' He could fight the case, take the School Committee to court. 'What will that achieve? More bad publicity for you and the school. You will win, but will Tabia, or Labasa for that matter, really accept you back? *Kaun faaida*, What's the use.'

'There are hundreds of Tabias around the country, villages steeped in wilful ignorance,' Mr Shiu Prasad continued. 'Our country needs us now. We have a big role to play, to get things right for the future. For our children. This is a small set back for you, Kali, but we all know the truth.' 'Except the Education Department,' Mr Charan replied. 'Well, that's the circus on top of things happening in this country. If I am to be honest with you Kali, this is a blessing in disguise for us, for the Indian community. You will achieve much more in Viti Levu than you will ever here.' He reminded Kali of President's Kennedy's stirring words at his inauguration. Then Mr Shiu Prasad recited a couple of lines of a Talat Mehmood song they used to sing at Nasinu: it was their motto:

> *E zindagi ke raahi, himmat na haar jaana*
> *Beete gi raat gham ki, badle ga e zamaana.*

> Oh traveller through life, do not lose hope
> This night of anguish will pass, the world will change.

Mr Charan was depressed and frustrated, but unbowed. He had done nothing wrong. There was nothing to hide. A couple of weeks later, he left for Lautoka.

A sad end to a promising career of such a dedicated man in Tabia I found distressing. It was Tabia's unlamented loss. 'Why didn't people speak up?' I asked our yaqona group. 'This place runs on rumour and gossip, Bhai,' Mohan said. 'Once the word spreads, it catches on like wild fire. *Koi ke muh men lagaam nahi sako lagao,*'can't clamp everyone's mouth. 'People are very protective about their girls. One whiff of scandal, and the family's reputation is ruined forever.' 'Teachers are like parents in our community,' Bhima said, *Baap-Mai.* 'We look up to them.'

Which is why rumours about Mr Charan and Jaswanti were godsend for Nanka. In no time, rumour was transformed into unassailable fact. 'This is not the only evil thing the headmaster has done,' he told people. 'It is better that you don't know the full story. Otherwise who knows what might happen.' Quietly, he let it be known that some female teachers had complained to him about the way Mr Charan looked at them, called them into his office at odd hours, stood close to them. Master Ram Prasad had complained of being a marked man, his well deserved promotion blocked. And so it went.

People believed Nanka. After all, he was their *agua*, village leader. He had been their eyes and ears all these years. Many attributed the village's undoubted progress to Nanka's tenacity and connection to the local officialdom. People appreciated his generosity, his willingness to donate money and goods for local causes. As a mark of respect, people never called him by his first name (no one knew his surname) but always addressed him as 'Nanka Boss.'

But Nanka, being Nanka, had his own plans. He had his eyes on Jaswanti as the wife for his son, a car mechanic in town. Jaswanti was the only child of Mangal, a big rice farmer in Laqere across the river. As soon as the rumours spread, Nanka approached Mangal and asked him to withdraw Jaswanti from school. *Keechad uchhade ke koi ke mauka nahi deo.* Don't give anyone a chance to throw mud at you. 'Jaswanti is like my own daughter.' Then he proposed marriage for his son to Jaswanti. Jaswanti left school before the final exams, and was married a few months later. All the six boys passed their Entrance Exams and went to Labasa Secondary and Sangam High for further education. One or two made it to university.

'Did Mr Charan ever talk about his Tabia days?' I asked Mr Shiu Prasad as we sat talking a few days after the cremation. 'Oh no, not Kali,' Mr Prasad replied. 'He was stubborn as a mule. Nothing could break his spirit. And nothing did. That is why he went on to become one of the most admired primary school teachers of this country.' 'And Jaswanti?' 'Yes, just before he left Tabia he said to me, 'Shivo, How many Jaswantis will we have to sacrifice before we come to our senses, before this place changes, before we break the shackles of the past? He was very idealistic in that way.'

'No feelings for Jaswanti?' I asked. 'Kali was Kali. He never re-married. I think losing his young wife and child haunted him. He blamed himself for their deaths.' 'Did you speak to Jaswanti?' 'Yes, I did.' 'And?' 'There was something there, but it is hard to say. I mean, this young bright girl in that god forsaken place, meeting a man who made her feel important, saw potential in her and encouraged her, tried to nurture her talents: it is only natural that she would appreciate the attention, don't you think?' I nodded in agreement. 'Yes, it is easy to fall under the spell of such a man.'

I wanted to meet Jaswanti. There was something about her that aroused my curiosity. I asked our yaqona group about her whereabouts. 'They left the village several years ago,' Bhima and Piyare told me. No one knew where. It was rumoured that Jaswanti had left her husband after leaving the village, but no one could be certain. After Nanka's death, the family squabbled about property and there was a court case. *Sab chittar bitthar gayin*, Badri said, they all scattered. That was the way things were with many Indo-Fijian settlements, wrecked by disputes about land boundaries, damage to crop caused by straying cattle, heated words about social trespass, the encroaching tentacles of village moneylenders. The comforting cohesiveness of old was disappearing.

Jaswanti was gone, but not forgotten. 'She started the first *Mahila Mandal* here,' Piyare recalled, village women's association. 'And the *Tabia Patrika*,' Bhima added, the monthly newsletter. The women held cooking and sewing lessons, talked about improving hygiene in homes and paying attention to the education of girls. She had even managed to get herself a place on the School Committee, the first and for years the only woman to do so. It was largely for the education of her own daughters that Jaswanti had left the village where old views and values about the role of women still held sway and unlikely to change anytime soon. 'I hear that one of Jaswanti's daughters is studying medicine in Suva,' Bhima said. That news would have made Mr Kali Charan very proud.

3
Marriage

Bhola and his wife Sukhraji were resting on the verandah of their lean-to house one hot afternoon when Nanka, their neighbour, dropped by. '*Ram Ram bhai*,' he said to Bhola, greetings, as he parked himself on a wooden crate. Sukhraji dashed to the kitchen to make tea as Bhola and Nanka engaged in small talk about village affairs. When Sukhraji returned with three enamel cups of red tea, Nanka turned towards her and asked, 'Can I say something *Bhauji*?' 'Yes, *Babu*.' Sukhraji never called village men by their name, always called them *Babu* or *Badkau*, husband's younger and older brother respectively. That was the village way. 'Dewa is ready for marriage,' Nanka said, adding mischievously, 'And you are not getting any younger either. Bhola *bhai*, you listen as well.' Bhola listened, but didn't say anything. 'You need someone besides Bhola *bhai* to look after you.' Nanka was what people in the village called a *muh-chutta*, a loudmouth, a harmless joker, an impotent flirt, not to be taken seriously.

'What are you people for,' Sukhraji replied instantaneously. 'He is your son too.' This was village talk. 'Why don't you people do something about it instead of putting all the responsibility on just the two of us.' 'Was waiting for the word, Bhauji' Nanka replied. 'All go now. But remember one thing, I will be the first to embrace the Samadhin,' the bride's mother. *Samdhin se chaati sab se pahile hum milaib.*'You can do whatever you want with her,' Sukhraji replied smiling. 'Just find us a good homely girl for our boy.'

Dewa's future had been on Bhola's mind for some time too, but he had not said anything to anyone. He himself had been married at seventeen, and Dewa was now nearly twenty. 'You don't want to be a grandfather to your own children,' Bhola remembered old timers saying. An unmarried man at that age caused comment, and Bhola had several younger children to think of. Besides, who knew when the passion of youth might lead him astray. Bhola thought of Asharfi's son Jhikka, who had made Dhanessar's daughter pregnant. The poor girl was sent away to another village, presumably to lose the child, but her brothers took their revenge. One night, as Jhikka was returning from a Ramayan recital, they ambushed him, beat him unconscious and threw him into the roadside ditch. No one said a word. No one volunteered information about the culprits to the police or the *panchayat*, the village council, and no one was ever apprehended. That was village justice. Rough and brutal and effective. Jhikka survived, but only as a chastened nervous wreck. Dewa was a good boy and Bhola wanted things to remain that way.

That night after dinner, Bhola and Sukhraji talked about Dewa. 'What Nanka Babu said is true,' Sukhraji said. 'I am getting on. We need another helping hand in the house.' 'Don't believe that flatterer,' Bhola replied, edging closer to his wife. 'He says that to everyone to make himself feel younger. You have at least another two sons in you.' '*Chup*. Hush. What if the children hear such talk.' The 'children,' teenagers, were sleeping in the adjacent room in the huge thatched house. 'I want a break from all this routine. I want to visit relatives I haven't seen for years. Before it is too late. And grandchildren would be nice too.' Everyone else their age in the village was already a grandparent.

Grandchildren! How fast time had flown Bhola thought. It did not seem that long ago that he himself had got married. They had suffered so much together: the death of two infant children, the disintegration of the joint household, the betrayal of family and friends, the poverty. But through all that the family had remained intact. His family was all that he had. He was immensely proud of that, and of his wife who had been by his side faithfully all these years. 'Remember when we got married and you came here as a *dulhain*, young bride for the first time?' Bhola asked Sukhraji. 'Do I remember? I remember everything as if it happened yesterday...' Sukhraji's parents lived across the Laqere river at the edge of the cane settlement by the sea. They had moved there a few years after the '*Badi Beemari*,' the influenza epidemic of 1918. No one knew much about them, because they were not cane growers. Her father, Chiriya, was a *girmitiya*. He had been a train driver for the CSR on the Tua Tua line, but that was all that was known about him. How he became a train driver, when he came to Fiji, from which part of India, were all lost. Like so much of the history of his people. (Her mother died when Sukhraji was still an infant). After her father's death sometime in the 1930s, she was raised by various distant relatives. They were good to her, but she knew her place in the family. She cooked, cleaned and worked on the farm to make herself useful and kept out of peoples' way.

If Bhola was worried about Dewa, parents of girls faced a much bigger problem. No fate was worse for a family than to have a girl who dishonoured its name. *Izzat* or honour is big among village people. Girls were married off soon after puberty. It was so in Sukhraji's case. One day, her aunt said '*Ladki badi hoi gai hai.*' The girl is ready for marriage. 'Ready' meant the beginning of menstruation. Ganga, the village leader, was approached. Feelers went out and Bhola was identified as a good prospect. The family had a good name: no thieves or scoundrels or jail birds in the family closet, and caste status was compatible: one was a Kurmi, the other Ahir, both 'clean' cultivators. Family elders met and the marriage pact was sealed with an exchange of gifts. Sukhraji was betrothed at thirteen, and married two years later. Sukhraji came into a family of complete strangers, married to a man, a boy really, she had never seen before. She carried on her innocent shoulders the hopes of her entire family, knowing in her innocent heart that she could never return to them no matter what her fate in the new home. No one would have her back. The gift of a girl-child, *kanya daan*, once given can never be returned. The break was final.

At first things didn't go well for Sukhraji. She was dark though with fine features, whereas Bhola was fair, like his mother. They called her *karikki*, the dark one, derisively. Her mother-in- law, whom she called 'Budhia,' 'old woman,' was a real terror, a real *kantaain*, Sukhraji remembered. What went through Budhia's mind no one knew. Perhaps in old age, herself uprooted and displaced, she was trying to recreate the remembered world of village India where mothers-in-law reigned supreme. 'Have you forgotten how you used to beat me so mercilessly as if I were a mere animal?' Sukhraji asked Bhola with a trace of bitterness. 'Cleaning and sweeping after everyone had already gone to bed. And getting up at four in the morning every day. Food had to be cooked just the way she wanted it, to perfection. One mistake and the terrible names she called me: *chinnar, kutia, haramin*.' Sukhraji turned directly towards Bhola, 'You never stood up for me, not once, even when I was innocent. You always took her side. Always the dutiful son. Remember how they taunted me when I did not become pregnant for three years? Barren woman, they said. Remember the day she gave me a piece of rope to hang myself so that you could marry another woman and have children. You stood there and said nothing.'

Bhola listened to this sudden, unexpected flood of memories with an aching heart. There was no reply to Sukhraji's bitterness and anger. She had spoken the truth. Yes, he was a dutiful son. He never stood up to his parents, especially his mother. He was her only son. Nothing, no abuse was worse for a man than to be called a hen-pecked husband. Keeping one's wife in line, even if it meant thrashing her occasionally, was one way of showing that he was the master of the house, the man in-charge, retaining his position in his mother's eye. Bhola reached for Sukhraji's bangled hands. 'Times were different, then. But all that is in the past now. We have built up our life together from nothing. This house, our children, our farm, our good name: all this we have done together. All this is just as much yours as it is mine. God willing, we will be together for a long, long time.'

Sukhraji was calmer now. The words had drained her. This was the first time, now that she herself was about to become a mother-in-law, that she had spoken so candidly about her traumatic past. This moment of release of the truth of their relationship somehow made her feel stronger, freer.

She was not bitter. Somewhere in her heart, she had forgiven her husband for his violent ways. Bhola had been a good husband and father. In any case, he was all she had.

A week later Bhola's older half-brother, Ram Bihari, came to visit him. Ram Bihari lived in Wailevu about seven miles away, but as the eldest, he was still the family leader. The family, the entire extended family all over Labasa, never took a major decision without his consent or involvement. He was there whenever he was needed. The family's public face and spokesman. After the customary cup of black tea, Bhola said, 'Bhaiya, time has come to get Dewa married. He is ready for a new life. If you know of any family...' Before he had finished Ram Bihari interjected. 'I know, I know. That is why I have come here today. Nanka told me about this in the market the other day.' Bhola was relieved. 'November might be a good time,' he said. 'By then, the rice will have been harvested and the cane cut with enough money for the expenses. And we will have about six months to make all the necessary arrangements.'

'I don't know anyone in Boca or Bucaisau,' Ram Bihari continued. 'There may be a few families in between I may have missed, but they can't be very important if I haven't heard of them. You know me.' Bhola did. Ram Bihari was well known throughout Labasa, knew everyone who mattered. He was president of his village Ramayan Mandali, member of the District Advisory Committee, patron of the Wailevu Primary School. He will find someone suitable for us, Bhola thought to himself and was relieved

'We are not looking for anyone special,' Sukhraji said from the back room, her head respectfully covered with a light shawl. Women always did that in the presence of strangers or family elders as a mark of respect and modesty. 'Education is not important. What will we do with an educated daughter-in-law in a home like ours? And money is not important either. Girls from rich homes expect too much and cause trouble.' What Sukhraji wanted was someone from a respectable family, who would be a home builder, knew about *ghar grhasthi*. And then she thought of something else. 'As long as she is not *langdi-looli*, deformed, we will be happy. Someone wholesome like Guddu's wife.' Guddu was Ram Bihari's eldest son.

Ram Bihari said after finishing his cup of tea. 'I have heard of someone in Dreketi,' he said. Neither Bhola nor Sukhraji knew much about the place or anyone there. There was no sugar cane there, and people lived a subsistence lifestyle. '*Ek dam Chamar tola*, a real backwater,' Bhola laughed. 'Don't laugh, Bhola,' Ram Bihari chided his younger brother in his characteristic big-brotherly way. 'I know the place, I know people there.' Bhola had forgotten. Ram Bihari's oldest daughter was married in Seaqaqa, half way between Tabia and Dreketi. 'It is just a matter of time before Dreketi goes places. Tabia will be nothing then. I have heard about sugar cane farms opening there in a few years time. Then the Chamars will become Brahmins!' '*Na bhaiya, khali khelwaar men bol diya*, I was just joking' Bhola said, slightly embarrassed.

Ram Bihari of course had his own agenda. Another family connection in Dreketi would be good for him, more *daru-murga*, alcohol-meat, parties. The people there had a legendary reputation for hospitality, happily hosting visitors for weeks on end. If there was a 'Friendly North,' it had to be Dreketi. And his daughter would have another family close by to visit. Ram Bihari had Kallu's family in mind. He knew them well. He went there whenever he visited his daughter in Seaqaqa. Kallu had five daughters, only the eldest of whom was married. Ram Bihari was smitten with Kallu's wife, Dhania. She was appropriately named after the spicy coriander plant, quick, witty, seductive and flirtatious. Openly so. She bantered, teased, and tempted with suggestive conversation. Dhania made men dance to the click of her fingers. Given a chance, I might be in luck, Ram Bihari thought to himself.

One day Ram Bihari pointed to the unploughed field next to the house. 'These fields haven't been ploughed for a while it seems. You could get a good crop of maize and lentils before the rainy season starts.' Dhania smiled without batting an eyelid. 'That's true. But what can I do? We have useless men here. They don't seem to have strong ploughs in the village any more. Maybe you could stay a few days and plough the fields.' The sensual innuendo was rustic and direct and arousing. Ram Bihari smiled at the thought. On another occasion, Ram Bihari remarked about the number of milch cows in the village. 'It's such a waste,' Dhania replied. 'Men here don't know how to drink milk.' Definitely good prospects here!

Once Kallu asked Ram Bihari about marriageable boys for his daughters. It was then that Ram Bihari had thought of Dewa. 'My daughters are my sons,' Kallu said proudly. They worked the fields, even ploughed the land, and cooked and cleaned at home. 'They know everything about homemaking'. What he didn't say was the daughters were also headstrong, independent and sensual free spirits. They were their mother's daughters. It was because of this reputation that people were reluctant to marry into the family. Ram Bihari overlooked this. 'I will do everything for you *bhai*. I feel like we are *rishtedaar*,' he said. Like relatives already.

'You should meet the family yourself, Bhola,' Ram Bihari told his younger brother. 'We will all go,' Bhola replied. Two weeks later they hired Mallu's car and drove to Dreketi, Bhola, Ram Bihari, Nanka and Chillar, a village friend. Sukhraji wanted to go as well, but Ram Bihari objected. Bhola said nothing. 'Arranging a marriage is men's business,' Ram Bihari said with the authority of a family elder. 'Besides, it is a long trip.' Neither was Dewa invited, which was not unusual on the first visit. 'This is just the first visit, beta' Ram Bihari told Dewa. 'Of course, you will meet the girl when things get firmer.'

The party received a great welcome. Kallu spared no expense to see that his guests received the very best. A goat was slaughtered. Kava and rum were in plentiful supply. Dhania maintained a discreet distance after greeting the guests but smiling glances and seductive winks were exchanged with Ram Bihari. Munni, the girl to be married, brought in tea and savouries. 'This is the girl,' Kallu said. No one looked up. It was not the thing to do. Besides, there was little to see. Munni's face was covered with a white shawl. 'God willing, she will be our daughter soon too,' Ram Bihari replied. As the *agua*, he did all the talking. He was in his element. Bhola, always a reserved man, hardly said a word. Things turned out exactly as Ram Bihari had hoped. A return visit was arranged 'to see the boy.'

Only when the marriage arrangements were almost finalised that Dewa got to see his future bride. Kallu, Dhania and Muni travelled to Nasea on the pretext of seeing their relatives. There was a remote, very remote, chance that Dewa might decline. For a girl to be rejected at that stage would be disastrous for the family. Questions would be asked and reasons for the failure speculated upon endlessly. Kallu did not want to do anything that might jeopardise the chances of his other daughters. Dressed for the occasion in tight new green terylene pants, red shirt and black shoes, Dewa was nervous. Over buttered bread and tea in Long Hip's cafe, he cast furtive glaces at Munni. She smiled shyly, showing her fine features. Wheat brown skin, full lips, perfectly proportioned nose and properly covered but ample bosoms. Dewa liked what he saw; he was hooked. Sukhraji, too was pleased. Munni, shy and dutiful-looking, would make the ideal daughter-in-law. The marriage pact was sealed. *Maarit pukka.*

Big wedding for the big boy,' Nanka said when Ram Bihari came to see Bhola a week later. 'The biggest the village has seen,' Ram Bihari promised. 'Big *dhoom dhadaka*. I will bring the whole of Wailevu down for the wedding. Then they will see what our family is made of.' Showing off the extended family was all a part of weddings. A display of family strength and solidarity. And it would do Ram Bihari's reputation no harm either. Bhola was anxious. He was not tight, but was not ostentatious either. Friends and neighbours in the village and extended family members was all that he had in mind for the occasion. A three-day affair, not a week-long celebration. He considered extravagant marriages a waste of time and money. He would have to borrow money to cover the expenses. And he had to think of his other school-age children. Yet Dewa was his eldest son, and this was the first marriage in the family. Besides, who was he to question his elder brother's decision?

The wedding was a big affair alright. Hundreds of people came. Three buses were hired to take the bridal party to Dreketi, with two taxis for the immediate family. For his part, Kallu too spared no expense. The best dancers and *qauwwali* singers were hired. Yaqona was in ample supply, and the food was plentiful and delicious: kadhi, puri, jeera dhall, kaddu, tamarind and tomato chutney. The guests were impressed, even seasoned wedding attenders. 'So when's the next wedding, Bhola *bhai*,' one said. 'You have struck gold. Everyone deserves a *rishtedaar*, relation, like this.'

Sukhraji was emotional all week, a little sad at the thought of 'losing' her son to another woman. But she was composed when the bridal party returned. Munni looked so pretty, she thought, dolled up in a red sari, her hands and feet decorated with *mehdi*, the parting in her hair covered with *sindoor*. Momentarily, her mind drifted to her own wedding all those years ago. Women and young girls and boys peeked at the bride. Village women gave small gifts to see the bride's face. They would later comment on her complexion, her clothes and jewellery, the amount of bridal gifts she had received: the stuff of village gossip.

Sukhraji was proud finally to be a *saas*, mother-in-law. She helped Munni cook *kichadi*, a simple traditional dish of rice and dhall. This was the first dish that a bride normally cooks. It is more a ritual than a test of cooking, to show the villagers and relatives that the daughter-in-law could cook and would be a good householder. In the evening a goat was slaughtered and beer flowed for all those who had helped with the wedding preparations.

Over the next few days as guests and relatives departed, the tin shed was dismantled and large cooking pots returned to the neighbours. Life began to return to normal in the Bhola household. Remembering her own ordeal, Sukhraji was gentle with her daughter-in-law. Like a patient teacher, she introduced Munni to the way things were done in the house. The way Bhola liked his food cooked. The amount of ghee on his roti, salt in the curry, sugar in the tea. She introduced Munni to the neighbours, took her along to weddings and birthdays in the village. She was in effect training her successor as the next 'mother' of the household.

Then things began to change. In small, petty acts of defiance Munni began to assert her independence. Munni washed her own and Dewa's clothes only. She ate her dinner alone in her separate house, without waiting for the menfolk to finish theirs. She hid away choice portions of meat for just the two of them. She refused to get up early to prepare breakfast for the family. Headaches and other mysterious ailments became increasingly common. Sukhraji noticed these things but was not worried. This was not how she had imagined things would work out but times were different and these were early days.

One day when Sukhraji asked Munni to massage her sore shoulder, Munni exploded. 'What's the matter with you? Ever since I have come here, you have been developing one sickness after another. Always expecting me to be at your back and call. Ask your husband to massage your arse. I am not your *naukarin*, servant.' With that, she huffed away into her house. Sukhraji was devastated, and began to cry. The complete unexpectedness of it all. The language, the temper, and the rudeness. Munni would have been skinned alive in days gone by. 'Maybe she is upset about something,' Bhola said to Sukhraji. 'I will speak to Dewa.' When Bhola spoke to him the following day, Munni had already told Dewa of the previous day's altercation. Dewa knew that Munni's complaints over work were exaggerated. He knew that his father always fetched water, and the boys chopped firewood. His mother washed her own clothes and that of his younger siblings. They all pitched in more than in most other households in Tabia. But out of a sense of solidarity with his wife he said nothing.

Dewa had something else on his mind. Tota, the next eldest, was in the first year of secondary school. Dewa resented that. He wanted Tota on the farm to do some of the work, so that Dewa could have free time of his own. 'Look at Tota,' Dewa said to Bhola. 'He is all suit-boot, and here I am busting my arse working for nothing. For whom? For what? What use would *his* education be for me? It will be good for all of us if he left school and worked on the farm.'

This hurt Bhola. He was speechless. He hadn't heard Dewa talk like this before. 'All this will be yours one day, Dewa,' Bhola said. 'You know this farm cannot support all of you. Educating the boys is not easy, I know. It is hard for all of us, especially you. But God willing, and with a bit of education, the boys will stand on their own feet. How can I can look in their eyes and stop them from going to school when we know there is no future for them here. God will not forgive us.' 'But what about me and my future,' Dewa asked? He was deeply embittered that he had been forced to leave school, although he was bright student, and made to work on the farm. 'You didn't allow me to complete my schooling,' he said accusingly. 'I would have made something of myself, instead of being a miserable menial.'

'I know, Dewa. But those days were different. Your mother and I wanted the world for you. But we were an extended family then. We couldn't decide things for ourselves on our own. Everything had to be considered properly. When they all decided that you should leave school, there was little I could do but go along.' He continued: 'I know you have been working hard recently. Why don't you and *badki* take a break. Go and visit Dreketi. Spend some time there. We will manage.' When Dewa mentioned this to Munni that night, she was ecstatic. 'The sooner the better,' she said, 'before they change their mind, or something happens to your good-for-nothing brothers.'

Three days later Dewa and Munni went to Dreketi. Dhania grilled Munni on all the gossip, from beginning to end, *poora jad pullai*. Munni was unhappy. Something had to be done. Soon. Kallu and Dhania came up with a plan. They had more land then was of use to them. Much of it was lying fallow anyway. They could transfer some of the wooded land, perhaps ten acres across the road, jointly to Dewa and Munni. Dewa would provide a helping hand, There would be another male in the house, and they could all keep an eye on things. Munni would be the mistress in her own house, not a slave in another.

Kallu mentioned the proposal to Dewa and Munni the next morning. Munni could not believe her ears. Her own piece of land. Her very own house. She would be her own boss. 'This is a God-send,' she said to herself. But Dewa remained subdued. His lack of enthusiasm surprised everyone. 'What do you think, *beta*,' Dhania asked. 'This is good for all of us. You will have your own piece of land, your own peace of mind. And we will have a son we have always wanted.'

'This is wonderful' Dewa replied, betraying no emotion. 'It is a complete surprise. Let me think about it.' 'Take your time, *beta*,' Dhania said. 'There is no hurry.' Then she asked if Munni could remain in Dreketi a couple of weeks more. "We haven't seen each other for a very long time. Look at the poor thing. She desperately needs a break.' Dewa agreed.

Dewa knew from the very beginning that Dreketi was not for him. Hard work was never his suit. Clearing virgin land for crops would be no picnic. Getting by with as little physical exertion as possible was his motto. But lazy though he was,

Dewa was also a proud man. In Dreketi, he would be a *ghar damaad*, dependent son-in-law. His self-pride would be dented and freedom curtailed. He no longer would be a 'man' in his own right. And Dewa had his mind set on something else. To escape farm work altogether, he was taking driving lessons on Mallu's car to realise his ambition of becoming a bus driver. Easy work and the prospect of illegal income from short-changing illiterate passengers attracted him. Dreketi was a dead end for a driver.

Dewa mentioned the offer of land to his parents. They said little, hoping Dewa would remain in Tabia and eventually take over the running of the household. Besides, a *ghar damaad* was a lowly, despised figure in the community, much like a hen-pecked husband. But Ram Bihari encouraged Dewa to go. 'Times are changing, Bhola,' he said. 'Extended family under one roof with a common kitchen is a thing of the past. How long can you expect Dewa to remain with you? He will move one day, like my own sons. And he may not have an offer like this then.' But Dewa's mind was already made up.

In Dreketi Kallu and Dhania were doing their own scheming. They began to work on Munni, not that she needed extra persuasion. Tabia would always be a trap for her, they told her. Dewa's siblings were still of school age and she would have to look after them, and her own children when they came, for a very long time, perhaps for the best years of her life. And for what? When Munni mentioned the possibility of a separate household, Dhania countered, 'But where will you live? On a miserly plot of land, which won't be big enough even to grow baigan.' She continued. 'Yes, Dewa might one day inherit the land, but not while Bhola is till alive. He is fifty something now. Another twenty years. Another twenty years of hell for you. And there is no guarantee that the other boys will not want their share as well.' Dhania pressed on. 'Think girl. How many times have you been to the town, to the cinemas. When was the last time you bought clothes for yourself.' How many times have you come to visit us since you have been married?'

Listening to her mother, Munni remembered why the family had been keen for her to get married in Tabia in the first place. She had been sent there on a mission to look for suitable husbands for her sisters. Teachers, clerks, policemen and men like that, in cash employment. That would be easier from Tabia than Dreketi. And she had dreams of regular visits to the town, to the shops full of fancy goods, movies, visits to relatives in other parts of the island. But all she had in Tabia was the deadening routine of daily household chores of cooking, cleaning and looking after everyone else.

'Leave him,' Dhania implored Munni. Her sisters chorused support. Kallu said nothing. 'We will go to Social Welfare. I know a Babu there. I will explain things to them. You will get a good monthly allowance. If they can't pay that — and you know they can't — you will have Dewa living with you here. At last you will be your own boss.' All this made sense to Munni. She could not lose either way. When Dewa returned a fortnight later to fetch Munni, the old proposal came up again. Dewa could not tell the real reason why he could never live in Dreketi. He talked half-heartedly about the difficulty of having to start from nothing. The bullocks and farm implements he would have to buy and the building material for the new house.

'They are our concern, *beta*,' Dhania said. 'That is our responsibility.' Still sensing his reluctance, Dahnia continued.

'It is noble of you to think about your brothers and sisters. But what about you and Munni, about your children and family?' Like a gushing tap, Dhania continued, while Munni sat with her eyes glued to the ground. 'You are giving your life, and Munni's life, for people who won't be there for you when you will need them. There is no future for you there, *beta*' 'Some day,' Dewa said politely, hoping to diffuse the palpably mounting tension. 'By then, it might be too late,' Dhania replied. It was clear that Dewa was stalling, his mind made up. Dreketi would have to wait. 'Get ready, let's go,' Dewa said to Munni. 'The bus will arrive shortly.'

'No Dewa, you go,' Dhania said to her son-in-law, taking his name to his face for the first time. 'Go back to where you belong. Munni will stay where she properly belongs.' Dewa looked toward Munni who kept her face averted. Dhania had spoken for her. Dewa left thinking all this a minor hiccup. They will come to their senses. They didn't. A month later, a letter arrived from Shankar and Company. Munni had filed for divorce.

4

Masterji

> Some deemed him wondrous wise,
> and some believed him mad.

Six o'clock in the evening is a special time in every Indo-Fijian home. The clattering noise of cooking from the kitchen and the shriek and laughter of children at play cease abruptly as the entire family gathers around the radio set. The bell announcing the death notice rings three times. Then the voice intones sombrely: '*Dukh ke saath suchit kiya jaata hai ki...*' It is with regret that we announce the death of ... The notice, the last of the day, is often long. When it ends, the volume is turned down and normal conversation resumes. Children scatter, and women return to their kitchen duties.

In Tabia, without electricity, running water or paved roads, where nothing interesting ever seems to happen, people are puzzled about the strange names of places they have never heard of before. Dabota, Tavua: what kind of place is that? Or Moto or Mangruru or Field 40? People wonder about the kind of Hindi spoken there, the clothes people wear, the crops they plant, the food they eat. Simla and Benares cause confusion:

how did Indian place names travel to Fiji? Since no one in the family, possibly the entire village, has ever left Labasa, strange places remain strange, imbued with mystery, tantalizing at the edge of comprehension.

If the dead person is vaguely known, there will be endless talk about family history. Connections will be made to distant relatives living in remote parts of the island. Invariably, at the end someone will know someone related to the deceased. The connecting game provides relief from the chores of daily routine, reduces the sense of isolation and remoteness. The death of a relative, close or far, is another matter. Work will be re-scheduled and preparation made to go to the funeral. People are particular about death; saying the last goodbye in person is a habit that has persisted. It is still the right thing to do.

We were sitting on the verandah of Mr Tulsi's Store early one evening, drinking kava and talking about the impending Ramlila festival, when the death notice came over the radio. *dukh ke saath...*' One of the names mentioned was that of Mr Ramsay Sita Ram. His address was given as Bureta Street, Samabula, a lower middle class Indo-Fijian suburb of Suva. Listeners were asked to convey the news to close family members whose names accompanied the notice. '*Kripeya is khabar ko...*' Judging by the silence that accompanied the announcement, Mr Sita Ram might as well have been a resident of Tabia. Mr Sita Ram was an early teacher at the Tabia Sanatan Dharam School. After a few years, he transferred to Wainikoro, or was it All Saints? He returned to Tabia in the mid-1960s to end his teaching career just as I was completing my own primary education at the school. After all these years, he was still a respected household name in the village.

I had Mr Sita Ram in the penultimate year of primary school. He was one of my more memorable, not to say eccentric, teachers. He was short, five foot nothing, fair, bald with an eagle nose, and an incessant smoker. We mischievously called him 'Chandula Munda,' 'Baldie, Baldie,' because a bald man was a curious oddity in a settlement of men with full heads of hair. Mr Sita Ram did not live in one of the wooden tin-roofed teachers' quarters at back of the school but in Wailevu about five miles away. He arrived at school around eight thirty in the morning and left in his bottle green Morris Minor soon after the last school bell rang.

Mr Sita Ram was in his sixties when he taught us. To us he appeared very ancient, a relic of another time and place. Other teachers seemed to treat him with the mild affection reserved for a genial older uncle, past his prime, no threat to anyone's career, harmless but full of wisdom and an unrivalled knowledge of local history. To place children whose names he had difficulty remembering — Sukh Deo, Sambhu and Shankar Lal were all the same to him — he would ask us our fathers' or even grandfathers' names to establish our genealogy. His memory for this sort of detail was awesome (and awful) and frequently embarrassing. He would say 'Useless — *bekaar* — like your father and his father before him,' if someone got their sums wrong or could not spell a simple word or did not know who the prime minister of Bechuanland was. He knew all our secrets, our ancient family feuds, the disputes in the village.

When the mood seized him, he forgot whatever lesson he was teaching, and with the distant look of old men, focussed on something high at the end of the room, and talked about the past. We did not seem to exist. He was talking to himself, reliving his part of the vanishing past. Abruptly, he would walk out of the classroom, light up a Craven A, stand on the verandah with his back to us and take a long, lingering puff that seemed to restore his peace of mind. He would then return and resume teaching. Effortlessly. I remembered this about Mr Sita Ram when I heard news of his death.

'A very good man,' Jack — Jag Narayan — said after a long silence. Jack, now a farmer, was the village historian whom people nicknamed Magellan for his insatiable curiosity about world events. He was also one of earliest pupils of Tabia Sanatan when Mr Sita Ram first taught there. 'They don't have teachers like that anymore.' Moti, another old timer now a driver with the Public Works Department, agreed. 'Do you see any books in their houses now? Have you ever seen a teacher read for knowledge and pleasure?' Moti asked. The ensuing silence distressed me because it was books which had helped me escape the village, connected me to other worlds and pasts. Without them I would have been nothing.

'Can't blame them, can you, bro?' Jack said. 'How can you, with the way things are? Poverty, political troubles, the land question. Everyone trying to migrate. Another *girmit* here, if you ask me.' That word *girmit*, the memory of indenture and years of struggle and degradation that accompanied it, had been on peoples' lips quite a lot recently, reminding them of the glass ceiling in the public service, the blocked promotions, the imminent expiry of leases, and the end of promise.'Child Our Hope' they write on the blackboard,' Moti said cynically. 'What Hope? Hope is Joke.'

The talk of decline depressed me. It was the same wherever you looked. The quest for excellence, the passion for learning and adventure and exploration, the burning of the midnight lamp, had vanished. The insidious virus of mediocrity was quietly corrupting the nation's soul. I tried to steer the conversation back to Mr Sita Ram. 'A name like Ramsay: how did that happen?,' I asked. 'What was a Christian doing in a Hindu school? You couldn't possibly have that now, could you?'

'Mix another bowl' Moti said, scratching his leathery, kava-cracked skin as he took a long puff on his *suluka*, rough homegrown tobacco wrapped in newsprint. 'Master will pay,' he said. I nodded yes. 'His father was Ram Sahai, so he changed his name to Ramsay to sound like an English name. All so that he could get admission to All Saints,' Jack informed me. I was intrigued. This was news to me. 'You had to change your name to go to a European school?'

'The old days were different, ' Jack responded. 'It was British raj. There were just a few schools. One in Wainikoro, another in Bulileka, a few here and there. Children attended these schools for a few years, enough to read and write. That was it. But if you wanted to go on, you had to attend one of the Christian schools.' I was missing something. 'So what did people expect from the schools?'

'Our parents were illiterate, but not stupid, Master,' Jack said. 'They knew that without education we would be nothing but a bunch of coolies, good-for-nothings. Education opened doors to a good marriage. We could read the newspapers. We were frogs in a pond: how could we know about the world except through reading. Our parents could get us to read and write letters.'

Jack was beginning to hit full stride, when Moti interjected, 'Don't forget about the mahajans, bro.' That reference puzzled me. He continued, 'In those days, Master, our people did not know how to read and write. When people went to the shop, they let the Mahajan write the price of goods we bought in a book. We did not have cash. People bought things on credit. They settled the account at the end of the month, in some cases at the end of the cane cutting season. Then, when the time came to pay, they got this huge docket — for things they had never bought. You complained, but it was your word against the written record. The police could do nothing. That's the way it was. Why do you think our people remained poor after all that back breaking work in the fields?'

Blaming others for your own misfortune is always comforting, I thought, and the oppressed are very good at playing victims. There were other reasons for poverty as well — the small plots of land people had, the restrictions the CSR placed on what they could or could not plant on them, the absence of cash employment, our own nonchalant attitude to work. I realised, possibly for the first time, that our quest for education was driven by this grim reality, to escape the rapacity of our own kind rather than by some grand vision for cultural enrichment and intellectual exploration.

How could someone like Mr Sita Ram from this kind of background, growing up in the middle of nowhere, in the shadow of indenture, on the edge of everything, become a teacher in the late 1930s? It was an extraordinary achievement, when you think about it. It was just about the highest job you could aspire to. And teachers were the pillars of the community, respected for their learning and for their role as moral exemplars. Parents voluntarily handed over to them the responsibility for disciplining the pupils under their care.

Mr Sahai was the reason for his son's success. He had been a sirdar in the Tuatua sector. There were some dark secrets in his past, Moti hinted, but it was hard to know what or whom to believe. Some said he was on the 'the other side.' Meaning with the CSR. But he wouldn't have been the only one, playing the two sides to his advantage. Sirdars were chosen to extract the maximum amount of work from those under their charge, providing what someone has called 'lackey leadership.' When his indenture ended, Mr Sahai came to Tabia. He was one of the village's first residents. He knew the District Officer (a former employee of the CSR), and so was able to buy a large block of freehold land across the river by Shiu Charan's store.

In short time, Mr Sahai built up a big cane farm, employed people. Everyone called him 'Babuji.' Babuji could read and write. He wrote letters for the girmitiyas, read them, for a little something when they arrived. He arranged things for people, made connections with officialdom. He was the village agua, leader. From the farm and the gifts people gave him came the shop.

'You know how these people do business, Master,' Jack said. I didn't. 'Have you heard the story of the monkey and the cats?' No I hadn't. As I listened and reflected, I realised that I had assumed much about this place, but actually knew so little of its secret past.

'Once there were two cats,' Jack continued. 'One day they found a piece of roti. They decided to share it equally, but they couldn't trust each other to be fair. So they approached a monkey and asked him to divide the roti exactly in half. The monkey knew the trick. He deliberately split the roti into uneven sizes. Oh, this side is slightly bigger, he would say, so he would take a bite and kept on biting and adjusting until the roti was gone. 'That, Master,' Jack concluded, 'was how our Mahajans and Babus got ahead and moved about.'

'Don't forget Dozen and One,' Moti reminded him. 'Yes, Mr Sahai here was Dozen and One, too, along with Nanka

Boss in Laqere and Sukh Lal in Soisoi,' Jack continued. 'Well, Master, in those days, our people were not allowed to drink alcohol without a Police Permit. You had to be a man of good character, well connected and with money to get a permit. The permit allowed you to buy one bottle of spirit and a dozen bottles of beer a month. Mr Sahai himself was teetotaller, but he sold the liquor to people in the village. At twice the price. That is how he made his money. That is how they all made their money.' It was probably an exaggeration, but we had our share of rogues and swindlers, more than we cared to concede. 'Behind every success story is a secret story, Master,' Moti summed up with a laugh.

'Babuji was not keen to start this school,' Jack said. 'Why,' I asked? It seemed such an obvious thing to do.'Where will the teachers come from? Who will pay for the books? Where will you get land to build a school? Babuji asked these questions whenever people talked about education,' Jack continued.'You can't feed and clothe your own families. How will the people pay school fees and the building fund? We all want education for our children, but this is not the time. Plant more maize, rice, cane and vegetables. Have a few cows and goats and chicken. Poverty is our biggest enemy. This is our main problem. Schools can come later.'

People disagreed. They needed schools and educated children precisely to break the hold of people like Mr Ram Sahai and the unending cycle of poverty and hopelessness. A small start was made at the local kuti, community-cum rest houses, and rudimentary primary school started in 1945. From that came Tabia Sanatan.

Mr Sahai had other ideas for his own son. He enrolled him at All Saints Primary boarding school for boys in Nasea town.

Mr Sita Ram clearly remembered his father's words. 'Learn English good and proper, boy,' he had said. 'Learn the Sahibs' ways. See how white people rule the world. Learn their secrets. Open your eyes boy. Look. Farm work is coolie work. Make yourself a man. Keep our name high. Ram Sahai. Remember that.' Mr Sita Ram laughed when he finished recalling his father's words to me. The way the old man had pronounced it, Mr Sita Ram said, it sounded like 'Ram So High.'

But All Saints only accepted Christian pupils or at least those who did not object to Christian teaching. No problems for Babuji even though he was a regular speaker at pujas, marriages and funerals, knew the appropriate verses from the scriptures too, telling people that they must do everything to preserve their culture and identity. 'Without your religion, you are a rolling stone' he would say, bina pendi ke lotâ. In his own family, though, he was a different person. 'Religion doesn't put food on the table, boy,' he used to tell his young son.

And, so, Ramsay Sita Ram, at his father's behest, embraced the new faith though with no particular enthusiasm. He finished his grade eight at All Saints, passed the Entrance Exam and joined the Nasinu Training College to prepare for a career as a primary school teacher. His first posting was to Wainikoro Government Primary. After a few years, he came to Tabia.

Jack remembered Mr Sita Ram vividly. 'He taught everything: Hindi, English, Arithmetic, the whole lot. As a matter of fact, he was the only qualified teacher in the school.' 'Very keen on Indian history,' Moti volunteered. 'In those two or three years, we learnt by heart stories about Akbar and Birbal, about Jhansi ki Rani, about Shivaji, Tilak, Nehru, Gandhiji, Subhash Chandra Bose, the 1857 Mutiny.'

The list was impressive — and revolutionary. 'But weren't those books banned?' I asked, remembering how strictly the government controlled the flow of information, especially that which incited hatred against the British. The loyalty of the Indians was already suspect, and teaching about Bose and Gandhi would surely have been considered seditious.

'Mr Sita Ram got the stories from *Amrit Bazâr Patrika, Azâd, and Ghadr.*' Jack answered. His memory for names surprised me. It was for good reason that he was nicknamed Magellan! The parcel would be opened at the post office and its intended recipients put under surveillance, if not actually prosecuted and fined. I was perplexed how a teacher like Mr Sita Ram could get these papers, especially with a war on.

'From Chandu Bhai Patel, in Nasea town,' Jack said 'He got the papers smuggled in somehow.' In crates carrying pots and pans and spices and clothes. And a little baksheesh to the customs officials didn't go astray either. Say what you want about these Gujaratis, I thought, but they helped us keep our heritage alive at a time when we were down and out, at the edge, ridiculed and reviled, beasts of burden, nothing more. Without the Hindi movies, the newspapers, the music and the religious texts they imported, we would have become nothing, like the proverbial washerman's donkey, belonging neither here nor there. Na ghar ke na ghât ke.

Moti recalled another aspect of Mr Sita Ram's teaching. 'What did he say? All work and no play makes John a bad boy?' 'A dull boy,' I said. 'Something like that,' he continued. 'He taught us hockey, kabbaddi, rounders and soccer. Once or twice, we even took part in inter-school competition. Remember that Jack?' 'How can I forget!' Jack replied. 'Once Mr Sita Ram took our soccer team to Vunimoli. That was our first outing. Boy, they were rough.' 'Nothing has changed,' Moti laughed.

'One big fellow, fullback, he kicked me so hard in the shin that I thought I had broken my right leg. Swollen like a big football. When father saw my injury, he thrashed me with a *chapki*. I ended up having both a sore leg as well as a sore arse!' he laughed. But his father did not stop there. Jack continued, 'Father put on his singlet and went straight to the school. 'Masterji, I send my boy to school to learn not to get his leg broken. I don't have money to mend his broken leg. Who will look after him? You? Stop this nonsense before someone gets seriously hurt. That was the end of my soccer playing days.'

Mr Sita Ram also insisted that students in higher grades should learn the basics and practicalities of good husbandry. Hands on experience, planting radish, carrots, tomatoes, baigan, cabbage and lettuce. So he started a Young Farmers Club. A special part of the school compound, by the creek, was set aside for gardening. Each student, or a group of students were allotted a patch, which they prepared and planted and nurtured, watering it morning and evening, erecting scarecrows to keep birds away.

'That wasn't popular in the beginning,' Moti recalled. Some parents were actually angry at this 'waste time' activity. He remembered Mr Ramdhan coming to school one day telling Mr Sita Ram, 'I don't send my boy to school to learn how to plant beans. I can teach him that myself better than all of you put together. We have been farmers since before you were born.' Mr Sita Ram did not say much. He smiled gently, put his hands around Mr Ramdhan's shoulder and said, 'Come Kaka, Uncle, let's have a cup of tea.' I don't know what he said, but Mr Ramdhan calmed down, and walked away quietly.'

Some people thought that students would get to take home the vegetables they had planted. When they didn't, rumours spread that the teachers were keeping the vegetables for themselves, using school pupils for cheap labour. That was not true. Mr Sita Ram had other ideas. He used the money from the sale to buy books, pencils, writing pads for children from very poor homes, even uniforms, hiring buses for annual school picnics at Naduri or Malau. I could understand better now why his early pupils remembered Mr Sita Ram so fondly.

'So no one objected to a Christian teaching Hindu kids.' I returned to an earlier topic. 'Well, he wasn't really a Christian,' Jack said. 'He may have been,' Moti interjected, 'but it didn't really matter. He was a good man, a good teacher. As the old timers used to say, 'It does not matter whether the cat is black or white, as long as it catches the mice.' How things had changed. It would be difficult now to find a Muslim who is a principal of a Hindu school. And vice versa.

'This religious *jhanjhat* (trouble) is a recent thing,' Jack said. 'In those days, we were all one, like one big family. We ate together, played together, went to school together. We were all one.' He remembered the names of the different head teachers of Tabia Sanatan in its early days: Mr Munshi, Mr Ashik Hussein, Mr Mitha Singh, Mr Simon Nagaiya. 'Look at all this religious *katchkatch* (bickering) now. You call this progress, Master?' His voice betrayed regret and sadness at the way things had turned out. 'It is the price of progress, bro,' I answered feebly.

Over my remaining days in Labasa, I struggled with my own memories of Mr Sita Ram. I knew him when he was in his declining years, unconcerned about other peoples' approval or about the school's success rate in external exams by which its public worth was measured. My memory of that period is dim. 'History matters, boy,' I recall him telling me one day after class. 'Memory is such a precious thing.' Our people's lack of curiosity about themselves, their past, the world around them, their non-interest in anything creative or imaginative, their penchant for petty, back-biting politics and myopic self-interest, distressed him immensely. 'Every home should have a dictionary, the Bible, Koran and the Ramayana,' he once told the class. Even in old age, his passion for discovery and exploration had not deserted him.

Nor his mischievous sense of humour. One day, Mr Sita Ram asked the class, 'Which is the greatest empire in history?' 'The British Empire,' I answered 'Correct.' 'Why does the sun never set on the British Empire? Remembering all the red spots on the *Clarion Atlas*, I remarked about its global reach. 'No, boy. The sun never sets on the British Empire because God does not trust an Englishman in the dark,' he said with a huge chuckle that shook his jelly-like stomach. We were all puzzled. I remember Shiu, sitting next to me asking in a whisper, 'Is that true? Why doesn't God trust an Englishman?' I had no idea, although Liaquat volunteered that the reason might be that English people reportedly used paper, not water, when they 'did their business.'

On another occasion, he was talking about the great monuments of world history: the Empire State Building, the Tower of London and Big Ben, the Leaning Tower of Pisa, the Golden Gate Bridge, the Pyramids of Egypt. Then he pointed to the grainy, black and white picture of the Taj Mahal in our text book. 'That', he said, 'is the greatest Indian erection of all time, never to be repeated.'

Mr Sita Ram also took our singing lesson. We were taught songs that we were expected to memorise and sing in class every month. We all had to take turns. It was awful, the entirely tuneless and screechy rendition of beautiful words. Most of the time we could hardly stop laughing hysterically at some poor fellow making a mess of things. The standard song of last resort was 'Raja Kekda Re, Tu To Pani Men Ke Raja.... King Crab, you are the king of the sea... For the truly vocally and musically challenged — and there were more than you might think — there was 'Baa Baa Black Sheep,' and 'Humpty Dumpty' and 'Jack and Jill.' Mr Sita Ram himself had a deep rich voice. We beseeched him to sing during every singing lesson. He obliged with songs by CH Atma, Manna Dey and especially Mohammed Rafi. His favourite — our favourite — was 'Chal Chal Re Musafir Chal, Tu Us Dunia Men Chal... . Go Traveller, Go To That Other World... .

Mr Sita Ram was tolerant of potentially expellable misdemeanours. We all knew that Sada Nand and Veer Mati were sweet on each other. In class they exchanged coy glances and little hand written notes hidden in books: 'Roses are red, violets are blue...' that sort of thing. One day, someone reported this to Mr Sita Ram. Our hearts stopped. We knew that if he took this to the head teacher, Mr Subramani Goundan, Sada Nand would be severely caned (in front of the school assembly) and Veer Mati would be forced to leave school and married off soon afterwards. That was the way things were done in Tabia. But Mr Sita Ram settled the matter himself. He took the two aside one day after school and talked to them in a fatherly tone about their future and the foolishness of what they were doing at their age. When Sada Nand and Veer Mati married a few years after leaving school, Mr Sita Ram was the guest of honour!

Because Mr Sita Ram himself came from a relatively wealthy background — the Morris Minor was an undoubted symbol of prosperity — money did not matter much to him. On the contrary, he seemed acutely sensitive to the plight of others, especially bright children from poor backgrounds. He went out of his way to help them whenever he could, buying writing pads, pencils, paying school fees.

One day he talked about money and how our quest for it was so misplaced, leading us astray, away from the really important things in life, blinding us to its beauty. What he said remains with me. 'Money is not everything. Money can buy you books, but it can't buy you brain. Money can buy you the best food in the world, but it can't buy you appetite. Money can buy you the best cosmetics in the world, but it can't buy you beauty.' He went on like this for a long time, talking over our heads, talking to himself really. It was not until much later, after university, that I began to appreciate the profound truths of Mr Sita Ram's musings.

When we left the village for secondary school, and a few years later for university, we lost touch with our teachers and fellow students who had failed. But I ran into Mr Sita Ram in the Suva Market a couple of years ago. From a crowded distance, the bald, shrunken man sitting hunched on a wooden crate next to a vegetable stall, looked vaguely familiar. Coming closer, I knew it had to be Mr Sita Ram. When I spoke his name tentatively, he looked up, took a puff, and recognised me instantly. He stood up, even shorter than I remembered him, hugged me, slapping me gently on the back. 'Good work, boy, good work,' he said with the broad smile of a proud teacher.

'Have a bowl,' Mr Sita Ram offered. When I smiled in abstinence, he replied, 'You can have one now!' He asked about my parents and seemed genuinely sorry to hear that both had died. 'Good people they were,' he said, as he looked into the distance, recalling the past. As for the other boys, I had lost touch a long time ago, and so had he.

Mr Sita Ram told me he had retired a long time ago, and joined his children in Suva. Sometime in the late 1970s, the two boys had migrated to Australia and the daughter was married in Canada. His wife had died a long time ago. Mr Sita Ram had been to Australia a couple of times, but did not like it. 'A poked beehive,' he said, 'not a place for me.' 'Better at my age to be someone here than nobody there.' I understood what he meant.

I left Mr Sita Ram in the market, promising to keep in touch. But you know how it is: other commitments intervene and promises are forgotten. That was the last time I saw him. The news of Mr Sita Ram's death took me to a time and place I had nearly forgotten, reminded me of things that had quietly slipped into my subconsciousness, the kindness and generosity of people who paved our way into the world. People like Mr Sita Ram.

I went to Mr Sita Ram's basement flat in Bureta Street after I returned from Labasa. Why I have no idea, but felt it was the right thing to do. Perhaps the ancient urge to say the final goodbye in person. The landlord Ram Gopal invited me into the living room. After the customary cup of black tea, I asked about Mr Sita Ram's last days. Did he say anything? Were there any tell-tale signs of the impending end? Had he left any papers behind? 'Masterji seemed to be more reclusive in the last six months, more weighed down' Gopal said. 'What really killed him if you ask me,' he continued unasked, 'was the coup.' The committed multiracialist, Mr Sita Ram had joined the Alliance Party after retirement. 'We all have to live together,' I remembered him saying all those years ago. 'Masterji read all the newspapers,' Gopal said, 'listened to the radio, he knew what was happening, what was coming. Another *girmit*, he had once said to me.'

Listening to Gopal, my mind wandered back to Tabia Sanatan and I remembered a patriotic poem that Mr Sita Ram had us memorize from one of Pandit Ami Chandra's Hindi pothis:

Fiji Desh Hamaara Hai
Praano Se Bhi Pyara Hai...

The Nation Of Fiji Is Our Homeland
More Beloved Than Life Itself...

These words helped me understand why Mr Sita Ram had lost his will to live, why the coup had broken his heart. As I was leaving, Gopal remembered a piece of paper on the bedside table on which Mr Sita Ram had written the first few lines of a haunting Rafi song:

Chal Ud Ja Re Panchi
Ke Ab Ye Desh Hua Begaana...

Go, Fly Away Little Bird
This Place Is Not Your Home Anymore...

5

Across the Fence

> To meet, to know, to love — and then to part
> Is the sad tale of many a human heart

A new man has moved in across the fence. He walks past our shop every morning for his daily walk. Then around eight or so, he gets into his new four-wheel drive Toyota and goes to work. I presume it is to work. He is always immaculately dressed, in suit and white long sleeved shirt, wearing stylish green glasses. He must be either a lawyer or a doctor. Twice a week, he picks up a loaf of bread from our shop on his way back from his walk. There is just a barely perceptible hint of a smile as he says thank you and leaves. He is polite and graceful, softly spoken. He must be from abroad. His hands are soft, fingernails perfectly manicured. He is probably in his late forties or early fifties. Sometimes, I want to talk to him, just to get to know a little bit more about him, but he is shy and retiring. I want to ask his name, what he does, where his family is, whether he has a family, the sort of things neighbours want to know. But he may get the wrong impression that I am 'too forward.'

I am a stranger myself in Cuvu. We are from Labasa, from Wainikoro. Our lease was not renewed. Like so many others, we had to leave. But there was nowhere to go. My husband had a distantly related uncle in Cuvu. All his children had migrated, leaving only him and his elderly wife to look after the shop. They were making preparations to join their children in Vancouver, but they wanted to keep the shop, just in case things did not work out for them. We will run their store while they are away, and I will continue teaching, part-time, at the local secondary school until things settle down. If they ever settle down.

We have made a good start. We had established customers. People are friendly and curious about us. They admire our determination to make a go. If only people here worked as hard as you people, they say. There is something about Labasa people. People say we are humble and genuine, that we have kept our culture and language alive, untainted by Western influence. They invite us to their weddings and birthday parties. They try to make us feel welcome. Life settled into a routine after a few weeks. The novelty of welcoming new migrants wears off, and you are left alone to get on. It has not been easy since Vinesh, my husband, had a stroke about three months ago. The absence of close family and friends nearby during a crisis like this hurts deeply. There is no one to turn to, no shoulder to cry on. Sometimes, the loneliness can be overwhelming. I do everything by myself: manage the accounts, do the banking, keep track of the stock, make sure that Priya does her homework, prepare for class, and keep the household running. I often wish there were more hours in a day.

Early one morning, a little girl from across the fence comes to buy bread. So the man has a family. I ask the girl's name. 'Shirley,' she says. She speaks with a distinct Western accent. She probably has no Hindi at all. 'And you are from where, Shirley?' I inquire. 'Vancouver,' she says. 'And your parents, are they here with you as well?' 'No, just my mum and me. We are here for a holiday.' 'And that man is your?' 'Uncle. Uncle Viru.' 'And what does Uncle Viru do?' I have no idea why I am asking this little girl all this but I am getting curious about the man. 'He is a physician.' That's Canadian for doctor, I learn later. Now, his smart dress makes sense. 'Come back again sometime and meet my daughter, Priya. She is your age. I think you two will get along well.'

Later that afternoon, Shirley returns. 'Come over and play with me,' she says to Priya. 'Can I go, Mum?' 'Yes, but don't be too late. I have to go to town later.' A doctor from Canada, in Cuvu, all by himself? Like us, he is a newcomer to this place. Perhaps his wife and children will join him soon. 'Mum, you should see the inside of the house,' Priya says to me as soon as she returns. 'Yes.' 'The books. Sooo many of them. Big, thick books all along the wall. And DVDs and CDs. Must be billions of them.' 'Oh, come on now, Priya.' 'Mum, seriously.' Books and music and a medical doctor. That is a strange and rare combination of taste and talent. Here, even teachers don't read anything beyond the set texts. No time, they say. No time to spare from grog and gossip, that is.

A few days later, Shirley comes to the shop with her mother. A stylish woman, in her mid-thirties, short black hair, knee-length dress, floral top, probably from one of the tourist shops in Nadi. Not flaunty or flamboyant, but definitely someone who has lived abroad for some time, I realise. 'Lovely girl, Priya,' she says. Nice, soothing, slightly Western-accented voice. 'Thanks. She can be a real terror sometimes though.' I extend my right hand across the counter. 'Hello, I am Meera.' She reciprocates, her palm as soft as a baby's bum. She must be someone from a 'soft' occupation. 'Sorry, Hi, Geeta,' she says switching her handbag from her right to her left hand. Well spoken, educated. 'On holidays, Shirley tells me.' 'Yes, our second trip in five years. Holiday and to see Viren.' 'Shirley's uncle I take it?' 'Yes, her Mama. My cousin.'

'Time for a cup of tea or are you in a rush?' I ask hoping she will stay. I give her a pleading look. Geeta seems so vibrant, so full of life. 'Mum, remember lunch with Viru Mama,' Shirley reminds her mother. 'He's sending a car soon.' Geeta looks at me, shrugging her shoulders helplessly. 'Tomorrow will be perfect, if you are not busy,' Geeta volunteers. Busy! I wish. 'Tomorrow lunch then,' I offer. 'Nothing fancy, something very simple.'

I can only do lunches these days. Rural stores have a rhythm. There is a fairly heavy flow from around six to eight-thirty, nine. People come for the basic necessities: bread, butter, milk, eggs, onions, potatoes, kerosene, newspapers, lighters. There is hardly any activity around midday. Mid-afternoon, after school, the rush begins again, with schoolchildren buying lollies, ice-cream, ice blocks. By about eight, it is time to close shop. Thank God. By then, I am almost dead to the world.

The doctor, Viren, is on my mind. I feel confused and guilty. I want to know more about him. I know I shouldn't. It is not right for a married woman to look at another man, let alone think about him long into the night. Things haven't been easy since Vinesh's stroke. No woman should have the joys of her married life snatched away so cruelly, in the prime of her life — not even your worst enemy. All the dreams about travel, picnics at the beach, swimming in the sea, late-night parties, making love whenever the mood seizes: all gone. All the foregone pleasures when children come along cannot be revived. With a stroke, of course, it is longing and desire and passion with no prospect ever of consummation.

It wasn't always like this though. Once I truly loved and admired Vinesh. He had done the unthinkable for someone from his family background. He had married me, a South Indian. His father had threatened to disown him, hang himself if he married a 'Madraji.' The extended family had protested that he was setting a bad example for his younger siblings and cousins. 'Khatta Paani' is what they called us-dark-skinned people with little culture or class, an inferior type. But he had stood steadfast. I meant the world to him. He has never betrayed me, for which I am grateful. I have wonderful memories of love and lust together, the dark nights by the river and the cane fields, the excuses we devised to get away from people to be just by ourselves in bed, but they are just that, memories. They are not enough to carry me through the day.

I wonder if Geeta eats curry. That's the only dish I can cook properly. I won't make it too hot. Duck curry: that should be a delicacy. Mung dhall, tomato chutney, a bit of raita with cucumber, in case the food is too hot. Chappatis. For dessert, chopped watermelon and pineapples with a squeeze of lemon to cool things down. And masala chai to finish it all off. I haven't been nervous like this for years. I feel as though something important depends on the lunch. I want it to be a success. I want to make an impression. I can barely wait for Geeta and Shirley to arrive.

Geeta is punctual, neat in her hibiscussy dress and maroon top, her short wavy dark hair tied in a small bun, sunglasses across her forehead, her smooth face glistening gently with hints of perspiration. 'Here's something for dessert,' she says, handing me a large packet of rich Swiss chocolate. So sweet. 'You carry your Canadian custom too far for us country people here,' I said, but not actually meaning it. I wish our local people would show greater courtesy and consideration. 'Oh no, it's nothing.' Priya asked for a large bottle of soda before disappearing into her bedroom with Shirley.

Geeta and I sit on the back verandah, keeping an eye on the shop, and enjoying the cooling sea breeze off the coral coast. 'The place has changed a lot since you came here last?' I ask, trying to start a conversation. 'Heaps,' Geeta replies. 'Most of all, mobile phones. I can't believe that almost everyone has one, including taxi drivers. And they send text messages to the radio stations. Just the other day, I was amazed to listen to someone from Los Angeles requesting a song on at ext message!' Geeta had just returned from Nadi. 'That town is practically unrecognizable. The duty-free shops, the range of fab goods they sell, the exquisite handicraft. And you can get a decent cappuccino now. Five years ago, it was that dreadful black mud that passed for coffee.' 'It's all thanks to you guys,' I say. 'Keep coming back.'

'And you? Been here long?' Geeta asks. 'A couple of years.' 'From?' 'Labasa.' Geeta looks perplexed. The idea of people moving about within the country is new to her. 'That's another change then. We stayed put when we were growing up. For us Ba folks, Labasa was a strange country which existed only in name, where people spoke a strange language stranded in t he p ast, a nd v ery s imple.' 'I n a ni ce w ay,' s he c hecks herself, knowing that I am from there. I explain our situation. 'That's one thing I can't get over about this country. It can never be our home. We will never be allowed to claim it as our own,' Geeta says angrily. 'That's the way things are around here,' I say. 'No use complaining. Make the most of what you have, and hope for the best.'

Geeta was a nurse, which explains her soft, delicate hands. From Suva, she had married and accompanied her chartered accountant husband to Canada in the late 1980s. The marriage ended. 'I am sorry,' I say in sympathy. 'It's not the end of the world,' Geeta remarks in a matter-of-act way that is surprising as well as refreshing. 'It happens all the time.' She had her daughter, and she had an extended family which was close. None was closer than Viren. 'He's like an older brother to me,' she said, 'loving and protective. I don't know what I would do without him, especially Shirley.' I envy Geeta her freedom and opportunity — and most of all her closeness to Viren, and his warm sheltering of her.

'Viren moved here several months ago,' I say, 'but we don't really know him. He comes to the shop for the usual things, but that's about it,' I say, hoping Geeta will talk more. 'He's on the quiet side, unless he knows you well,' Geeta says. 'And then he is a non-stop chatterbox,' Shirley pipes up from the end of the verandah. What will make him open up, I wonder. I want to know more about Viren but should be careful not to show too much interest, nothing to cause suspicion at this early stage, to send the wrong signal.

'Duck curry!' Geeta almost shrieks. 'I haven't had one in years.' 'Yum,' she says, as she takes a piece of meat between her thumb and forefinger and sucks on the gravy. 'You're a great cook, Meera,' she says appreciatively. 'Really.' 'It's a hobby and a habit,' I say. I have been doing this all my life, but it is good to get appreciation, to get noticed. Vinesh, well, he hasn't noticed or done anything for years. My domestic work is taken for granted, but that is nothing unusual around here. Women's fate, they say. Any excuse will do. Taking your partner for granted can be the cruellest cut of all.

'Shirley is so fond of her uncle,' I say, hoping to prod Geeta to talk about Viren. 'Is he from around here?' Geeta took the bait. 'Viru is from Ba, but he grew up in Canada. His parents [my Mama and Mami] migrated there some time in the late 1960s. They were among the earliest Fiji migrants to Canada. Viru is their only son. He did medicine and worked at the local hospital in Surrey, which is where most of our people in Vancouver live. He has been a practising physician for nearly twenty years. He could have climbed the ladder, gone places, but Viru is not like that.' I am happy that we are on the right track now.

'So what is he like?' I ask nonchalantly, trying not to give too much away. 'He's a free spirit, always seeking that extra something in anything he does. He works five days a week at the hospital, but runs extra free consultations on the weekends. He volunteers for the St John's Ambulance, is with the Red Cross. He plays and sings at fundraising events for charities — you know, Blind Society, Handicapped Children, that sort of thing. And, of course, he is my closest friend. Shirley spends all her spare time with him. I don't know what we would do without him.' Those words again. He seems too good to be true, but maybe there are people like him out there in the world that I don't know about.

'Never married?' A delicate question, I realise, but not out of place in the flow of the conversation. 'He was, to Kala.'

'From Fiji?' 'Yes, but like Viru, raised in Canada. A beautiful girl, so talented.' So there is a past, a history. 'What happened?' 'She was killed in a skiing accident in Banff. That's the main winter resort in western Canada. They were married twelve, maybe thirteen years.' 'No children?' 'No. Kala had life-threatening complications and they both decided not to risk her health.' He would have made a great daddy, I say to myself. What a great loss. I feel for Viren.

'So, how did this Fiji thing come about?' I ask as we sip masala chai. 'Canadian doctors have a volunteer scheme for developing countries. There is always demand for doctors in Africa, Latin America, parts of Asia. You put your name forward, fill out the forms, indicate your country of preference and wait. Viru chose Fiji. He got it. For many the really exotic places are Central America and Africa. You know, the Albert Schweitzer thing.' I had no idea who this person was, what he had done, why he was popular among doctors, but nodded knowledgeably, hoping she wouldn't ask me about him. 'And so he is here. Actually, your Medical Department chose Sigatoka for him.'

'I wonder why he chose Fiji when he could have gone to so many other places. I mean, Fiji? Everyone is leaving Fiji.' All the violence and turmoil, and this man wants to come here? 'But he has always wanted to come to Fiji, and this was the perfect opportunity.' I couldn't help wondering loudly, 'Why?' 'He is from Fiji, but like so many of us, he hardly knows the first thing about the country. How did we get here in the first place? What was *girmit* all about? Why is there so much trouble in this country? You can read about all this in the papers, but it is not the same thing, Meera.' Return voyage of self-discovery. Sounds so airy-fairy to me. 'I suppose you can afford it if you have the money.' Luxury of the rich. My curiosity increases.

'What about you, Meera?' Me? What about me? The question takes me by surprise. 'One day at a time, I suppose. We'll run this store for a while. It's not much, but at least we get by. People are friendly. Priya likes her school.' 'And Vinesh?' She had noticed him lying on the bed on the back verandah. I wish she had not brought his name up. Sometimes, it is good to escape the grim reality of our lives, think of happy things and forget about unhappy moments. 'A stroke. There is some movement in his right leg, but the left side of the body is gone. It is not like overseas here. And we don't have the money to take him overseas for treatment. We will just have to live with it. That's life, isn't it?' I hope I did not sound too depressed or despairing.

Time flew as our conversation ambled on. By the time we had had tea, it was nearly five. Just as we were getting up, there was a knock on the shop door. It was Viren! 'I am sorry, ma'am, but I am looking for Geeta. We had planned to go to Natadola this evening.' 'No, I haven't forgotten,' Geeta says as she rushes to the front door. 'Come on, Shirley, Mama is here.' 'Viru, you have met Meera, haven't you?' 'Well, yes, sort of. Hi, I am Viren,' he says, shaking my hand. 'Hi,' is all I am able to manage. Soft hands, gentle squeeze. I avert my gaze.

'Mum, can Priya come with us. Pleease!' Shirley pleads. Geeta looks at me. 'We'll be back in about two hours,' Viren says encouragingly. Priya was tugging at my hand, looking into my eyes for permission. 'Can I, Mum?' The little girl hardly goes anywhere, has no one to play with after school. Really, this place is like a prison for a small child. 'Only if you promise to behave.' 'Promise! Promise!' 'Would you...' Geeta asks me. But before she could complete her sentence, I said, 'No, no,

I can't. This is a very busy time of the day, and I have to give Vinesh a bath. Piyari, the house help, as taken the day off. But thanks. May be another time,' I say knowing that another time is a dream.

Natadola. It's ages since I have gone there although we live just half an hour away. Picnics and swimming and walking were never big with Vinesh. Beer with the boys was more his scene. But now all that's gone. Getting him out of bed is a challenge; getting him to go anywhere is a major expedition. He gets irritable, angry, frustrated, as if saying: why me, what have I done to deserve this? Why indeed, the poor man. My normal outing is from this place to the town, occasionally to the mandir or a puja during day-time. You have to be careful in this place. A poor man's wife is everyone's sister-in-law. Our reputation is all that we women have.

Priya was ecstatic. 'Mum, it was so good. Uncle Viru is so much fun.' 'Oh, Uncle Viru, eh? Since when? And what did this Uncle Viru of yours do that you are all ga-ga about him.' 'We swam. We splashed water on each other. We played soccer on the beach. We had coconut and ice-cream on the way back. He's such a kind man, Mum.' I am glad that Priya likes Viren. I sincerely hope she sees more of him. I hope he likes her too. This beautiful girl deserves all the fun she can have. Kind man, yes, but also probably very lonely. I wonder whether he misses his family, what goes through his heart as he tries to find himself in this place.

Geeta must have told Viren about Vinesh. Next day, early in the afternoon, they came over. 'Will I be able to see Vinesh?' Viren inquired. No pleasantries. Pretty direct, very doctor-like. 'Go right in,' I said as Geeta and I went into the kitchen to boil the kettle. Half an hour later, Viren returns and sits at the kitchen table. Both Geeta and I are all ears. 'CVA — sorry, Cerebrovascular Accident — that's the technical name for stroke of a fairly common kind. It is called schaemic stroke.'

'Translate, please,' Geeta teased Viren. 'Stroke occurs because the blood supply to part of the brain is totally or partially blocked through build up of a clot or through particle or debris from one part of the body travelling in another where it should not be,' Viren explains. Very much the doctor. No emotion. 'People with diabetes are particularly at risk. There are other more severe types of strokes, such as haemorrhagic stroke caused by bleeding in and around the brain, but fortunately, that is not the case here.' Then Viren asks me about Vinesh's pre-stroke health. 'Heavy smoker, fatty food, drinks, you know, the good life.' Viren shook his head. 'That's what they all think.'

'It must be hard on you,' Viren said to me. There was touching concern and sympathy in his voice. He was the first one in a long time who had spoken to me like that. Tears well up in my eyes. I am embarrassed, but I can't help it. 'With all that physical disability and emotional highs and lows and low self-esteem, the sleeplessness, the sores, the irritability, the panic attacks, the irregular bowel movement.' Viren was choosing his words carefully, almost clinically. He is a doctor after all. 'Complete recovery is impossible, but Vinesh can improve.' Yes, I live with that hope, but sometimes hope is not enough. I want a miracle.

I look straight into Viren's eyes, asking how? He reads my mind. 'Through occupational therapy, relearning daily activities such as eating, drinking, bathing, dressing, toilet, help with language and speech, returning as much as possible to the routine of daily life. Regular monitoring of temperature, blood pressure and sugar level. Emotional support is very important. Post-stroke depression can be very dangerous, fatal even. You must not make the person feel as if he is a burden.' I hope to God that I haven't.

Then checking himself, making sure he had not come across as a doctor talking to a patient, Viren said, 'I am sorry to sound so formal. I can see that you have been taking good care of Vinesh. Things can only improve from here on. He is a very lucky man.' Luck: what price, I think to myself. If only Viren knew the hell I go through every day just to keep us afloat. And Vinesh is not the easiest of men to please. Nothing is ever good enough for him these days. I should be at his beck and call twenty-four hours. He grills me whenever I go out to buy goods for the store: who I have seen and talked to. He throws a tantrum when he sees me speaking to male customers at the shop. He thinks I am having affairs. God, I sometimes wish that were true. 'I will send some antidepressants tomorrow,' Viren says as he leaves the house. I am sad to see him leave. It is so good to have adult conversation.

A few days before she returns to Canada, Geeta invites me to lunch at Viren's. Just the two of us. It is salad, sandwiches and soup. 'Something different,' Geeta apologises. 'Wouldn't dare try curry with you around.' I am flattered. We get along so well. I feel there is an unspoken bond between us. She understands my situation and feels for me, without any hint of pity or condescension. She knows that she will leave and return home. She has a place to go back to, to look forward to: friends, family, job. And I will go on as always, on my treadmill of daily routine.

The rooms are full of books and music as Priya had said, books along the wall, foreign magazines and newspapers, clippings friends have sent scattered on the floor of the reading room. CDs of music with Western names I don't know — Mozart, Beethoven, Schubert, Vivaldi — and dozens of Hindi ones by Lata Mangeshkar, Mohammed Rafi, Mukesh, Talat Aziz, Mehndi Hasan, Chandan Das, Jagjit and Chitra. I recognise all the songs on the covers, of course, songs of love, loss and longing, of times and places long forgotten, lodged deep in the memory. 'Books and music keep Viren going,' Geeta says. 'A hopeless romantic at heart, he is.' Nothing wrong with that, I say to myself. God, we could all do with more romance in our lives.

'Viren will miss you,' I tell Geeta. 'Shirley more than me,' she replies instantly. 'That girl means the world to him. She can do no wrong in his eyes. Spoils her rotten. She sleeps in his bed, they often eat from the same plate. It's a strange bond, very special.' So Viren has a warm heart as well. 'Viru is also very fond of Priya, you know. He says she's cute, very bright.' 'That's so nice of him.' 'And he admires you too, you know.' I look straight into Geeta's eyes, searching for any hints. 'The way you run the shop, look after Vinesh, the way you are raising Priya. It's not easy, especially for a woman.' Pity, sympathy, probably more than admiration, I think. I was hoping for something more, but then he hardly knows me.

'Can I go to Viru Mama's house?' Priya asked me a week or so after Geeta and Shirley had returned to Canada. 'He is not your Mama.' 'But Shirley calls him Mama.' 'That's different.' I don't have sisterly instincts towards Viren. Far from it. I am confused, but there is a deeper desire and longing that I can't quite describe, a desire for closer attachment perhaps, even romance. To sit together in the unlit night listening to syrupy songs, picnics at the beach, long walks in the mountains, movies. 'Call him Chacha.' Father's younger brother or cousin with whom a joking or even a sexual relationship is permissible. That way, no roads are closed. 'Or simply Uncle. But not Mama.'

Priya and Viren get on like a house on fire, as they say. 'Chacha said this, Chacha did that.' She was almost possessive about him. 'My Chacha,' she would say to children at school. She once invited him to school to give a talk about Canada. She was so proud. Everyone adored him and the girls envied Priya. The two go swimming together at the beach, to the town on Saturdays. He cooks for her, and they watch movies together. Once or twice she has slept over. After years of neglect and the physical absence of fatherly attention, Priya is beginning to blossom. A child's innocent heart and pure love are truly wonderful things to behold. I often wonder about Viren and Priya, what they talk about, the games they play. I sometimes desperately want to be a part of that company, but Vinesh would disapprove. He disapproves of so many things these days. Besides, I don't have the time.

I now look forward to seeing Viren on his early morning walks, his sweaty athletic body striding in the distance, head covered with a baseball cap. He picks up his bread and morning papers, smiles his innocent smile, asks after Priya and Vinesh and then leaves. He is concerned about Vinesh. That much I can see. The other day, he brought some antidepressant pills along with a small booklet explaining the different kinds of stroke, thrombotic and embolic and others I forget, and their diagnosis and therapy.

The two have struck up a chord. Vinesh can be (and recently has been) irritating and stubborn, but he is not dumb. The two talk mostly about the past. Viren is keen to know how things were done in the 'old days.' The marriage ceremonies, the funeral rites, the celebrations of festivals, the text books students read. 'Try some of the retired head teachers for the books,' Vinesh advises, but there is no luck. 'We don't have a sense of the past,' Viren says to Vinesh one day. I agree. Getting by or getting on top by hook or by crook is the story of our people. Vinesh now looks forward eagerly to his talks with Viren. It is good to have him around, just his physical presence.

Next morning, Viren was up for his walk as usual. 'I am having a party for some friends this Saturday. I would like you to come, Meera.' This was the first time Viren had ever taken my name, and he looked straight into my eyes, unblinking. My heart missed a beat. Inside, I felt as if I was meeting a man I had always wanted to meet. Something is happening, but I can't put my finger on it. It is something I felt all those years ago when I first met Vinesh, the same flutter, the same anxiousness, the self-consciousness whenever Viren was around, wishing always that he would prolong his visit, any excuse to talk to him.

'Of course,' I replied excitedly. 'Not sure about Vinesh, but Priya and I will be there.' 'No, Priya is coming over on Friday!' says Viren. 'You two are something else. Lately you seem to be the most important person in her life,' I say. That is the truth. I am of course delighted with the developing bond between the two of them. Viren smiles, still looking at me as he prepares to leave. Saturday is two days away. 'What's on the menu?' I ask hesitatingly. I don't want to appear intrusive. 'I will think of something. There is still time.' 'Leave that to me.' 'I can't possibly do that.' 'This is Fiji, not Canada, doctor-ji. We could go shopping tomorrow afternoon.'

We do, just the two of us. Priya is still at school. It is so good to be driven, not to have to worry about all the crazy drivers on the road giving you the dirty looks, not to have to bother about parking. Viren is a polite, careful driver. Nice aftershave. 'Nice day,' Viren says to me, looking ahead, his hands firmly on the steering wheel. We are both avoiding eye contact, both acutely self-conscious of being together in a confined space, but I like being physically close to him. There is something reassuring about that. 'That time of the year,' I say. It is May. We head for *Rupa's Fresh Foods*. Viren pushes a rattling wayward trolley. 'Like your cars,' he says to me and laughs. 'I thank our potholes and mechanics,' I add smilingly. We buy three kilos of fresh goat meat, two kilos of king prawns and from the vegetable section, garlic, onions, ginger, coriander leaves, tomatoes and hot chillies. We don't say much to each other. We don't need to. That is the beauty of it all, the understood silence.

Mid-morning Saturday, I walk over to Viren's to cook. Everything is properly stacked: the plates, the bowls, the kitchen towels, the stove squeaky clean. He hasn't done this just for me, has he, I wonder. He makes me a coffee as we plunge into the cooking. Viren cuts the onions in thin strips, and crushes ginger and garlic. 'Medium hot?' I ask. 'Oh, the normal.' 'No one eats goat in Vancouver,' Viren says, 'but it is so delicious. So lean.' He's trying to create conversation. I smile. 'Well, you will have to come to Fiji more often, won't you?' I add. 'I would like to,' he says. There is touch of hesitation in his voice. I look straight at Viren, but he averts his eyes and moves away from the kitchen. By mid-afternoon, the cooking is all done. 'See you around seven,' I say as I leave. 'It's our party, yours and mine together,' he says gently as he opens the front door.

What to wear? I feel like a girl about to make an appearance at an important or glamorous party. Red Salwaar, orange *dupatta* will look good and red *bindiya*. A dash of Opium. Gold bangles and my favourite gold necklace, a gift from our wedding so many years ago. I tie my hair neatly in a bun, and lightly brush with powder the faint worry lines on my forehead. 'Mum, you look great,' Priya says, hugging me. 'Chaccha will be really pleased.' 'Will he?' Why am I asking a little child this, I catch myself thinking. 'How do you know?''C'ause I know,' Priya replies with a mischievous smile. 'Yes, always the know-it-all, eh.' I stroke Priya's hair.

'Don't be late,' Vinesh says from his bed. 'I am not feeling well.' When do you feel well, I say to myself angrily. Can't I have a moment of fun without you spoiling it for me? Lately, he has been behaving strangely. He disapproves of Priya sleeping over at Viren's. And he does not like me talking to him much either. He doesn't say much, but his body language gives him away. No doubt, he thinks I am having an affair with Viren or something close to it. He knows I have never betrayed him. Sometimes, his sullen looks get too much. Then, I wish I were actually having an affair. But it is always a guilty, fleeting thought. Nothing, no one in the world, is going to spoil this evening for me.

Guests are already in the verandah when I arrive. A European couple, a Japanese medical consultant and a doctor from India. People compliment me on my dress. 'That's the thing about this place,' Mrs Lansdowne says, 'so splendidly, joyously, colourful.' 'Fiji: a resplendence of colours' would be a nice description of this beautiful country,' David, her husband adds. 'How long have you known Viru,' Mrs Lansdowne asks me. I note the hint of familiarity. 'A few months.' 'Related?' 'No, just good neighbours.' 'We miss that here, friends dropping by for an afternoon cup of tea or just a chat.' Viren is a great host — polite, playful, courteous — and good at light conversation. When he goes to the kitchen to fetch a bottle of wine, Mrs Lansdowne says, 'He is a most wonderful man, you know.' I know. Looking at David, she says with a wink, 'Lucky you came before him.' 'Ah! Lucky is my middle name, dear.'

Viren behaves as if I am the hostess of the party. I like the attention. I haven't felt like this for years. The banter, the easy laughter, the lightness of touch, the familiarity of friends, wide-ranging conversation, the welcome attention. It is a special evening. Once or twice, I catch Viren looking at me from across the head of the table. Unresisting, I return his gaze. There is a gentle smile in his eyes. I feel warm all over. Yes, it is our party together. It is our secret.

Guests leave around midnight. Priya is asleep on the couch in the living room, the remote control still in her hands. I envy her innocent peace. I wash the dishes and Viren dries them. It all feels so natural, as if I have known Viren for ages. Then we return to the veranda with our cups of coffee. The night is soft, silent, except for the occasional croaking of frogs, and the moon is caressed by gentle, passing clouds. I wish Viren would touch me, hold me close to him. It has been a long time. He is in an easy chair, gazing into the moonlit distance, sipping coffee.

'So how have you found this Fiji of ours?' I ask. 'Your first trip?' 'Yes, actually.' This takes me by surprise. People travel so much these days, and Viren is not short of money. 'Any reason?' 'My father didn't want to return, and we didn't persist. I know many families which have never returned.' The hurt perhaps, the guilt of leaving desperate relatives behind, the struggle in the new homeland. I had heard similar stories from returning relatives before. 'Why now?' I ask. 'The Canadian volunteer scheme provided the perfect opportunity.' 'Like the Peace Corps? We have some Peace Corps teachers at school. 'Yes, something like that, but more professionally oriented: doctors, engineers, those sorts of people.'

'Any relatives in Fiji?' I ask. It is then that Viren tells me about his visit to Ba, which had splintered his heart. He had gone there for a week, to Vatia, in 'search of my roots,' as he put it. His father, Ram Shankar, once a primary schoolteacher turned insurance agent, had worked there. Younger people at the Ba Hotel, where he stayed, had no knowledge of local history. No one knew his father. Inquire with the rural shopkeepers, someone suggested. He did. At first people seemed reluctant to talk, or tried to change the subject or pretended ignorance. Viren persisted. Then one day, the story seeped out, slowly at first and then in torrents. Ram Shankar, the insurance agent, had blackened his name through a notorious series of arson cases in Ba about thirty years ago. Several shops in the town burned down over four nights. Arson was suspected. The shopkeepers, all Gujarati, were supporters of the cane strike so they could get the farmers in greater debt than they were in already. In retaliation, so it was said, a group of incensed anti-strikers burned down the shops. No one was ever caught. The shopkeepers claimed insurance from Ram Shankar's insurance company.

The true story emerged years later. The wooden structures were old and rotting. The shopkeepers wanted them pulled down. They bribed Ram Shankar. He got their insurance papers in order, overestimating the value of the houses by thousands of dollars. And then he hired his cousins to torch them. Everyone knew the truth but was too afraid to report it to the police. Ram Shankar had everyone in his pocket or under his thumb, not a man to be crossed or treated lightly. If he himself didn't intimidate people into submission, he had friends who did. It is difficult to believe this story that such a gentle and caring man as Viren could have such a brutal father as Ram Shankar.

Ba was Ram Shankar's place in more than one way. He belonged to a group of wealthy and well-connected men — big landlords and moneylenders — for whom the village women from poor homes were playthings. They could have anyone they wanted, and they did. Ram Shankar made one of them pregnant, but denied paternity. No one could do anything about it. Reporting the matter to the police was out of the question; that would bring only more trouble. And the local village advisory committee was in Ram Shankar's pocket. The girl was hurriedly married off into a poor home. 'You should meet your illegitimate brother,' an old man had remarked acidly, spitting out rough tobacco. 'He could do with some help, the poor fellow.'

Parmesh lived on the outskirts of Moto, a poor casual labourer, a hired cane cutter in the cane harvesting season. Viren was bitterly ashamed of his father, leaving a woman pregnant with his child, just like that. 'How cruel can you be?' he said. 'Even animals acknowledge their offspring.' Viren said nothing about who he was. 'It broke my heart to see my Parmesh in a state of abject poverty, torn clothes on his body, his children working as hired labourers even at their tender age. The look of desperation in their eyes. Their future is dead.' 'Did you say anything?' 'What could I say? There was so much I wanted to know about my brother's background, his journey, whether he knew who his real father was. Perhaps he didn't. It was better to leave the past in its grave. I gave him the hundred or so dollars I had on me, and promised to send him funds regularly. Why this generosity from this complete stranger? he must have wondered. Or did he, like me, know the truth but thought it best not to bring it up? It would have been too painful to find out.'

Parmesh was not Viren's only discovery in Ba. He also learned that his mother was his father's second wife. He had divorced his first wife with whom he had two daughters. 'Divorce was worse than death in those days,' Viren says. You became an outcast for life, living in suffering and sufferance, a free domestic helping hand, little more. His wife and daughters were packed off to their parents' place near Vaileka. She never remarried and died a few years ago of tuberculosis. 'A whole life destroyed, and no remorse, no regret,' Viren says. 'My father never said a word about all this. What a stone-hearted man.' 'What about the daughters?' I ask. 'I wish I knew.' No one in Ba knew when or where they were married, whether they were still alive. 'A part of my past is lost forever, gone' The visit to Ba explained to Viren why his father had so few friends in Canada. Even close relatives had kept their distance from him. It made sense to him now why all these years Ram Shankar had refused to return to Fiji, to connect Viren to his roots. The door was slammed shut on Fiji, secrets kept from the family until now.

Viren is devastated by his father's secret past. Fiji has lost its charm for him. I touch his forearm. 'All this has nothing to do with you, Viren,' I say in sympathy. 'We all have skeletons in our closets.' What hurt Viren most was that the memory of his father's deeds were still remembered and recalled bitterly by the older generation in the village. And the discovery of his half-brother and his step-sisters had overwhelmed him. 'They don't deserve this,' he said. 'I wish I had known about this earlier.'

'I will be leaving the day after tomorrow,' he says after a long silence. His words strike me like lightning. 'For how long?' I ask, dreading the answer. 'For good.' 'I see,' is all I can manage. 'Nice to have met you. Priya will miss you a lot.' 'I will miss her. And I will miss you too.' 'Me? What have I done?' I ask, looking into his face. 'I don't know where to begin. Perhaps it is better not to say anything,' Viren replies. 'We don't have much time. And knowing the truth won't hurt.' 'I admire the way you juggle so many things: the store, Priya, Vinesh.' Is that all he thinks about me? I feel irritation welling up. 'I can do without pity. We women are not as helpless as you men think or believe.' 'I did not mean it that way. You are a very attractive woman, Meera. Just because I didn't say anything to you doesn't mean I did not notice you. I noticed you the moment I first saw you. What man wouldn't?'

I am touched but feel a 'but' coming. 'I wish times were different, things were different,' Vinesh says in a voice choking with emotion. 'Yes, it is always like that, isn't it?' Why does it have to be me? 'Vinesh loves you. More, he needs you. I couldn't possibly hurt Vinesh. He does not deserve that, not in his present state. He doesn't have anyone besides you. You are his everything.' I have my needs too. What about my needs? Does anyone ever think of that? 'I truly wish things were different, Meera, but they are not.' I see tears welling up in Viren's eyes. 'You will always be in my heart.'

I will be very sad to see Viren leave. He gave me hope, made me feel special. I felt young again, full of life. I looked forward to his morning walks like a girl in love. The comfort of his presence, the vague anticipation of better things to come. His gentle, caring ways. But it's all in the past now. It is best for him to leave. Fiji will always haunt him, and he will be destroyed by it. He doesn't deserve that. There is nothing I can say or do that will lessen his pain. We both stand up spontaneously and hug each other. A long, warm hug. Viren's shoulder is wet with my tears. I feel his strong athletic chest against mine. I can almost hear his heart beat. I must leave.

I see a strip of glowing light appearing on the horizon. Another dawn is breaking. Soon the bread truck will arrive and it will be time to open for business.

6

A Gap in the Hedge

> We go back a long way, you and I,
> through a gap in the hedge, across a field,
> through a gate we forgot to close...
>
> Hugo Williams

Ram, my best friend, is unwell. High blood pressure, failing kidneys and rampant diabetes, have all taken their toll on his health. 'Not long to go, Bhai,' he said to me the other day, managing a characteristically resigned smile. He is living by himself, alone, in a one bedroom rented apartment in Bureta Street, a working class suburb of Suva. I visit him most evenings, have a bowl of grog, and talk long into the night about the old days. Both he and I know that the end is near, which makes each visit all the more poignant. As Ram often says, repeating the lines of Surendra's immortal fifties' song, *Hum bhor ke diye hain, bhujte hi ja rahe hain*, we are the dawn's candle, slowly going out (one by one).

Ram and I go back a long way. We were fellow students at Labasa Secondary in the late sixties. He was easily the best history and literature student in the school. He knew earlier than anyone of us what *Lord of the Flies* and *Lord Jim* were about, the two books we were studying for the exams. I often sought his assistance with my English assignments, and helped him with geography, at which he was curiously hopeless. I still have in my library the final year autograph book in which he had written these lines: *When they hear not thy call, but cower mutely against the wall, O man of evil luck, walk alone.* 'Ekla Chalo,' in Mahatma Gandhi's famous words, "Walk Alone".

We both went to university on scholarship to prepare for high school teaching in English and History. I went on to an academic life while Ram, by far the brighter, was content to become and remain a high school teacher. One day we talked about Malti. 'I wonder where she is now,' I asked. 'Married and migrated,' Ram said. 'No contact?' 'No. There was no point. It was all too late.' Ram and Malti were an 'item' at school. Their developing love for each other was a secret we guarded zealously. We knew that if they were caught, they would be expelled, just like that, no compassion, and no mercy. Labasa Secondary was not for romantics. It was a factory which prepared students for useful careers, its self esteem measured by the number of A graders it had in the external exams and where it ranked in the colonial educational hierarchy with other notable secondary schools: Marist Brothers, Suva Grammar and Natabua High.

Malti failed her university entrance exam, and her cane growing parents were too poor to support her at university. Jobs in Labasa were few, so Malti stayed at home. Ram was distraught, but there was little he could do but go to university. At the end of the first year, he received a sad letter from Malti telling him that she was getting married to an accountant at Morris Hedstrom. After all these years, Ram still had the letter, quoting lines he had once recited to her. *You will always be my light from heaven, a spark from an immortal fire.* 'Byron, did you know?' I didn't. 'You are the poet, man. I am a mere garden variety academic.' Then Ram recited Wordsworth's Lucy poem: *A violet on a mossy bank, Half hidden from the eye.* Such aching pain, endured through the years.

After completing university, Ram married Geeta. Both were teaching at Laucala Bay Secondary. Geeta came from a well known Suva merchant family. She married Ram not out of love but convenience, I always thought, after her long love affair with a fellow teacher had come to an abrupt end. Ram was a good catch, a university graduate, well spoken, handsome, employed, and well regarded. Geeta was stylish, opinionated and ambitious. But Ram was in no hurry to get anywhere soon. He was happy as long as he had his books and his music. Whatever money he could spare, he would spend on books ordered from Whitcomb and Tombs in New Zealand and Angus Robertson in Sydney. He was probably the most deeply and widely read man in Fiji, a far better student of poetry than some of the post-modern pretenders at the local university.

In 1984, Ram was transferred to Lamolamo Secondary. Geeta tried hard to persuade him to reject the offer. Her father interceded on their behalf with the Chief Education Officer (Secondary), but without success. Even a bottle of *Black Label* failed to get the desired result: teachers were in short supply and, worse, the new fellow, too earnest for his own good, seemed strangely impervious to importunities of any kind, including the *daru-murga* variety (dinner-drinks). Ram feigned disappointment to Geeta, but was quietly pleased at the prospect of spending some time in the west, among country people whom he liked so much, away from his intrusive in-laws, away from the soul-destroying, incestuous 'socials' on the Suva teachers' cocktail circuit. He told Geeta that the transfer was just another step to better things and before they knew it, they would be back in Suva.

Lamolamo was a rural hinterland, smack in the middle of the cane belt of Western Viti Levu. The living quarters at the school were spartan, the water supply and electricity erratic, roads unpaved, food cooked on open fire, clothes washed by hand in the nearby river, drinking water fetched from the well. 'Living hell,' is how Geeta described her new home to her parents and friends in Suva. The slow rhythm of village life was well beyond her. The other teachers at the school were from western Viti Levu and spent their weekends with their relatives attending weddings and birthday parties, but Geeta had no close relations nearby, no one she could properly socialize with. 'Rurals' was how she contemptuously described the village people, rough, lacking in elementary social graces, plain. '*Tan ko sahoor nahin haye.*' No manners whatsoever.

Ram revelled in the village environment, re-living the vanishing world of his rural childhood in Labasa. In no time, he had made friends in the village. He loved attending Ramayan recitals in the evenings and having a bowl of grog or two with the people at Sambhu's store. People asked him for favours: filling forms, writing letters to families who had migrated, giving advice about education. Ram was a regular and much honoured speaker at weddings and funerals. '*Masterji aye gaye haye,*' people would say, Master has arrived, sending shrieking school children into immediate respectful silence. 'You should stand for election, Master,' Kandasami suggested one day. 'We will support you, no problem.'

A political career was furthest from Ram's mind, but he appreciated the invitation. '*Retirement ke baad men dekhe khoi.*' We'll see after I retire. The topic kept returning.

Geeta resented Ram's after-school life. He would often return late, usually with a few friends, for an evening of grog and bull session. She would be expected to cook dinner. 'I also work, in case you have not noticed,' she would tell Ram after his friends left. She would often retreat to her bedroom and Ram would heat up the food himself. The silences between the two were getting longer, more sustained, eye contact averted, conversation more and more strained. The physical intimacy of the early years was long gone.

'You have been stuck in this job all this time. Why don't you apply for promotion?' Geeta asked. She had in mind head of department, assistant principal, and then finally the top job at some decent suburban school near Suva. 'But I love what I am doing. I love being in the classroom,' Ram replied. 'Geeta, you should see the way the children's eyes light up when they finally get something. Today, we were reading 'The Snake.' Such a beautiful poem, don't you think: Lawrence gets the cadences, the nuances, the slithering subtleties.' Ram usually spoke about literature the way he wrote prose: complete sentences, words carefully chosen. Poetry was the last thing on Geeta's mind.

All the pressure, the nagging, finally did it. Ram gave in and accepted the headship of the Social Science Department. Soon afterwards, all his horrors of headship materialised. One of his teachers was having an affair with the head girl. This had been going on for sometime, but Ram being Ram, was the last one to know. Charan Singh, the principal, was adamant: the offending teacher would have to go. 'One rotten potato can ruin the whole sack,' was how he put it. 'But where will he go? He will be finished for life. We can put a stop to all this. Just give me one chance.' Ram remonstrated. 'Too late for that, Ram,' Charan Singh replied with a firm tap of the finger on the desk, signalling the meeting was over. 'He should have thought about his future beforehand, kept his trousers zipped.' 'Come on, it hasn't gone that far, Mr Singh' Ram reminded him. 'Could have! Then what?'

Reluctantly, Ram broke the news to Prem Kumar, who had just turned twenty two. The head girl was eighteen. He had to go, and he did. 'I am sorry Prem,' was all Ram could manage. Ram was troubled for a long time. 'It's so unfair,' he thought aloud to himself. 'One mistake, just one, and your life is over in the blink of an eye lid.' He decided there and then that he would not apply for further promotion. 'If I want power, I will become a bloody politician,' he resolved to himself.

'This is my kind of place, Geeta,' Ram said when she asked him again to seek a transfer from this 'rural hell hole,' as she put it. There was a vacancy at Nadera High for a vice-principal. 'I am at home here, at peace. Look at those mountains.' He was referring to the craggy Nausori Highlands in the background splitting Viti Levu in half. 'The play of light on them at dusk. It's majestic. After this, who would want to be in Suva with all the rain and the dampness and the mosquitoes? 'But I will be closer to my parents.' 'That's what holidays are for, Geeta.' 'It is not good enough. You have your friends here. I have nobody.'

Before Ram and Geeta could resolve the deepening impasse between them, Sitiveni Rabuka struck with the first of Fiji's four coups on May 14 1987. The school closed for a month. Ram and Geeta returned to Suva to be with Geeta's parents. There were unconfirmed reports of gangs of thugs terrorising Indo-Fijian areas of the city. In Geeta's parents' house, there was turmoil. Once the talk was of promotion and transfer, now it was migration. 'Everyone is leaving. Just look at the long queues in front of the Australian and New Zealand Embassies,' Geeta's father said. Ram had seen the long lines, and been moved by the look on the faces of people in the scorching May sun. 'This place is finished. *Khalas sab kutch.* We Indians have no future here,' Geeta's mother chimed in. 'We have talked to Sudhir, and he has agreed to sponsor you. We will come later.' Sudhir was Geeta's older brother living in Auckland.

Ram was torn. He knew he could not leave Fiji, yet he also could not ignore Geeta's wish. The closeness between the two had gone, but he still wanted to be with Geeta, more out of habit and obligation than anything else. But the faces of the villagers in Lamolamo also haunted him. 'Where will they go?' he kept asking himself: no means, no connections, unskilled, tethered to their farms all their lives, coping without help or hope. 'I can't leave them now when they need me most,' he told Geeta one day.

Geeta was unmoved. 'That's the problem with you Ram. You always put others before me, before us. *Sab ke pahile, aapan ke sab roj baad men.* I don't know what magic have the village people done to you.' Time was of the essence. David Lange, the New Zealand prime minister, was quietly allowing Fiji people to enter New Zealand without the usual stringent visa requirements. 'We have to do something now before it is too late. Who knows when the doors will be shut?' 'You go and I will follow later,' Ram said unconvincingly. 'If that is what you want,' Geeta replied, knowing full well that Ram would be the last person to leave Fiji. She knew in her heart that their married life was over.

Ram returned to Lamolamo as soon as the school reopened. He taught his share of classes, but he was far more troubled by what was happening to the country and to his community, being gradually wrapped in the descending veil of darkness and despair, as he put it. People in the village peppered him with questions when they met for their usual grog sessions at Sambhu's store. A state of emergency was in force, the newspapers were censored, and radio news in Hindi bland amidst funereal music and sad songs. But in the countryside, *Rumour Devi and Messers Fact and Fantasy* were running wild. There were reports of people being picked up at night and interrogated at the military barracks, forced to walk bare feet on scorching tar sealed roads for miles, made to drink drain water, forced to crawl on rough pebbly ground, masturbate in front of others. Ram had heard the rumours, too, but did not know the truth.

Then, one day in town, quite by accident, he came across a copy of *The Fiji Voice* at Master Mohan's place. Mohan, a retired head teacher, was in contact with the union people in Suva. The newspaper, the brainchild of Sydney journalist and trade unionist Dale Keeling, printed hard hitting news censored in Fiji, especially news about the rampant abuse of human rights. Ram became a regular and avid reader, and related its troubling contents to the villagers at the shop in the evenings, to the slow shaking of heads in utter disbelief that such atrocities were taking place in Fiji. *Biswaas nahi hoye ki aisan cheez hiyan kabhi hoye sake*, people said. Sometimes, he used the school photocopier to make copies for people in neighbouring villages. The more sensational abuses reported in the newsletter were translated into Hindi. People were confused and bewildered and helpless, powerless witness to their own paralysis and guilty impotence.

'You are banging your head against a rock, Ram,' his colleague Satish had remarked. 'Don't get me wrong, bro. I know the coup is wrong and all, but sometimes we have to accept reality too.' 'Yes, that's what they all say,' Ram replied, slightly irritated. 'That is what they all want us to accept, commit political suicide voluntarily.' He continued 'Where would we be if we had accepted that the Britishers were going to be here forever? Where would the world be if they had accepted the 'reality' of Hitler's master plan?' Ram had thought about this and rehearsed his arguments carefully. 'No, the reality thing does not do it for me. It's a cop out, man, and you know it.'

'All that the Fijians want is to control the government, Ram,' Satish said calmly. 'That's all. You give them that and they will leave us alone. These are not a bad people, you know.' 'Not at the point of the barrel of a gun. No. Do you really think they will leave us alone? An inch today, a foot tomorrow. Today they take our government away, tomorrow it will be our homes and businesses. We have to stop this cancer now before it destroys us all.' 'You are an idealist, Ram,' Satish said. *Unsudharable*. Unchangeable. 'Better that than a neutral — or shall I say neutered — armchair 'realists' like you folks, Satish.' Ram remembered Gandhiji's words: *A no muttered form the deepest conviction is better and greater than a yes muttered merely to please, or what is worse, to avoid trouble.*

'Remember, all the guns are on the other side, and you know who will be killed first when the shooting starts, don't you?' Satish continued. 'Just look around, Ram, and tell me how many of these *chakka panji* (hoi-polloi] will follow you into the battle: a handful, if that. Your problem, man, is that your head is always in the clouds, lost in lofty thoughts. Get real for once. *E kuaan men panni nahi haye, bhaiywa.*' This well has no water, my friend. 'It is easy sitting here in our cushy chairs with our monthly salaries and long holidays and pontificate, do nothing, accept things as they are,' Ram said. Well that is not good enough for me.' There were times when Ram felt like Sisyphus rolling his stone up the mountain, but there was nothing else he could do. The struggle had to go on. *Still we persist, plough the light sand, and sow/Seed after seed where none can ever grow.*

The people of Lamolamo were incensed at what had happened, ready to erupt like an overheated furnace. The village was a close knit community. It spoke as one on most things. It was known far and wide for its single-minded solidarity. This was also Labour heartland. For many Mahendra Chaudhry, the Labour leader, was their guardian angel. They had waited for so long to be in government, only to thrown out after a month. One day at Sambhu's shop, they decided to form a small committee to map strategy. *Ek dam kuch kare ke padi.* We absolutely have to do something, all the villagers resolved. Ram Baran, the village *mukhia*, headman, was on it along with Shafiq Ali, the owner of several lorries, Buta Singh, a large cane grower, and Chinnappa Naidu, the leader of the South Indians. Every cultural group was represented. Ram was invited to join. In fact, he was the one who had mooted the idea.

In the months after the coup, things went from bad to worse. Rabuka's belligerent Christian rhetoric compounded fears. His words on Radio Fiji sounded ominous. *I appeal to all Christian leaders to concentrate on evangelising Hindus and*

Muslims' he thundered. That was the only way for permanent peace in Fiji, if everyone believed in the one God, Jehovah. Hindu and Muslim festivals might not be celebrated as national holidays. Fijians must do what the Christian missionaries had done: convert heathens to Christianity. *I would be guilty in the face of God if I did not do that, if I did not use my office, my influence, to get the Church, those who believe in Lord Jesus Christ to teach his love and what he stands for.*

Wild rumours spread in the village about forcible conversions, especially of children. Ram tried to calm fears. 'It's all talk, cheap talk,' he told people at the shop one evening. 'The white missionaries tried this before during *girmit*. No success. Think: if they did not succeed, will these fellows? Converting cannibals was one thing. Us? Never.' People nodded amidst bowls of kava. 'We are Sanatan Dharam, *bhaiya. Koy khelwaar ke baat nahi haye*,' said Bhola. Eternal, without beginning or end, indestructible, nothing to trifle with. 'What will Christians give us that we don't already have?' '*Patthar*, useless stones, rubble,' Ram Jiwan piped up from the back.

Within a week, talk of conversion had turned sinister. One night, while people were meeting at the shop, the *Shiv Mandir*, the main village temple, was trashed and about $25 in donations stolen, the prayer book burned and idols smashed. The radio reported more desecrations in Tavua and Rakiraki, including the desecration of a mosque. 'How low can these *kuttas*, dogs, Go, Master?' Mahavir said to Ram, 'What have our gods done to Fiji that they deserve this?' He began sobbing. It had taken him and a few others a very long time to build the *mandir* from scratch, with hard-earned donations collected at *Ramayan* recitals. Now all gone.

Ram was ropeable. 'No use crying, bro. We have to do something.' People looked in his direction as he spat out the words in embittered anger. Like what? 'We should torch one of their bloody churches,' Piyare suggested. *'Jaraao saale ke.* I will do it myself.' 'No,' Ram advised. 'No, we should guard the mandir and our homes with physical force. We should form a group and take turns every night.' A vigilante group is what Ram had in mind. 'They touch one finger, we chop off their hands. These people only understand violence. If they want to fight, we give them a fight.' *Cowards die many times before their deaths; The valiant never taste of death but once.*

These were fighting words from a man of peace whose first love, preceding and leading to Malti, was English poetry. Something deep had stirred in Ram. Reports of daily humiliation, petty discrimination, the taunting and the threats, the steady drift of the community into the limbo between life and death, had had their effect. He was like a man possessed. 'How dare these bastards do this to us,' he said to Satish one day. 'Our forefathers built this place up with their bare hands. This is our home too. And they think they can take away our rights, just like that, and we would do nothing. Hell no. Over my dead body.' 'There will be many dead bodies before this evil saga is over, Bro,' Satish replied. 'This is *Kalyug,* after all, remember.' The cosmic Dark Age.

People were with Ram. Young men armed with polished mangrove sticks and sharpened cane knives patrolled the village. They protected the temple and would have beaten to pulp anyone caught attempting desecration. Some of the young men described themselves as members of the *Bajrang Dal,* soldiers of Lord Hanuman who had single-handedly rescued Sita from the clutches of Ravana. *'Dekha jaai ka hoye.'*

'We are prepared for whatever happens,' the young men said. Nothing happened for months. The attacks had been condemned by leading church leaders, even by Rabuka himself. The thugs had made their point, their anger subsided. People relaxed and went back to their old routine.

But just as one crisis was over, another emerged. The Sunday Ban came into force, banning all sports and work on Sabbath. There was no public transport on Sunday. You couldn't bury the dead, wash clothes in the open, organise weddings or social gatherings without official permission, or work in the fields. Opinion in the village was divided. For Ram, as always, it was a matter of principle. 'No one has the right to tell me when to rest. This is a free country. And since when has Sunday become our day of rest?' There was the farming angle to consider as well. 'If we don't harvest on Sunday, what happens when the wet weather starts? The mills won't operate after December.' Suruj Bali said. 'Forget about harvesting *yaar*,' Bhola chimed in 'we won't have taxis on the roads, no buses, nothing. What if we have to go to hospital?' 'Once again, we poor people get caught in the middle,' someone added. *Phir garib log ke upar sala museebat aaye*. But some of the casual labourers who usually kept quiet, actually welcomed a rest on Sunday. They had nothing to lose. *Is me hum log ke ka kharabi haye?*

One day, Bansi organised a large Bhagvata Katha at his place to mark the first anniversary of his father's death. The entire village was invited to the ten day affair. It was not an act of defiance, though Ram thought it was. It was thought that such a harmless religious activity would be of no interest to the authorities. They were wrong. Late on the second day, a truck load of soldiers arrived. After making enquiries, they took Bansi and his eldest son Jamuna away. Both returned home late in the evening in a hired cab, their bodies bloodied and bruised, lips swollen from punches, pants soiled. 'Next time we catch you,' the soldiers had warned them, 'you will find yourself in a morgue.'

How did the military find out what was happening at Bansi's house in the middle of nowhere? Ram wondered. Obviously, there were spies among them. But who? Ram suspected Jumsa, an excessively deferential unemployed young man, who attended all the meetings, listened intently to everything that was spoken but never said a word. Often he volunteered for anything the village committee decided. But there was no proof. Only much later it was revealed that Ram Baran, whose spy Jumsa was, had quarrelled with Bansi over a land boundary and lost the court case. This was his opportunity to take revenge and gain favour with the military chief for western Viti Levu, Aisake Mualevu. Unknown to anyone, this respected leader of the village, the chairman of the village coup committee, in whom everyone reposed trust and confidence, was also the military's eyes and ears in the settlement. A sheep without, a wolf within. *Haraamzada*. The labyrinths of betrayal and deceit ran deep in the roots of our community. *Is there not some chosen curse, Some hidden thunder in the stores of Heav'n, Red with uncommon wrath, to blast the man, Who owes his greatness to his country's ruin?*

With no signs in Suva of the crisis resolving, talk increased of putting more pressure on the military regime. The leaders decided that there should be a boycott of the cane harvest. 'We must bring this illegal regime to its knees,' one of them said. 'Why should we pay these bastards to put their boots into us?' 'When we ask for sanctions from overseas, we must be prepared to pay a price ourselves.' 'Sacrifice begins at home.' 'We broke the CSR's back with our strikes,' someone said 'what is this?' *Saalan ke nas maar de khoi.* Well shall teach the bastards a lesson, reduce them to impotence. Brave talk of defiance and determination began circulating in the village. Ram was quietly pleased at the way people were beginning to stiffen. His occasional doubt about their resolve began to dissolve.

A meeting of the village committee was convened to firm things up. The usual pro-harvest boycott arguments were rehearsed. Ram took the minutes. Buta Singh, the biggest cane farmer in the village, who had remained quiet through out the meeting, spoke when everyone had finished and a vote was about to be taken. 'Why is it that whenever there is any problem, the farmers are the first ones to be asked to make sacrifices? No one comes to help us when we are down, when there is a drought or a flood or hurricane or fire.' All eyes were on him. 'Will the trade union babus making so much noise now sacrifice a single cent from their salaries? Will the big businesses, which suck our blood, close their shops for even one day? Will they? Then why ask us to be the first ones to be in the frontline?' *Kahe khaali hum kisan log ke sab se aage pahile bheja jaaye haye?*

'*Hum log ek chota kund ke megha haye*, Sirdarji,' We are frogs in a small pond, Ram Samujh responded after a long, stunned silence following Buta's blunt words. 'Our leaders will never ask us to make sacrifice unless there is no other way. They are one of us. *Hamai log ke admi to haye.* We have complete faith in them. Cent per cent.' 'Buta,' Shiu Ram said sharply, 'you are worried about saving your pennies when the whole country is going to the dogs. All these nice buildings, nice farms, tractors: what's the use having them when we have no rights in this country? Fighting this evil regime must be the first priority of every Indian in this country.' 'Think back, front, right, left, before you decide. ' *Aage, peeche, daayen, baayen, dekh ke bichaar aur faisala karna.* Buta Singh said as he left the meeting. In the end, the meeting decided to boycott.

Buta Singh had made sense, Ram thought and said as much. 'We must bring this illegal regime down,' he told the meeting, 'but everyone should shoulder his share of the burden.' He himself was prepared to sacrifice part of his salary for the cause. 'There should be a national strategy for a national boycott. Everyone should chip in. Traitors should know what will happen to them. We will boycott their shops. 'Burn them down,' someone said. 'Yes, if we have to.' 'Talk is cheap, Master,' Raghu said sharply. 'We need action now.' Then, 'What have you got to lose? Here today, somewhere else tomorrow. Like a bird' *Aaj hiyan, kal huaan. Ek chirai ke rakam.* That was a cruel cut: for Ram, for there was no other place he would rather be, but he did not say anything.

Ram was genuinely distraught to learn next morning that a large part of Buta Singh's cane farm had been burnt down. It was a clear case of arson, punishment for speaking his mind. Ram was amazed at the technique the arsonists had used to avoid being detected. They had tied kerosene-soaked cloth around the tails of a dozen mongoose, lit them and set them lose in the cane field. The terrified mongoose ran for their lives in every which direction, leaving behind a trail of burning tinder-dry cane leaves, making it difficult to put the fires out. The village was split down the middle. Ram thought to himself, 'Here we're fighting for our democratic rights, and this is what we do to a man who had the courage to speak his mind? We must rid ourselves of what we condemn.'

A week or two after Buta Singh's farm was burnt down, a couple of government caterpillar bulldozers arrived to upgrade the village road. That surprised everyone: why their village, why now? Who had approached the government? That evening, all was revealed at the shop. Shafiq Ali, the owner of trucks, had asked the public works minister through a well-connected relative, to see if the badly pot-holed and at places eroded road could be repaired for a little something. What that 'little something' was no one knew, but 'gifts' up to five hundred dollars for these sorts of favours were not rare. No one could do much to Shafiq. They needed his lorry to carry cane. There was no point thinking of ostracizing him: Hindus and Muslims had always kept social interaction to the minimum any way. And Shafiq was more attuned to what leaders of the Fiji Muslim League were saying. 'Keep quiet and work with the Fijians. This is not our fight.'

Ram was saddened at the religious rift. Although Muslims and Hindus in the village were not socially close, relations were still cordial. But ever since a Muslim delegation had told the Great Council of Chiefs that they accepted the coup and would support Fijian aspirations in return for four separate Muslim seats, relations had soured. A local Muslim academic had even said that it was the Hindus who were opposing the Fijians, not Muslims. As far as he was concerned, Muslims and Christians were people of 'The Book,' Hindus were not. His own grandmother had been a Hindu converted to Islam. 'What has religion got to do with the price of *aloo* and *piyaj*?, potatoes and onions, Ram had asked. 'Do these arseholes know the damage they are doing to our people here? These bloody city slickers are lighting a fire they won't be able to put out.'

Once or twice, Ram thought of talking to Shafiq, but saw no point: the damage had been done. And Shafiq had said so many times before, *Jamaat ke baat kaatna haraam haye*. It is a sin to disobey your community. When Shafiq's wife died a few months later, not a single Hindu attended the funeral. Except Ram. But Shafiq did not escape completely unscathed. For a long time, he was mystified why his cane-carrying lorries had so many punctured tyres. The reason, ingenious when you come to think of it, was that people hammered nails into dozens of stalks of cane and scattered them randomly on roads used by the lorries! They lay unnoticed among all the other cane stalks that had fallen from trucks and were being flattened into cane carpets on the cane belt roads.

Shafiq, though, was not the only one who was having second thoughts about joining the resistance. One day, Chinappa Naidu told a meeting at the shop that Fijians were very agitated, in a vengeful mood. '*Maango, maango, nahi maango, jao.*' 'Want, want, don't want, go.' If you want the lease on our terms fine, they were saying, if not, leave. Their demand was clear: One thousand dollar goodwill payment upfront, and no opposition to the coup. '*Fiji hum log ke jamin baitho. Hum hiyan ke raja hai.* Fiji is our land. We are the kings of this place. There was nowhere Chinappa and other evicted tenants could go. Fijians knew our vulnerability, knew our pressure points and they were determined to have their way. '*Vulagi Can't Be Taukei. Sa sega sara.* Immigrants can't be Natives, Never, was the common refrain. It was the same everywhere in Viti Levu, this talk of vengeance and retribution and expulsion. 'Where will I take my family?' he asked simply. Kahan laye jaaib sab ke? He had three children in high school, with a daughter about to be married. The ten acre plot of leased land was all he had, the sole source of livelihood for the family. Everyone sympathised with Chinappa, because they knew that their turn would come one day, sooner rather than later. What Ram had feared most was taking place right before his eyes, his dream of uniting the village and stiffening its spine was dissolving almost even before it had begun. *So bees with smoke and doves with noisome stench, Are from their hives and houses driven away.*

The worst victims of the coup without doubt were the young people in the village. Those who had passed their exams with good marks — a handful — had gone on to form seven and some even to the university and the local technical institute, but many had failed to make the grade. Their fate was sealed. There were no jobs in the towns, none in the village, no prospect in sight. 'My heart broke,' Ram said to me, 'to see these kids from simple homes, decent, well behaved, wanting to make something of their lives, but with nothing to do, no where to go, victims of blatant racism.' 'Our time was different,' he continued. 'You had a decent education, you got a job. But now, Form Seven is nothing. A university degree is what everyone is looking at.' A lost generation, I thought to myself, promising young lives cut short so early. Ram had found a few of the brighter boys jobs as part-time tutors for the children of business people in town, while some eventually found employment as taxi and bus drivers. That was all he could do. Still, they remembered him with gratitude and affection, like a kind younger uncle, still calling him 'sir' whenever they ran into him. *I would never have thought I would be born here, So late in the stone, so long before morning.*

A few of the girls found employment in one of the tax-free textile factories that had sprung up after the coups.

Thirteen year tax holidays and other concessions had attracted a few foreign companies. The government wanted to kick start the economy by whatever means it could. This seemed an easy and promising option. The government turned a blind eye to the working conditions in the factories. Most women working in them were single mothers from broken homes, widows, young unemployed girls just of school.

One day, Ram received a visit by one of his former students, Kiran. She was working at a garment factory in Lautoka. Ram already had a reputation as a champion of the underdog among the students, the teacher to whom students confided their problems, sought advice, knowing that their confidence would be respected. 'Sir, you must do something about this. How long will these atrocities go on?' *Kuch karana padi, sir, kab tak aise atyachaar chalte rahi*, she said handing him a blue manila folder full of loose handwritten sheets. He promised to read the file that night and get back to her.

What he read in the files enraged him, hand written evidence of example upon example of utter merciless exploitation of women. There was the case of Sheela Kumari, divorced, who worked for a garment manufacturer on probation for six weeks. All she got paid was her bus fares of two dollars, and no pay for the work she had done producing the garments. Then there was Uniasi Marama, in the packing department, who had worked in the factory for 14 years and she still earned only seventy two cents an hour. 'It takes this lady 14 years to earn seventy two cents an hour. She was fourteen years only when she started work,' Kiran said. Meresimani Tinai and Senata Tinai's pay was 50 and 55 cents respectively. Ameila Sukutai did ironing and packing but was paid only 50 cents an hour. 'You can see on this one, sir,' Kiran said, 'that she is performing two jobs but is being paid only for one.' None of the workers got overtime even though many worked beyond their normal working hours.

Shobna Singh was brave enough to have her experience written down. Ram read the report aloud. 'Work starts on the dot at 8 am. After that, no one is allowed to even look around. The neck stiffens, eyes water and burn and a headache starts, nose gets blocked with cotton dust and back and legs begin to ache. The machines themselves are not in proper working condition yet any delays are blamed on the worker. Hard chairs and poor ventilation add to the discomfort. Few minutes late starting means a deduction in the wage. There is no such thing as sick leave pay. No overtime paid. No benefits for long term service. No insurance to cover any health hazard that may confront a worker while at work. No leave or leave pay. No emergency exits or drills to deal with emergencies. No fire extinguishers in sight. At break, nobody is allowed to leave a second early. Morning break from 10am–10:15: no one is allowed outside the premises. Lunch break is limited to 30 minutes, 12pm–12:30. And at 3 pm there is a 15 minute break where nobody is allowed out again. An hour's break in all that 8 hours of work. No calls are passed on or calls allowed to be made. No one is allowed visitors. In a caged atmosphere workers are urged to work faster and faster.'

Ram asked Kiran to arrange a meeting with one of the workers to get a better feel of the situation. Kiran fetched Anshu. They met at Ram's quarters late on Sunday. Anshu related an incident involving her at the factory the previous day. 'During lunch hour I had gone to the toilet when the alarm bell rang. As soon as I came out, the security guard came and said to me 'What are you doing inside the toilet?' I said,

'Don't you know what a lady does in a toilet.' He said 'Don't talk cheeky, you just go in.' Anshu then went to her desk. As she was punching time off at the end of the day, the security guard came up to her and asked, 'What is in the plastic bag?' I said 'Apples and milk.' The guard grabbed the plastic bag and tore it to look inside. Then he threw the bag and its contents outside the gate. A hard-earned $6.59 cents worth of food destroyed. Then he swore at her. 'Fuck off you bastard, take your plastic and go,' he said, threatening to punch her. Anshu was saved from assault by a Fijian security guard who picked up the apples and milk and put it inside the plastic bag, apologetically.

'You must do something about it, Sir.' Kiran's words kept reverberating in Ram's head. But what? How? Ram began by compiling a list of abuses and transgressions as accurately as he could. With Kiran's assistance, he would meet the garment workers late in the evenings, during weekends, taking care not to be seen in public with his informants. He tracked down Shobna Singh and talked to her at length. Over the next month, Ram compiled a detailed report on the working conditions in the garment factories in the Lautoka area.

Ram then travelled to Suva to give the report to Ema Fulavesi, the trade union activist. Ema was a rolly-polly woman with a passion for her cause. 'This is dynamite, *Bhaiya, ek dam julum*' she told him, very good indeed, brother. 'We have the buggers by the balls. *Magai Chinamu*. Sorry, *Bhaiya*, don't mind my language. Big catch, this one! Blerry bastards.' Several months later, Ram received in the mail a small printed paper containing the news of a demonstration in Sydney against the garment industries in Fiji. The demonstration was against the Fijian Garments Exhibit Apparel Expo at Darling Harbour, outside Hall 5, Sydney Exhibition Centre.

It was organised by the Clothing Trades Union, at the request of the Fiji Trade Union Congress. The leaflet announcing the demonstration read: 'The garments being promoted are made in Tax Free Zones by workers earning as little as 50 cents an hour in sweat shop conditions. Many of the companies are Australia and New Zealand employers who have moved part or all of their operations to Fiji to avoid labour laws and trade unions.' A Garment Workers Union has just been registered in Fiji after a long struggle. But workers are still denied a living wage. And some workers caught organising for the Union have been victimised, dismissed, and even physically assaulted.'

The response was swift and effective (though in the long run ineffectual.) The government promised to establish a Garment Training Centre with a factory and a training division, for about 150 to 200 students, with the better students to be retained full-time with full pay to run the company's production factory. The Centre would be run by nominated representatives of the government and the garment industry. Ram was quietly satisfied at the result all the after-school sleuthing had produced. He was even more grateful to Kiran and Shabnam. They had so much to lose, but showed so much courage, more than the kava-sodden, scrotum-scratching men, meeting him at odd hours, providing detailed data on the working conditions, all the while keeping out of the public gaze, seeking no credit or glory for themselves. *Truth is like a torch,* Ram remembered from something he had read along time ago. *The more you shake it, the more it shines.*

The garment industry was furious. How had such damaging 'inside' information gone public? A hunt was on for a mole in the factory, but no one suspected Kiran. She was always quiet and outwardly obedient and punctual, always calling her boss 'Sir,' averting his gaze, getting along with everyone. But again, it was Jumsa who spilled the beans. He had kept a close eye on where Ram went, who he talked to and reported it to Ram Baran, his uncle. It did not take Ram Baran long to put two and two together.

One day while Ram was teaching his class on 'Literature and Society,' the principal came around and told him that Ram Baran, the chairman of the School Management Committee, wanted to meet him urgently. 'I will complete the class for you,' he said. Judging by the urgency in his voice, Ram knew something was askew. He walked towards the Committee Room with words from an Auden poem ringing in his ears. *The sky is darkening like a stain, Something is going to fall like rain, And it won't be flowers.*

'Masterji, we should talk,' Ram Baran said, beginning the proceedings 'About what?' Ram enquired cautiously. 'Oh, small things, big things, about you and the School.' That all seemed mysterious to Ram. He waited for Ram Baran to continue. 'People have been talking, Master,' he said. Ram looked at him straight in the eye, waiting for him to continue. 'About you and the girl.' 'What girl? What are you talking about?' 'Master, you know the girl, the one who works at the garment factory.' 'You mean Kiran?' 'Yes.' 'What about her? She was my student once and she now works at the garment factory.' 'You two have been seen together at odd hours and strange places. *Jamin ke pas bhi kaan aur ankhi haye.*' Even the land has ears and eyes. 'So?' 'We have the reputation of the school to think of. When married teachers have affairs with their former students, it does not look good, Master.'

Ram was stumped for words. His marriage had been over a long time ago. Geeta was seeing some one else. It was an amicable separation. The two were not meant for each other, they both knew, and always deep in Ram's heart, there was Malti. But Ram had not seen any point in publicising his divorce. His close friends knew but made little of it. Marriage failures were common enough; Ram's was no exception. Ram had not been having affairs, certainly not when there had been so much else to do. To be accused of having an affair with Kiran, attractive though she was, was simply preposterous.

'Kaka [Uncle], let me say this once and once only. I am not having an affair with Kiran or anyone else. Kiran and I have been working on a research project.' He then described the data the two were collecting on the working conditions in the garment factories. 'So it was you, then,' Ram Baran said, 'who gave all that dirt to the trade unions.' 'Kaka,' Ram replied firmly, 'you should see things for yourself. It's worse than what you can imagine.' He went on to talk about women having to get permission to go to the toilet, male guards posted outside women's toilet, the musty, filthy conditions inside, the sexual advances, the threat of violence. 'And to think that this is our own people doing it! Here we are fighting this coup regime, and look at what these bastards are up to. *Kitna gira jaat haye hum log.*' What a low-down people we are. Ram Baran said nothing.

The following week, the Management Board convened. It had been a busy week for Ram Baran. Jason Garments had contributed to the refurbishing of the school library and he was keen to make sure that future funds did not dry up. What better way to ensure that than to ingratiate yourself with the factory owner. Ram Baran told Ravin Dhupelia, the owner, what Ram had been up to, the damage he had done. 'Get rid of him now, Ram Baran. Now. Get rid of that rotten egg. That arsehole of a bastard.' *Sala, Chutia, Gaandu.* How dare he bite the hand that feeds him?' 'Leave that to me, Boss,' Ram Baran said as he left Duphelia's office. He then contacted all the members of the Management Board, one by one, and told them about Ram and how his immediate firing was necessary for further funding from Jason Garments and other business houses in town.

At the meeting attended by the full Management Board, Ram Baran spoke at length and on behalf of everyone. 'Master, we are not satisfied with your performance. You seem to be more interested in politics than teaching these days.' That was not true, Ram said. He hadn't missed a single day of class. And wasn't it true that the highest number of A Grade passes in Fiji Junior were from his class? Ram Baran ignored him and proceeded with his rehearsed speech, reminding Ram of every thing he had done and said since the coup: organising the village committee, using the school printing machines to circulate newsletters, putting strange ideas about 'dignity and self respect' into the heads of children, and now this: rocking the garment industry. 'You are risking the future of our children. Do you know how many girls from this school the garment factories employ?' Many, Ram knew, but at what cost? 'We don't want to kill the goose that lays the golden egg,' Ram Baran said. Some golden egg, Ram thought to himself. 'We have reached the decision — and it is unanimous, if you must to know — that you should leave the school immediately. *Baat aage tak pahunch gaye haye.* We have already informed the Education Department. *Your tongues are steeped in honey and milk, Your hearts in gall and biting despair.*

'I thought of many things to say,' Ram said to me 'but in the end chose not to. Their minds were already made up. There was no point confusing them with facts. I packed up and left.' Not a single person on the Board spoke up for him, no one in the village came to farewell him. This most idealistic of men with a brave heart and noble vision having to suffer this kind of petty humiliation saddened me immensely. All that selfless work, standing up against the coup, organising people, helping the victims of the garment industry, had in the end come to naught, undone by the duplicity and deviousness of his own people and by his high principles clashing with a rotten world gone strangely awry. *Love, fame, ambition, avarice — 'tis the same, Each idle, all ill, and none the worst — For all are meteors with a different name, And death is the sable smoke where vanishes the flame.*

Ram returned to Suva. His heart had gone out of teaching. He took up a job as a part-time sales representative at a hardware store in Samabula, and spent the rest of his time by himself, reading, alone, in his musty, dingy book-strewn rented flat in Bureta Street, a battered but unbroken man, living in flickering hope. Last night when I visited him, reminiscing as usual about our distant youthful days, he sang a Talat Mehmood song:

Phir wahi shaam, wahi gham, wahi tanhaai hai
Dil ko samjhaane teri yaad chali aayi hai

Once again that evening, that sadness, that anguish.
Your memories have returned to soothe my heart.

7
In Mr Tom's Country

I seldom visit Tabia now, the village of my birth and childhood. The place is a labyrinth of haunting memories of happier, more innocent times better left untouched. But on the rare occasion I do, I always make an effort to see Arjun Kaka. Now in his late seventies, he is the only one in the village who has a direct connection to my father's generation, the last link to a fading past. He knows my interest in history and we talk endlessly about past events and people at every opportunity. Kaka is illiterate and a vegetarian and teetotaller. Everyone in the village knows him as a man of integrity, a man with a completely unblemished reputation. His wife died about a decade ago and he now lives on the farm with the family of his deceased son. The other three boys, bright and educated, migrated to Australia after the 1987 coup. He misses them desperately, for this is not the way he had wanted to spend his twilight years. He now wished one of them had remained behind. There is no telephone in the house and the letters from his children are rare. He wonders about his grandchildren, how old they are, what they look like, if they remember him, ruminating like old men usually do.

A few years ago, covering a general election, I went to Labasa and visited Kaka. 'Why don't you visit Krishna and the other two boys, Kaka' I said after he had mentioned how badly he missed his children. 'At my age, beta, it is difficult,' he said sadly. 'You know I cannot read and write. Besides, my health is not good.' 'Kaka, so many people like you travel all the time,' I reminded him. 'Look at Balram, Dulare, and Ram Rattan.' Formerly of Tabia, they had moved to town when their cane farm leases were not renewed. Kaka nodded but did not say anything. Then an inspired thought occurred to me. I was returning to Australia a few weeks later and could take Kaka with me. When I made the offer, his face lit up, all the excuses forgotten. They were excuses, really, nothing more. He has a deep yearning to travel but not knowing how. '*Beta, e to bahut julum baat hai,*' he said, this is very good news indeed, son. He embraced me. 'You are like my own son. Bhaiya [my father] would be very proud of you.' If truth be known, since dad's death, I regarded Arjun Kaka as a father.

'Have many people left Labasa in recent years?' I asked Kaka. There was a time when going to Suva was considered 'going overseas,' an experience recounted in glorious and often embroidered detail for years. Australia and New Zealand were out of the question. 'The place is emptying day by day, especially since all the *jhanjhat* [trouble] started.' He meant the coup. 'There is no growth, no hope. Young people, finishing school, leave for Suva. No one returns. There is nothing to return to.' '*Dil uth gaye,*' Kaka said, the heart is no longer here. Kaka's observation reinforced what I had been told in Suva. There was hardly a single Indo-Fijian family in Fiji which did not have at least one member abroad. 'The best and the brightest are leaving,' a friend had remarked in Suva. Only the *chakka panji* [hoi poloi] remain.' The wealthy and the well-connected had their families safely 'parked' in Australia and New Zealand, he had said. An interesting way of putting it, I thought, suggesting temporariness, a readiness to move again if the need arose. I had heard a new phrase to describe this new phenomenon: frequent flyer families. Those safely abroad talked of loyalty and commitment to Fiji, of returning one day, but it was just that, talk, nothing more. I felt deeply for people who were trapped and terrorised in Fiji, victims of fate and racial hate.

As the news of Kaka's planned trip to Australia spread, people were genuinely happy for him. At Tali's shop the following evening, Karna bantered. '*Ek memia lete aana, yaar,*' bring a white woman along with you.' '*Kab tak bichari patoh tumhar sewa kari.*' How long will your poor daughter-in-law continue to look after you?' Learn some English words, Mohan advised. 'Thank you, goodbye, hello, how are you, mate.' He was the village bush lawyer. 'Make sure you are all 'suit-boot,' [well dressed], not like this,' referring to Kaka's khaki shorts and fading floral shirt. 'We don't want others to know that we are country bumpkins.' 'Which we are,' Haria interjected to mild mirth. Bhima wondered whether some of the *kulambars* [CSR overseers] were still alive and whether Arjun Kaka might be able to meet some of them in Australia. Mr Tom, Mr Oxley, Mr Johnson.

Mr Tom: now there was a name from ancient history. He was the first white man I ever saw. Tall, pencil-thin, white hard hat, his face like a red tomato in the midday sun, short sleeve shirt and trousers, socks pulled up to the knees, the shirt pocket bulging with pens and a well thumbed note book. The overseers had a bad reputation as heartless men driven to extract the maximum from those under their charge. Was that true, I wondered. 'Well the Company was our *mai-bap*,' Kaka said, our parents. 'You did what you were told.' Bhima chimed in: 'The *Kulambars* were strict but fair.' So it wasn't all that bad? I wanted to know more. Bhima continued. 'As far as they were concerned, we were all the same, children of coolies. They didn't play favourites among the farmers. Look at what is happening now.' I had no idea. 'Look at all the *ghoos-khori* [corruption]' He went to explain how palms had to be greased at every turn — to get enough trucks to cart cane to the mills, to get your proper turn to harvest. 'In the old days, if you did your work, you were left alone.' Nostalgia for a simpler, less complicated time perhaps, I wondered, but said nothing.

People in the village had very sharp memories of the overseers. Mr Tom drank kava 'like fish,' Mohan remembered. 'And chillies,' Karna added, 'A dozen of those '*rocketes*,' no problem. '*Chini-pani, chuttar pani.*' We all exploded with laugher. *Chini-pani* in the cane belt meant 'sugar has turned to water,' the sugar content is down, which is what allegedly the overseers at the mill weighbridge told the farmers, cheating them of a fair income. *Chuttar pani* refers to washing your bum with water after going to the toilet, a reference in this case to Mr Tom's probably agonizing toilet sessions after eating so many hot chillies.

Overseers, I learnt, were expected to have some rudimentary Hindi because the farmers had no English. But sometimes their pronunciation of Hindi words left people rolling with laughter. Bhima recalled Mr Oxley once asking someone's address. '*Uske ghar kahan hai.*' Where is his house? But the way he pronounced '*ghar*' — gaar — it sounded like the Hindi word for arse: 'Where is his arse!' Kaka recalled Mr

Tom visiting Nanka's house one day wanting to talk to him. But Nanka had gone to town. Mr Tom asked Nanka's son whether he could speak to his mother. Instead of saying 'Tumar mai kahan baitho,' where is your mother (mai), he accidentally added the swear word, chod, to fuck: a common swear word among overseers, 'Tumar mai-chod kahan baitho,' where is your mother fucker! Which left Mrs Nanka tittering, covering her mouth with orhni, (shawl), and scuttling towards the kitchen. Mr Tom practically sprinted to his landrover as soon as he realised the faux pas he had just committed, his face flushed and covered in sweat.

This warm reminiscence of aging men from another era brought back memories which until now had vanished. I recalled the excitement of the visit every three months or so of the CSR Mobile Unit coming to the village. On the designated evening, the entire village would gather in the school compound, sit on sheets of stitched sacks (paal), cover themselves with blankets in the colder months and watch a tiny screen with grainy pictures perched at the end of a land rover. At the outer edges of the compound would be placed a put-put-put droning generator to provide power to the projector. Sometimes, the documentary would be about a model Indian family, sometimes about some aspect of the sugar industry or good husbandry. 'This is Ram Prasad's family,' the voice-over would announce in beautifully cadenced English. Then we would see an overseer, in hard white hat, his hands on his hips, talking to Ram Prasad, in short sleeves and khaki pants, his amply-oiled hair neatly combed back, his hands by his side or behind his back, not saying much, avoiding eye contact with the overseer. Ram Prasad's wife would be at a discreet distance by the kitchen, wearing lehenga and blouse, her slightly bowed head covered with orhni, while school children, in neat uniforms with their bags slung around their shoulders, walked past purposefully. The moral was not lost on us. We too could be like Ram Prasad's family, happy and prosperous if only we were as dutiful, hard working and respectful of authority as them.

Occasionally we would see documentaries about Australia. We did not understand the language, partly because of the rapid speed at which it was spoken, but the pictures remain with me: of vast fields of golden-brown wheat harvested by monster machines, hat-wearing men on horseback mustering cattle in rough hilly country, wharves lined with huge container carriers, buildings tall beyond our imagination and streets choked with cars crawling ant-like. Pictures of parched, desolate land full of rock and rubble, dry river beds and ghost gums puzzled me. It seemed so harsh to us surrounded by nothing but lush tropical green. I sometimes wondered how white people, who seemed so delicate to us, could live in a place like that. But the overwhelming impression remained of a vast and rich country. It was from there that all the good things we liked came: white purified sugar we used in our pujas, the bottled jam, the Holden cars. The thought that we would one day actually live there was too outrageous to contemplate. And we did not.

I also remembered the annual school essay competition. The CSR would send the topics to the school early in the year. Usually, they were topics such as 'Write an Essay on the Contribution the CSR Makes to Fiji,' or 'How the Sugar Industry Works.' The brighter pupils in the school were expected to participate and turn in neatly written and suitably syrupy pieces. I was a regular contributor. One day during the morning assembly, our head teacher, Mr Subramani Gounden, announced that I had done the school proud by winning the *third* prize in the whole of Vanua Levu! The first one ever from our school, and the only one for several years, I was later told. I vividly recall trooping up to the front to receive my certificate scrawled with a signature at the bottom. Such a success, such thrill. It was at university that I realised how unrelenting and tough-minded the CSR was in the management of the sugar industry, but at primary school, we were immensely grateful for the tender mercies that came our way. We were so proud that on the prize giving day, we had an overseer, no less, as our guest of honour. Mr Tom was a regular and much honoured presence.

One day I asked Arjun Kaka what he thought Australia would be like. '*Nahin Jaanit, beta.*' I don't know. 'There must be a lot of people like us there,' he said. 'Why do you say that?' I asked somewhat perplexed. 'You know white people. They can't plant and harvest sugar cane, build roads or do any other hard physical work like that. All that is our job. They rule, we toil.' Kaka spoke from experience, but I assured him that white people did indeed do all the hard work in Australia. They planted and harvested cane and wheat, worked as janitors and menial labourers, drove trucks, buses and cars. Kaka remained unconvinced. 'It must be cold there?' he enquired. I tried my best to explain the seasons in Australia. Knowing the Canberra weather in summer, I said 'Sometimes it gets hotter than Fiji. 'But how come then white people there don't have black skins? Look at us: half a day in the sun and we become black like baigan [eggplants].' 'You will see it all for yourself, Kaka,' I said and left it at that. This old man is in for the shock of his life, I thought to myself. His innocence and simplicity, his complete lack of understanding of the outside world was endearing in a strange kind of a way. I made a mental note of things I would have to do in the next few weeks: get Kaka's passport and visa papers ready, ask Krishna in Sydney to purchase the ticket. Then I left for Suva, promising to inform Kaka of the date of travel well in time. I would see him in Nadi.

Kaka was relieved to see me again in Nadi. This was his first visit to Viti Levu, the first out of Labasa actually. In the late 1990s, the Nadi International Airport resembled a curious atmosphere of a mixture of a marriage celebration and a funeral procession as people arrived in the busloads to welcome or farewell friends and family. Men were dressed in multi-coloured floral shirts and women in gaudy lehengas and salwar kamiz and saris. I noticed a family huddled in one corner of the airport lounge. One of them was leaving. I could quite imagine the scene at their home the previous night. A goat would have been slaughtered and close family and friends invited to a party long into the night. The puffed red eyes tell the story of a sleepless night. A middle-aged woman, presumably the mother, prematurely aged, with streaks of grey dishevelled hair, was crying, a white hanker chief covering her mouth. And the father, looking anxious, sad and tearful, chatted quietly with fellow villagers, passing time.

This was a regular occurrence in those days: ordinary people, sons and daughters of the soil, with uncertain futures, leaving for foreign lands. A trickle is turning into a torrent right before our eyes. To an historian, the irony was inescapable. A hundred years ago, our forbears had arrived in Fiji, ordinary folk from rural India, shouldering their little bundles and leaving for some place they had not heard of before but keen to make a new start. A hundred years later, there were children and grandchildren on the move again: the same insecurity, the same anxiety about their fate. No one seemed to care that so many of Fiji's best and brightest were leaving. Some Fijian nationalists actually want the country emptied of Indians. Kaka noticed my contemplative silence. He had read my thoughts. He asked, 'Beta, desh ke ka hoi?' What will happen to this land? It was an interesting and revealing formulation of the problem. He hadn't said 'hum log' a communal reference to the Indo-Fijians. He had placed the nation — desh — before the community. I wished Fijians who were applauding the departure of Indians could see the transparent love an unlettered man like Kaka had for the country.

Arjun Kaka seemed nervous as we entered the plane: this was only the second time he had ever flown in a plane. The first time was when he flew from Labasa to Nadi to catch the flight to Sydney. Kaka was watchful, nervous. 'So many seats, beta,' he said. 'Jaise chota saakis ghar,' like a mini theatre. Not a bad description, I thought to myself. 'And so many people! Will the plane be able to take off?' I watched him say a silent prayer as the plane began to taxi. 'Everything will be fine, Kaka,' I reassured him. 'Yes, beta, I just wanted to offer a prayer,' he said smiling. Sensing my curiosity, he said, 'Oh, I was just saying to God that I have come up this high, please don't take me any higher just yet.' We both smiled at the thought.

Half an hour after take off, the drinks trolley came. I asked for a glass of white. Knowing that he was teetotaller, I asked Kaka if he would like anything soft. 'No, Beta, I am okay. Sab theek hai.' 'Nothing?' 'What about soft drinks: tomato or orange juice, water?' 'At my age, you have to be careful,' Kaka said to me some minutes after the trolley had gone. 'I have to go to the toilet after I have a drink. Can't contain it for too long.' '*Bahut jor pisaap lage.* 'But there is a toilet on the plane, Kaka,' I reassured him, gently touching his forearm. 'Actually there are several, both at the front and back of the plane.' That caught Kaka by complete surprise. A toilet on the plane? 'You can do the other business there, too, if you want,' I continued. But Kaka was unwilling to take the risk. Later I realised a possible reason for his hesitation: if he did the other business, he couldn't wash himself with water — toilet paper he had never used.

When lunch was served, Kaka refused once again. He was a strict vegetarian, a *sadhu* to boot. 'You can have some bread and fruit, Kaka,' I said. He still refused. 'You don't know what the Chinese put in the bread,' he said. In Labasa, all the bread was made by Chinese and a rumour was started, probably by an Indo-Fijian rival, that they used lard in the dough. I did not know but it did not matter to me. In the end, Kaka settled for an '*apul*' and a small bunch of grapes. 'I am sorry, Kaka, but I have ordered chicken,' I said apologetically. '*Koi bat nahin,*' he said, don't worry. Everyone in his family ate meat, including his wife. He was its only vegetarian.

My curiosity was aroused. How did Kaka become a vegetarian and a teetotaller? Most people in the village were not. I noticed that the palm of his right hand was deformed, his skin burnt and his fingers crooked. 'Kaka,' I said, 'if you don't mind my asking, how did that happen?' 'It is a long story, Beta,' he said. 'But we have three hours to kill,' I replied. This is what Kaka told me. Soon after he got married, he had a large itchy sore on the back of his right palm. Someone had obviously 'done' something. Magic and witchcraft, *jadu tona*, were an integral part of village life. One possibility, he said, was his neighbour, Ram Sundar, who might have spread the rumour that Kaka had leprosy, the most dreaded social disease one could imagine, a disease with a bad omen. If Kaka went to Makogai Hospital (for lepers, in the remote Lomaiviti group), the whole family would be ostracised, no one would think of marrying into it, no invitations to marriages and festive occasions. Social pressure would force the family to move to some other place to start afresh, as far away from established settlement as possible. If Kaka had leprosy, he would have to move from the village and Ram Sundar would then finally realise his dream of grabbing Kaka's ten acre farm. Such cunning, such heartlessness, and here was the outside world thinking that warm neighbourly relations characterised village life.

The extended family — because their reputation would be singed too by this tragedy — decided that something had to be done soon about Kaka's condition. Rumour was spreading fast. Instead of going to a doctor — no one in the village did or really believed in the efficacy of western medicine — his *girmitya* [indentured] father sent him to an *ojha*, a sorcerer, in Wainikoro some thirty or so miles away to the north. The *ojha*, Ramka, was famous — or dreaded — throughout Vanua Levu. He had once saved the life of a man, Ram Bharos, who had gone wild, squealing like a mouse sometimes and roaring like a lion at others, clenching his teeth and hissing through closed lips, because he had faltered trying to master magic rituals which would enable him to destroy people and cattle and property, even control the elements. To acquire that power, Ram Bharos was told — by whom it was not known — that he would have to eat a human heart sharp at midnight. Nothing was going to deter Ram Bharos from realising his ambition. He killed his own aged father. At night, he went to the graveyard, opened his father's chest with a knife and put the heart on a banana leaf. After burying the body, he walked to a nearby river, with the heart in his hands, and waded chest-deep into the river. Then something frightening happened. He saw a man shrouded in white walking towards him. Suddenly there was a blinding flash of light. Ram Bharos stumbled, forgot the names of deities he was supposed to invoke. He went mad. Ramka cured him partly, restoring a semblance of normalcy to Ram Bharos' damaged personality. This sounds like an improbable story, but I believed Kaka. Labasa, dubbed the Friendly North, has its dark side as its residents know only too well.

It was to this famous Ojha that they had taken Arjun Kaka. In a dimly lit room, Ramka did his magic. He rubbed Kaka's damaged palm with fat and turned it over the over the fire for a very long time, chanting words in a language that was incomprehensible to him. By the time he had finished, the skin had been charred. A few days later, the bones had twisted. But Kaka was 'cured,' he did not have leprosy, the family's honour was saved, and the farm remained intact. Ramka asked Kaka never to touch meat and not have pork cooked at his home. That was how Kaka had become a vegetarian.

Magic, witchcraft, sorcery, belief in the supernatural, the fear of ghosts and devils, blind faith in healers and magic men: it all recalled for me a world which the *girmitiyas* had brought with them and of which we all were a part, but which now belonged to an era long forgotten, for the present generation nothing more than stories from a twisted imagination. And this man, from that world, was going to Australia! 'I have forgotten the details, Beta,' Arjun Kaka apologised. 'You are the first person to ask me.' I am glad I did. After Kaka had spoken, I recalled the pin-drop silence of eerie unlit nights, in the thatched bure — *belo* — where we slept, the scrotumshrivelling fear of strange nocturnal animals scurrying on dry leaves around the house, stories of swaying lights in the neighbouring hills, soft knocks on doors at odd hours, the mysterious aroma at night of perfumes usually sprinkled on corpses, streaking stars prophesising death somewhere, wailing noises across the paddy fields and shimmering figures in the mangrove swamps. We dreaded nights.

At Sydney airport, Krishna met us. I gave him my phone number and promised to keep in touch. Kaka had a three month visa and I told him that I would visit him in Sydney. After we embraced, I headed for Canberra, determined that I would do everything I could to give Kaka a memorable journey to Mr Tom's country. About a month later, Krishna phoned me. Kaka wanted to talk to me. 'Beta, I am going back soon. I would like to see you before I return.' 'But you have a full three month visa.' 'Something inside tells me that I must return as soon as possible.' A premonition of some sort? His world of magic and sorcery came to mind, and I realised there was no point arguing or trying to persuade him to change his mind. I left for Sydney the following day.

Krishna and his wife had gone to work and the children were at school when I reached the house. It was immediately clear to me that Kaka was a lost man, uncomfortable and anxious. I reminded him of his promise to tell me the full story about his Australian experience. '*Poora jad pulai.*' Everything. What he missed most, Kaka said, was his daily routine. In Tabia, he would be up at the crack of dawn, feed the cattle and have an early breakfast before heading off to the fields. Even at his age. In the evening, after an early shower at the well, he would light the wick lamp — *dhibri* — and do his *puja*. He missed his devotional songs on the radio, the death notices in the evening. He would not be able forgive himself if someone dear to him died while he was away. Kaka often wondered how Lali, his beloved cow, was. He treated her tenderly, almost like a human, a member of the family. For him not looking after animals, especially cows (*gau-mata*, mother) was a crime.

In Fiji, Kaka was connected, was part of a living community. He had a place in the wider scheme of things. But not here. 'I sit here in the lounge most of the day like a deaf and blind man. There is television and radio, but they are of no use to me.' What about walk in the park, a stroll in the nearby supermarket? I asked. Kaka recalled (for him) a particularly hair-raising experience. One day Krishna had left him in the mall of a large supermarket and had gone to get his car repaired. At first Kaka was calm, but as time passed, surrounded by so many white people, he panicked. What if something happened to Krishna? He did not have the home address or the telephone number with him. How would he find his way home? He tried to talk to a young Indian man — who was probably from Fiji — but man kept walking, muttering to himself. 'He probably thought I was a beggar or something.' From that day on, Kaka preferred to remain at home. For a man fond of the outdoors, active in the field, this must have been painful. 'It is torture, beta. Sitting, eating, pissing, farting. That's all I do all day, everyday.' I felt his distress.

Did Krishna and his wife treat him well, I wanted to know. It was an intrusive question, I know, but I wanted to be helpful. 'Oh, they both are very nice. *Patoh* makes vegetarian dishes and leaves them in the fridge for me. I have a room to myself. My clothes are washed. On the weekends, they take me out for drives.' But there was something missing, I felt. 'Beta, it is not their fault but I don't see much of them. Babu

[Krishna] goes to work in the morning and *patoh* does the evening shift. By the time she returns, it is time for bed.' The 'ant-like life,' as Kaka aptly put it, was not his cup of tea. 'Getting established in this society is not easy Kaka,' I said. 'But things improve with time.' 'That's true, but by then, half your life is over. These people would have been millionaires in Fiji if they worked as hard as they do here.' 'They do it for the future of their children, Kaka.' He nodded. 'I know, I know.'

Kaka felt acutely conscious of himself whenever he did anything, constantly on the guard. Back home, he would clear his throat loudly and cough out the phlegm on the lawn. Everyone did it. Here his grandchildren giggled and covered their mouths with their hands in embarrassment. In Tabia, Kaka always wore shorts at home. Here, on several occasions, he felt undressed, half naked, when Krishna's friends came around. 'I could see that both Babu and Patoh were sometimes uncomfortable.' Sometimes, the people he met at pujas and other ceremonies, especially people from Viti Levu, laughed in jest at his rustic Labasa Hindi. 'They find us and our language backward. '*Tum log ke julum bhasa, Kaka,*' they would say to me mockingly, uncle, you folk (from Labasa) have a wonderful language: '*awa-gawa,* [come and gone, when they say *aya-gaya*], *dabe* [flood, *baadh*], *bakeda* [crab, *kekda*]. They find it funny, but after a while I find the mocking hurtful. So I don't say much, not that I have much to say these people anyway.' In Tabia, Kaka had his own *kakkus* (outhouse) where he could wash himself properly with water after toilet, but here he would sometimes spill water on the toilet floor or accidentally leak on it, causing mustiness and foul smell. He would then feel guilty and embarrassed. Kaka found the accumulation of small things like this making him self conscious, ill-at-ease in the house. No one ever said anything, but he felt that he was a bit of a nuisance for everybody, especially when Krishna's friends came around.

Kaka was desperate for news from home, any news. There was nothing about Fiji, let alone Labasa, on television and only brief snippets on one or two radio stations, which he invariably missed because he did not know how to use the dial. 'At home, I knew what was happening in Fiji and the world, but here I sit like a frog in a well. It is as if we do not exist.' I understood his puzzlement. Fiji — Labasa — was all he knew. His centre of the universe was of no interest and of no consequence to the rest of the world. 'That is the way of the world, Kaka,' I tried to assure him. 'We are noticed only when we make a mess of things, or when there is a natural disaster or when some Australian tourist gets raped or robbed.' Some of the people he had met, especially the older ones, hankered for news from home, but the younger ones were too preoccupied with life and work to bother.

Television both entertained and embarrassed Kaka. He couldn't watch the soapies with the entire family in the room. The scantily clad women, the open display of skin, the kissing, the suggestive bedroom scenes, the crude advertising (for lingerie, skin lotions) had him averting his eyes or uttering muffled coughs. Sometimes, unable to bear the embarrassment, he would just retire to his room on the pretence that he was tired, and then spend much of the night sleepless, wondering about everything. He liked two shows, though, and enjoyed them like a child. One was David Attenborough's natural life programs. He did not understand the language but the antics of the animals and creatures of the sea did not need words to enjoy. These programs brought a whole world alive for him.

He remembered the animals his *girmitiya* father used to talk about: *sher* (lion), *bhaloo* (bear), *hathi* (elephant), *bandar* (monkey). He had seen pictures of them in books, but to see live animals on the screen was magical. And he liked cartoons, especially the Bug's Bunny shows. They made no sense to him at all — nor to me — but that was their charm, characters skittering across the screen speaking rapid-fire '*gitbit gitbit*.' He would laugh out aloud when no one was watching.

These were the only programs Kaka could watch with his small grandchildren. Otherwise there was no communication between them. The children were nice: '*sundar*' is how Kaka described them. They made tea for him and offered him biscuit and cookies, but they had no Hindi at all and Kaka knew no English. He would caress their heads gently and hug them and they would occasionally take him for walks in the park nearby, but no words were exchanged. '*Dil roye, beta*' Kaka said to me, the heart cries, 'that I cannot talk to my own flesh and blood in the only language I know.' 'I hope they will remember me and remember our history.' Krishna was making an effort to introduce his children to Indian religion and culture through the weekend classes held at the local *mandir*, but it was probably a lost cause. History was not taught in many public schools, certainly not Pacific or Fijian history and I wondered how the new generation growing up in Australia, exposed to all the challenges posed by global travel and technology, would learn about their past. I did not have the heart to tell Kaka, but I know that his world would go with him, just as mine will, too. Our past will be more than a foreign country to children growing up in Australia.

Once or twice, I took Kaka out for a ride through the heart of Sydney, pointing out the monuments, Hyde Park,

Circular Quay, the Museum and the Mitchell Library, but Kaka had no understanding and no use for the icons of Australian culture. For him, the city was nothing more than concrete and glass chaos, one damn tall building after another. I took him for a ride in the country, playing devotional Hindi music in the car (which he enjoyed immensly). Kaka had imagined Australia to be clogged with buildings and people, but the long, unending distances between towns both fascinated and terrified him. In Labasa an hour's journey was considered long; the idea of driving for a couple of days to get from one place to another was alien to him. And the geography too fascinated Kaka: the dry barren countryside wheat-brown in December, the bleached bones of dead animals by the roadside, the rusting hulks of discarded machinery and farms stretching for thousands of hectares. 'How can one family manage all this by themselves,' he wondered. 'How can you grow anything in this type of soil?' And he wondered how, living so far apart on their farms, the people kept the community intact. I said little: he was wondering aloud, talking to himself. On our return journey, Kaka said sadly that he wished my Kaki [his wife] could have seen all this with him. I wished that too. I could sense that he was missing her. Kaka remained silent for a long time.

I was still unsatisfied that Kaka was happy with all that Krishna and I between us had been able to show him. Then it came to me that Kaka might like to visit the Taronga Zoo. It was an inspired thought. Kaka was like a child in a garden of delight. The animals he had seen on the television screen he saw live with his own eyes: giraffe, rhino, tiger, leopard, lion, cobra, and elephant. I was so glad that he was enjoying himself, pointing out animals to me, saying: 'look, look,' with all the excitement of an innocent child. As we approached the monkey section of the zoo, Kaka stopped, joined his palms in prayer and said *Jai Hanuman Ji Ki*, Hail to Lord Hanuman, the monkey god, Lord Rama's brave and loyal general, who had single-handedly rescued Sita from Ravana's clutches. He was excited to see a cobra. 'Nag Baba,' he said reverentially, the snake god. When I looked at him, Kaka smiled but I couldn't tell whether his display of quiet reverence for the monkeys and cobras was for real or was it for my entertainment! I knew that the old man certainly had an impish sense of humour.

As we were having a cup of tea at the end of the zoo visit, sweetening it with white sugar, Kaka wondered where that was manufactured. The next day, I took Kaka to the CSR refinery. He was thrilled. We considered white sugar 'pure,' enough to offer it to the gods in our *pujas* and *havans*. A supervisor gave us a good informative tour when he found out that Kaka was from Fiji. Kaka was impressed with how clean the place was and how new the machinery was, nothing remotely like the filthy, stench-ridden sugar mills in Fiji. We also visited an IXL jam factory on the way. Jam and bread were a luxury for many poor families in rural areas of Labasa, to be enjoyed on special occasions, such as birthdays. The standard food in most homes was curry, rice and roti, with all the vegetables coming from the farm itself.

The visit to the sugar refining factory re-kindled Kaka's interest in the CSR. He wondered whether any of the *kulmbars* were still alive. 'We could find out,' I offered. It would mean a lot of research, but I wanted to do it for this man who meant so much to me. I rang the CSR head office in Sydney. There was nothing on the overseers. Evidently, once they finished with the Company, they disappeared off the record books, a bit like the girmitiyas about whom everything was documented when they were under indenture, and nothing, or very little, when they became free. Was there ever an association or club of former Fiji overseers, I wondered. The lady did not know but promised to find out. She rang an hour or two later to say that I could try Mr Syd Snowsill. He was the leader of the Fiji pack in Sydney. The name seemed vaguely familiar; he was, from memory, the spearhead of the Seaqaqa Cane Expansion project in the early 1970s. A gruff voice greeted me when I rang him. When I explained the purpose of my enquiry, he became relaxed. '*Bahut Accha*,' very good. 'Who are you after? Anyone in particular?' I volunteered three names: Mr Tom, Mr Oxley and Mr Johnson. 'I see,' Mr Snowsill said chuckling and with some affection, 'all the Labasa *badmaash* gang, eh,' the Labasa hooligans. He did not know the whereabouts of Mr Oxley and Mr Johnson, but Mr Tom — Leslie Duncan Thompson — was living in retirement in Ballina. 'His name will be in the local telephone book,' Mr Snowsill said as he wished me good luck. '*Shukriya ji. Namaste or should I say Khuda Hafiz!*' 'Both are fine.'

If you do not know it, Ballina (Bullenah in the local Aboriginal language) is one of the loveliest places in Australia. A rural sugar cane growing community of fewer than twenty thousand in sub-tropical northern New South Wales, by the enchanting bottle-green Richmond River and surrounded by sea of rippling cane fields for as far as the eye can see, tidal lagoons and surf beaches nearby. It was the kind of place I knew that Kaka would like: a rural cane country since the 1860s, the people, friendly and genuine, in the way country folk generally are. And he did, as we drove on the Princess Highway through small, picaresque seaside towns, beaches, thickly-wooded rolling hills along the roadside, across a gently gathering greenness in the distance.

Mr Tom was certainly in the phone book when I checked the next morning. His address was a retirement home on the outskirts of the town, on a small hill overlooking the river. I didn't ring but drove to the place to give Mr Tom a surprise. My mental picture of him remained of a tall thin man, barking orders. Kaka was smiling in anticipation, perspiring slightly. We waited in the wick chairs in the veranda as the lady at the front desk went to get him from the dining table across the room. As he walked towards us, I knew it was Mr Tom: tall, erect, with a bigger waist now, face creased and the hair gone, but not the sense of purposefulness. 'Yeash,' he drawled. When I explained why we had come and told him Kaka's name, he beamed and hugged him, two old codgers meeting after decades, slapping each other gently on the back. '*Salaam, sahib,*' Kaka muttered. '*Salaam, salaam,*' Mr Tom replied excitedly. '*Chai lao. Jaldi, jaldi,*' bring some tea, quick-fast, he said to no one in particular. Perhaps he wanted us to know that he still had Hindustani after all these years. '*Tum kaise baitho,*' Mr Tom asked, Kaka, how are you?

Before Kaka could reply, Mr Tom said, '*Hum to buddha hai ab,*' I am an old man now. I translated for Kaka. After a while, the names came to Mr Tom: Lalta, Nanka, Sundar (he pronounced it Soonda). He especially asked after Udho, the de facto head man of the village, who was one of the few from Labasa to volunteer for the Labour Corps during World War Two. He had died some years back. 'Too bad,' Mr Tom said. 'He was a good man.' He asked after Kaka's family, about the school. 'I haven't been to Labasa since leaving, but hear it is a modern place now, not bush place like it used to be. They tell me the roads have been tarsealed and people have piped water. No longer a *pukka jungali* place, eh. You people deserve every bit of it.'

'*Seaqaqa kaise baitho*, Arjun? How is Seaqaqa? Mr Tom asked Kaka. That was the project on which he had worked with Mr Snowsill. It had been launched with great hope of getting Fijians into the sugar industry. Half the leases were reserved for them. When Kaka told him that many Fijians had left their farms or sub-leased them to Indo-Fijian tenants, Mr Tom seemed genuinely sad to learn that all the effort that he and other overseers had put in had gone to pot. 'It was done all too suddenly. They wanted to make political mileage out of it. Win elections. All that *tamasha* (sideshow). That's no way to run this business. We needed to have proper training for them, proper husbandry practices in place. You can't just pluck them out the bush and make them successful farmers overnight. Ridiculous.' 'Farming is a profession, son,' Mr Tom said to me, 'just like any other. It is not everyone's cup of tea.' Mr Tom said that the CSR should have remained in Fiji for another five to ten years to effect a good transition, train staff properly, and mostly to get politicians to see the problems of the industry from a business angle. 'But no, everything had to be done in a rush. You got your independence and you didn't want white men around telling you what to do anymore. Fair enough, I suppose.'

Then Mr Tom asked about the current situation. He had read that the industry was in dire straits. 'I am afraid it is true, Mr Tom,' I said. Most leases in Daku, Naleba, Wainikoro, Laga Laga — places Mr Tom knew so well — had not been renewed, and the former farms were slowly reverting to bush. Mr Tom shook his head. 'Sad. So much promise, shot through so early.' He asked about the farmers. Those evicted were moving out, many to Viti Levu, starting afresh as market gardeners, vegetable growers, general labourers and domestic hands. 'Girmit again, eh? Unnecessary tragedy. Why? What for? We have all gone mad.'

I asked Mr Tom about something that had been on my mind for many years. 'Why didn't the CSR sell its freehold land to the growers when it decided to leave Fiji? It would have been the right thing to do, the humane thing to do.' Mr Tom acknowledged my question with that characteristic drawl of his, 'Yeash.' And then bluntly, 'We couldn't give a rat's arse about who bought the land. All we wanted was *nagad paisa* [cash].' Fijian leaders understood very well that land was power and didn't want the CSR to sell its freehold land to Indians. Over two hundred thousand bloody acres or so. Indian leaders in the Alliance went along, trying to please their masters, hoping for some concessions elsewhere. The Fijians and the Europeans — Mara, Penaia, Falvey, Kermode, that crowd — had them by the balls. We in the Company watched all this in utter incomprehension and disbelief, but it wasn't our show. We were so pissed off with the Dening Award.' He was referring to the award by Lord Denning, Britain's Master of the Roll, which favoured the growers against the millers and which led eventually to CSR's departure from Fiji in 1973. 'And then there was the Gujarati factor, did you know?' I didn't. 'Some of your leaders feared that if Indian tenants got freehold land, Gujarati merchants would get their hands on them by hook or crook. To some, the Gujaratis were a bigger menace than Fijians and Europeans. Such bloody short-sightedness. Son, some of your suffering is self-inflicted. Harsh thing to say, but true.'

After a spell of silence, Kaka wanted to know about Mr Tom's life after Tua Tua. From Tua Tua he had gone to Lomowai and did the rounds of several Sigatoka sectors (Kavanagasau, Olosara, Cuvu) before moving to Lautoka mill as a supervisor. Taking early retirement, he returned to Australia and after some years of working in Ballina's sugar industry, he 'went fishing,' as he put it, travelling, taking up golf and lawn bowling. I vividly recalled lawn bowling as the game white people, in white uniforms and white shoes played at Batanikama. Wife and children? Kaka wanted to know. The wife had died a few years back, which is when he moved to this place. The children were living in Queensland. 'There is nothing for them here.' Kaka wondered if Mr Tom still had that fearsome taste for hot chillies. '*Nahin sako*, Arjun,' can't do it anymore. '*Pet khalas*', the stomach's gone. 'And what do you do, young man?' Mr Tom asked me. When I told him that I was an academic in Canberra, he smiled. '*Shabaash*, beta,' well done, son. 'Boy from Labasa, eh! Who would have thought! From the cane fields of Fiji to the capital of Australia! And you joined the bloody know-all academics at the tax payers expense! Good onya, son.'

We had been talking like this for an hour or so when the topic of the coups in Fiji came up. Mr Tom had been outraged by what had taken place. There was broad sympathy in conservative Australia for the coups, who saw them as the desperate struggle of the indigenous community against the attempted dominance of an immigrant one. But Mr Tom was different. 'I wrote letters to the local papers, gave a few talks and interviews on the radio. No bloody use. Look, I said, you don't know the Indian people. I do. I have worked with them. I understand them. They made Fiji what it is today. They have been the backbone of the sugar industry. You take them out and the whole place will fall apart. Just like that. What wrong have they done? How have they wronged the Fijian people? Their only vices are thrift and industry.' He went on like this for sometime. I was not used to hearing this kind of assessment from people in Australia. Mr. Tom was refreshingly adamant, defiant.

'Yours must have been a voice in the wilderness, Mr Tom,' I said 'Bloody oath, yes. You talk about immigrant people ripping natives apart. Bloody well look at Australia! Look what we have done to the Aborigines. Snatched their land, made them destitute, pushed them into the bush, robbed them of their rights. Bloody genocide, if you ask me. What have the Indians done to Fiji? They worked hard on the plantations so that the Fijians could survive. What's bad about that? If I had my way, I would bring the whole bang lot here. We need hardworking people like you in this country.' Mr Tom had spoken from the heart. 'Let me not go on, because all this hypocrisy lights me up.' 'Mr Howard would not approve,' I said. 'What would these city slickers know,' Mr Tom said dismissively. 'They don't know their arse from the hole in the ground, if you ask me.' I had heard many a colourful Australian slang — blunt as a pig's arse, cold as a witch's tits, all over the place like a mad woman's shit, slipperier than snot on a brass doorknob — but this one was unfamiliar. I smiled, and appreciated Mr Tom's unvarnished directness.

It was time to go. Once again, Kaka and Mr Tom hugged. 'Well Arjun, *nahi jaano phir milo ki nahin milo*,' don't know if we will ever meet again. 'Look after yourself and say salaam to the old timers.' With that we headed back to Sydney. I told Kaka all what Mr Tom had said. 'Remember beta what I told you: many kulambars were tough but fair. We were not completely innocent either: *Chori, Chandali, Chaplusi*,' thievery, stupidity, wanton behaviour. I was impressed, even touched, by Mr Tom's directness and his principled uncompromising stand on the Fiji coups. I had not expected this sort of humanity in a former kulambar, whose general reputation in Fiji is still rotten. Talking to Mr Tom and driving through the cane country brought back memories of growing up in Tabia more than a half century ago — of swollen brown rivers, the smell of pungent cane fires reddening the ground, cane-carting trains snaking through the countryside, little thatched huts and corrugated iron houses scattered around the dispersed settlements, smoke from cooking fires rising in the distance, little school children in neat uniforms walking Indian-file to school. 'You are a godsend,' Kaka had said to me when I had offered to bring him to Australia with me. In truth, Kaka was a godsend for me. With him, I had revisited a world of which I was once a part but no longer am.

I dropped Kaka at Krishna's place and returned to Canberra. I was going to Suva for a conference in a couple of months' time and promised to see him then. Tears were rolling down his stubbled cheek as he hugged me. '*Pata nahin beta ab kab miliho*,' don't know son when we will meet again. I didn't know it then, but it was the final goodbye. A month after Kaka returned, Krishna rang to say that he had died – of what precisely no one knew. I was speechless for days. The last link to my past was now gone, the last one in the village who had grown up in the shadows of indenture, lived through the Depression, the strikes in the sugar industry, the Second World War. I felt cheated. I still feel his loss.

When I returned to Fiji, I knew that I had to go to Labasa. Perhaps it is the ancient urge to say the final goodbye in person. I wanted to know the exact circumstances of Kaka's death. Only then could I finally come to terms with my grief. He was very happy to return home, back in his own house, back to his routine, people told me. Then one day, all of a sudden, Lali, the cow, died. Kaka was distraught; she was like family to him. Lali was his wife's gift to him when their first grandchild was born. He used to talk to her, caress her forehead, religiously feed her para grass every morning and afternoon, wash her once a week. People said that Kaka talked to Lali as if he was talking to wife, telling her his doubts and fears. Using her as a sounding board for his ideas and plans. Now a loved link to that past was gone. He was heart broken. In fact he had died from a massive heart attack. The last words Kaka spoke before he collapsed, one of his grandchildren remembered, was 'Sukhraji, *taharo, hum aait haye*,' Sukhraji, wait (for me), I am coming.

8

A Change of Seasons

> But it was all over too soon
> When somebody decided you'd
> Better move on.

Aap kab aawaa, the boy asked, when did you come? He meant, 'How long have you been waiting.' Tall and dark, perhaps sixteen or seventeen, he was a car wash boy at the Laucala BP Station. I used to go there every second weekend to have my car washed and polished, tyre pressure checked, oil changed. The boy, Vinay, was a new recruit at the gas station. He looked startled, almost frightened. If I had been waiting long and his boss found out, he would be fired, perhaps slapped around the ears for slacking off, being negligent. He looked at me pleadingly and then gazed at the ground expecting to be told off, sworn at. Anything would be better than to be reported. He had been cramming for his exams at the back of the garage.

'Just this minute,' I said, although I had been waiting for about ten. Vinay knew the truth. 'I will do a special job for you today, sir,' he said. 'The usual will do, son,' I replied as I tapped him gently on the shoulder with the smile of a benign uncle.

A word he had spoken had given him away and made me feel warm and curious about him. *Aawaa*: that was pure Labasa, a rustic word long forgotten in Viti Levu, a signifier of our primitive country origins, a badge of inferiority in their eyes. *Aayaa* is what they say, a politer word, more literary. Vinay and I are *kaivata*, as the Fijians might say, people from the same place and so somehow distantly related.

I read the weekend papers sitting on a tree stump under the lanky acacia tree while Vinay goes about his work. Cakes of mud dislodge from the mudguard under pressurized water, the sides are splashed and then rubbed with cloth, the hubcaps cleaned, the inside vacuumed, and mirrors wiped. Vinay's speed and precision suggest he is a practised hand at this. Occasionally he throws a furtive glance at me to see if I am watching. I wave back gently. His dark face glistens with sweat in the hard sun and unbearable humidity.

The heat and the humidity, the look of desperation on Vinay's face, that haunting and hunted look in the eyes of a boy ageing before his time, are familiar, and bring back memories of a distant past. I recall early rainy mornings when Mother and I went to work for Santu, our neighbour. Mother received five shillings for a day's backbreaking work in knee-deep dirty water transplanting rice seedlings and I, a 'mere child,' one shilling. There was no break from the wind and the pelting rain; a specified number of rice seedling bundles had to be planted by the end of the day before we were paid, much like the daily task under *girmit*. We return home around dusk, but mother's day was not finished. She had to prepare dinner, before we all went to bed only to start all over again the next morning.

Then there was work at Ram Dayal's cane farm. Mr Dayal had been promised our labour during the school holidays, for what amount we didn't know. But there we were, just children in primary school, hoeing and fertilizing cane, cleaning the outer edges of the farm of weed and overgrown grass, braving hornets, feeding the cattle, sometimes fetching well water for their cooking. No money passed through our hands. It went straight to Father, who used it to buy books, clothes and food for his young family. We didn't ask any questions; that was the way things were done. We were all grateful just to get by, happy to contribute whatever we could to our perennially strained household budget.

Our routine at home was set before and after school: regular work in the mornings taking cattle to the fields, feeding them cut para grass in the evenings, tending vegetable gardens, gathering firewood from the neighbouring hills, fetching water from the well, keeping the compound clean. And the same repetitive meals in the evenings: dhall, rice, pumpkin or jack-fruit curries, ground chillies, mint and garlic for chutney. Once, for some reason, we had an abundance of pumpkins, so much so that we had it for breakfast, lunch and dinner. My younger brothers got so fed up that one day they secretly poured a pot of boiling water on one of the plants. It died soon afterwards. Mother was perplexed, and Father wanted to find the culprit, who would then get the thrashing of his life, but not a word leaked out until years later by which time we could have a good laugh.

Our experience was common. Tabia was a poor village on the outer edges of prosperity. There were no paved roads, no running water, no electricity, just thatched huts for homes and wells for water. Attending school by the late 1950s had become the norm, though completing primary schooling was another matter. And no one had any idea of a possible future career. Working at the local banks was the most prestigious job we could aspire to. We all longed for some employment outside the village, anything that would take us away from the local rut. One of my fondest memories of those years is of watching planes flying from Waiqele airport over our village. I would gaze at the plane until it dissolved into a blip and then disappeared from sight. Then for a long time afterwards, I would think about the plane, the people who might be in it, where they were going, whether one day I too might get to fly to strange, unknown places. Paradise was always somewhere else, deepening the aching desire to leave.

All this was more than forty years ago. Now, Tabia is a changed place. A modern tar-sealed highway connects the village to other parts of Vanua Levu, there is electricity, piped water and television in most homes; the village has a vibrant primary school and well-regarded secondary college to which students come from all parts of the island. People from the village have travelled widely, and some have children abroad. Tiny tots when I was there, Tabia boys and girls have done well, joined the professions, gone places, made something of themselves. I had myself moved on and returned only intermittently, for wedding, funerals and rare family get-togethers, until the death of my parents practically severed the link. Tabia is now an evanescent memory.

Vinay reminded me of the world from which I had come, but it hurt that this child now, all these years later, through no fault of his own, was undergoing a misery I thought had long ceased. I knew about the non-renewal of leases and of the general exodus from the once flourishing cane farms in northern Vanua Levu (Naqiqi, Wavu Wavu, Daku, Lagalaga, Wainikoro). Among the refugees, for that is the right word, were members of my own extended family, though my contact with them had long been broken through years of absence and short returning visits. For many of them, I was a 'name,' a good name, to be sure, but just a name. There was something about Vinay that aroused my curiosity about things I had heard and read about, but never really considered.

'You go to school, right?' I asked him after he had finished washing the car. 'Yes, sir,' he answers politely. 'From Labasa, right?' 'Yes, sir.' He looked perplexed, wondering what he had done or said to give away his identity. People from Labasa, I learn later, are not always welcome in Suva. Regarded as unrefined country people at the best of times, the butt of jokes about the way they talk and walk and dress, they are now derided openly for being diligent and hardworking, taking any and all jobs for pay which Suva people consider beneath them.

'How long have you been here, Vinay?' I ask. 'Since last year, sir." With your family or by yourself?' It was not an empty question. There was a time when some of the wealthier and well-connected families sent their sons for a bit of high schooling in Suva to improve their chances of securing a good job. 'My father, mother and my younger sister, sir.' 'She goes to school too?' 'Yes, sir, she is in Form Five.' 'And you are in?' 'Form Seven, sir.' 'I would like to meet your family some time,' I said.

Vinay seemed horrified by my request, as if this was the most unusual thing anyone could have asked him. 'Sir?' he asked, saying, in effect: why in the world would you like to do such a thing. 'Yes, some day, Vinay, I would like to meet them.' With that, I handed him a five-dollar note as a bonus. No one was watching. Vinay looked into my eyes with a sadness that burnt deep into my memory. 'Get something for yourself and your sister, beta,' I said, patting his head gently. 'Thank you very much, sir,' he said as he turned away wiping tears from his eyes.

The following Saturday I again went to the gas station to meet Vinay. He was courteous and respectful. 'Ram Ram, sir,' he said. 'Ram, Ram,' I replied. 'Will tomorrow be all right for me to visit you?' 'Sir?' 'Tomorrow. Just a short visit to meet your parents. I am from Labasa too, in case you don't know.' 'Sir, my father knows you. He says you are a very famous man.' 'You know us Labasans. We are all famous,' I said. Vinay smiled. 'Tomorrow at ten, then?' 'Yes, sir,' Vinay replied hesitantly. I understood the reason for his reluctance. He was a proud boy who did not want me to see his desperately poor family circumstance. His pride would be injured in case I thought any less of him because of his background. But I was determined.

Newtown Mini Market is where Vinay arranged to meet me. It is towards the higher end of the Khalsa Road that links Kinoya and Tacirua. The road dissects a congested corridor. The Kinoya end is the more settled part. The concrete houses are bigger, more substantial, set apart from each other by respectable distance, closer to the shopping centre, bread shops and churches. The Tacirua end is clogged, full of sardine-can tenements of rickety roof iron and stray wood, one on top of another, some perched precariously on a ridge leading to a gully, many partly shielded from view from the road by tall grass, some without electricity, many without water, all testimony to human misery.

I arrive about ten minutes early. 'Mini Market' is a serious misnomer. The place is empty, deserted, strewn with garbage. All that survives is a crumbling corrugated iron shed resembling a chicken coop, full of rotting, crumpled cardboard boxes and bits and pieces of wood. Once this place would have been a bustling local centre, selling vegetables, eggs, root crops, perhaps even a live chicken or two to the surrounding neighbourhoods. But all that must have been a long time ago. As with so many things in Fiji, temporariness is the order of the day here. I wonder who its owner was. Probably some evicted Indo-Fijian tenant who was here for a while and then moved out to something better elsewhere.

Behind the chicken coop is a well maintained house painted dark blue. A Fijian man, fresh from a shower and wrapped in a floral sulu walks towards me. He has probably seen me leaning against my car, waiting, for some time. 'You looking for someone?' he asks. 'Yes, a boy named Vinay.' 'The thin fallah who wash car here?' 'Probably.' 'He live on the other side of the road, over there,' the man says, pointing me to a collection of tin huts on top of a grassy hill. 'Thanks, Bro, but I will wait here for just a bit longer.' 'Come, have some chai *Bhaiya*,' have some tea, brother, he says. 'Thanks, but I have just had breakfast.' This typically generous Fijian offer to share food and drink, so common in the villages, still survives in this depressed corner of Suva.

Vinay apologises for being late. We walk along a muddy path to his 'home.' Barely clothed curious children look silently in our direction. They are not used to seeing well-dressed, important-looking strangers coming to their settlement. Both sides of the path are overgrown with grass. and fresh dog shit is all over the place. There is a foul smell in the air, a mixture of burning kerosene and urine. Vinay's place is a typical squatter settlement structure, a one-bedroom, rusting corrugated-iron shack.

Vijay, Vinay's father, greets me at the front door with both hands and invites me in. He has none of Vinay's unease or embarrassment. Inside, I sit on a wooden crate covered with piece of white cloth. Around forty or so, Vijay is prematurely aged, his skin dry and leathery from prolonged exposure to the sun. His wife, Vimla, returns from fetching water from the communal tap outside. 'Ram, Ram *Bhaiya*,' she says as she covers her head and walks past me shyly. A village girl in single overflowing dress she too looks worn out, her unkempt hair greying at the edges. *Thoda chai banaao*, Vijay tells his wife, make some tea. 'Vinay, get some *biskut* from the shop.' Such hospitality amid this squalor feels incongruous. I kick myself: I should have brought something along. I hand Vinay a five-dollar note, which he accepts reluctantly after a nod from his father.

The room is spartan, small, probably ten by twelve, very much like the rooms in the lines during *girmit*. A rolled up mattress is stacked against the wall. I imagine the whole family sleeps on it. A couple of tin crates and musty cardboard boxes contain all the family's possessions. Vijay's wife is boiling water on an ancient darkened stove, and the room reeks of kerosene and smoke. A dozen or so cups and plates are heaped in a large enamel bowl. From the open spaces of a rural farming community to this cramped, sooty and smelly place must have been quite a traumatic journey.

Vijay mixes a bowl of grog. *Bas ek dui piyaali*, just a bowl or two. That is an euphemism as well as an excuse. Vijay, I can tell, is a seasoned kava drinker. His skin is cracked and the corners of his mouth sickly white from excessive indulgence. Vijay begins by making family connections. In no time, it is established that he is distantly related to me by marriage to one of my cousins about whom I know nothing but pretend familiarity. He is from Naleba, one of the early cane districts of

Labasa, notorious during indenture for rampant overseer violence. The place was emptying out as cane leases were not renewed. Vijay was a part of the exodus. 'It all came as a shock,' he says. 'One day, a Land Rover arrived. Three Fijians got out. They had some papers in their hands. One of them said that our rent was in arrears. Unless we paid up in a week, our lease will end.' *Poth bharo nahin to jameen khalaas. Khali ek hafta bacho.* 'Just like that?' 'Just like that!'

Vijay needed about two thousand dollars, but that kind of money was not around. There were no money lenders left in the village, and the banks in town would not come to the party. With so many leases expiring and the future of the sugar industry shaky, the risk was too great. Besides, the ten-acre plot was held jointly in the name of Vijay and his brother. And Vijay was already in debt. 'Father's illness cost us a lot. Several months in the hospital. We gave him a good farewell.' *Achhha se bida kiya gay.* Then there was the expense of the children's education: building fees for the school, books and uniforms for the children. Vijay was not alone: nearly everyone in the village was teetering on the verge of bankruptcy.

'Did you try and find the Fijian landlord to see if you could strike a deal, maybe get into share-cropping or something?' I had heard of similar arrangements in parts of Viti Levu. '*Bhaiya*, I didn't know who the landlord was. *Maloomen nahin.* There were no Fijians in the village. We had no idea who owned the land. We got this lease a very long time ago, when my father was a child. We never had any dealings with Fijians. We only knew the [Native Land Trust] Board.' The creation of that organisation had brought about a semblance of order and stability in the system of land leases. Instead of dealing with individual landowners, the tenants dealt only with the NLTB. But it also extinguished personal relations between the landlord and the tenant. There was no human face, no human contact to mediate in times of crisis like this.

'Have you found out the name of the landowner now?' 'No,' Vijay replied. 'It will be no use. They always take money and demand other goods. This *kerekere*, the borrowing business never ends. A chicken today, a goat next week, money for funerals and weddings the week after. Bottomless well. These young fellows are greedy. Easy come, easy go. The older generation was different.' Rapacity among landowners in Fiji is not uncommon although it has increased in recent decades of relative prosperity in the farming community.

But there was another motivation to move. It was clear that there was no future on the farm for the family. 'There was a time when the farm was all we had,' Vijay said. 'We all grew up on it. Our parents raised us on the farm. That was our world. But now, the income is not enough for all of us. There is always someone working outside, which keeps us going. 'Otherwise we will be finished.' This, too, is a recent phenomenon: the farm principally as a place of residence, not as a source of livelihood.

Vijay was concerned about his children's future. 'There is nothing for them here,' he says. 'What will they do?' he asks. 'We live for our children.' It was for that reason that Vijay, like so many others, had decided to leave Labasa for good once the lease was not renewed. In Suva, there was some hope; in Labasa, there was none. 'I am glad it is happening now, when I am still strong and can work. A few years later, I might not have been able to do this.' *Wahi pinjada men bund rahit.* 'We would have remained trapped in that place forever. We should have seen this coming a long time ago and left then.'

I asked about Vijay's neighbours. He pointed out the tenements belonging to former Labasans. There were at least a dozen around Vijay's place. 'We have all become family,' Vijay tells me. 'We look out for each other.' They were the new *jahajibhais*, brothers of the crossing like their *girmitiya* forebears, facing the same hurt and humiliation, the same levelling fate. Everyone there was a refugee. Whether you were from Nagigi or Naleba, Daku or Dreketilailai, a Madrassi or a Kurbi, Hindu or a Muslim, you were a Labasan first and foremost. There was no going back: the rupture was final.

'What do people do around here?' I ask. 'Anything, *Bhaiya*. We will take any job. A job is a job. It is the question of our livelihood.' *Pet aur baal bachhon ke sawaal haye.* Casual labouring, house-help, grass cutting, car washing, nightwatchman. Some had taken to carpentry and others to bus and taxi driving. The more skilled ones found jobs as sales assistants in the bigger supermarkets while a few women found employment in the garment factories. The old entrepreneurial spirit still exists, I realise, now fuelled by desperation and a very real fear of descending into debilitating destitution among strangers in this alien place.

But the Labasans' enterprising spirit, their willingness to make a go of things, has made them targets for many Suva residents. Not knowing that I too was from Labasa, people were free with their prejudices. Labasans are prepared to work for dirt, I am told. They have no ethics, no sense of responsibility. Greedy 'like hell,' they take on work beyond their competence, making a mess in the process. 'No one who wants good work ever hires these fellows the second time around,' a man says to me. 'They are so clannish, so uncouth,' *ek dam ganwaar*. A few weeks back, I was reminded, a small car repair garage owned by a Labasan in Kalabu was burnt down. The police did nothing, they probably had a hand in it. No charges were ever laid. 'What would you expect in this cut-throat business,' man says. 'We have to earn our living somehow too.'

'*Bhaiya*, these people are jealous,' Vijay said to me. *Bahut bhaari jalan bhav.* 'They won't do the work themselves and they make threats against us. They look down on us. They call this place *Chamar tola*,' the place of untouchables, the lowest of the low. As Vijay spoke, I realised the people from Labasa were the new pariahs, on the outer fringes of society. We were the butt of many a joke. Our speech was mocked, our preference for simpler things ridiculed. We were tolerated as country bumpkins.

Anti-Labasa prejudice goes back a long way, and is not without reason, although Labasans find hard to admit it. Vijay's words recalled my own first trip to Suva. It was in 1969. I had come to Suva with my uncle, my father's elder step-brother, to get glasses for my deteriorating eyesight. The stories I heard about the visitors have remained with me. In the mornings, men from Labasa looked for *datoon*, raw twigs, preferably the *bariara* stem, to clean their teeth. Most had never used a toothbrush in their lives. But twigs were not easily found, so men took long walks in the evenings searching for them. Much to the amusement of the locals, Labasa people made slurping noises as they drank their tea and belched loudly in appreciation of a good meal. They thought nothing of clearing their throats and coughing the phlegm out on the lawn. Used to letting go in the open, they frequently took a leak on the toilet floor and urinated while having a shower, causing a foul smell. They used water (from empty beer bottles) after toilet, not toilet paper, which they thought unhygienic, leaving behind a mess which women and children hated cleaning.

People tried to create a sense of community in this place of chaos and anxiety. There was a *Ramayan mandali* in the squatter settlement, and people took turns hosting recitals at their homes. Unlike many Suva residents, Labasa people were punctilious about rituals and protocols. Just as they had done back home for decades, they did not have meat or alcohol at home for a prescribed number of days before the event. This was very familiar to me. In the Tabia of my childhood, people were fastidious about rituals. *Hanuman Katha, Satyanarayani puja, Shiva Ratri, Ram Naumi* and many others were performed with excessive religiosity. Once I was impatient with this sort of thing; religion was the opiate of the masses, I believed in my radical, irreverent youth; education, I was convinced, was the true liberator of humanity.

But I realised as I looked around how few outlets there were for social interaction and entertainment. Regular gatherings encouraged social cohesiveness and provided the people with a sense of community. They gave life amid all this dreariness a certain rhythm, purpose and identity, something to do outside work. And the story of Lord Rama held a certain resonance in the lives of an uprooted group. Rama had been exiled from his kingdom of Ayodhya through no fault of his own, in deference to his distraught father's wish to fulfil a promise to one of his wives, but he did return, after fourteen years, a triumphant prince. Good had in the end triumphed over evil. Their agony too would end one day, people consoled themselves, for they too were innocent victims of circumstances beyond their control. The *Ramayan* had provided great spiritual and emotional comfort to the *girmitiyas* at a time of great distress and disruption in their lives. I imagine it is providing solace to these people as well.

Still, glimpses of hope and escape from this wretched place were rare. 'My main concern is my children,' Vijay said again. Their future was weighing on his mind. 'I feel so sad that I can't give them what they deserve, what every child deserves.' *Bachpana ek hi baar aawe haye.* You have only one childhood. 'But you are giving them what every parent should and what every child deserves — an education.' I meant it. Vijay nodded in approval, but I suppose he had in mind good clothes, money for the occasional outing, video games. 'Yes,' Vijay said, 'it is mainly because of Vinay and Shivani that we decided to move here.' Such beautiful, evocative names in this empty, shattered place, I thought.

Vijay was doing what Indo-Fijian parents had always done: sacrificing whatever they had to educate their children. That, more than anything else, was the reason for our success. The story was familiar to me; I was a part of it. At an early age, we were told that there was no future on the farm for all the six boys. We would have to look for other opportunities. Education was the only way out. We pursued it single-mindedly and succeeded. The path we trod all those years ago, alone and often without a helping hand, was now being pursued by a new generation at a time when the sky should have been the limit for them.

With one difference. We grew up in a settled environment and in a home which we proudly called our own. We were poor, but a home was a home. The routine and rhythms of village life, deadening at times, defined the parameters of our existence. We knew that we belonged in the village, that we had a place in it. The village gave us an identity. We felt secure. We said proudly that we were from Tabia. With no idea about the outside world or of the changes ahead that would disrupt our lives irreparably and take us to unimagined places, we cherished the idea that Tabia would always be our home. It would be there for us always, welcoming. That sense of attachment has diminished with time, but it once had a powerful hold on our youthful emotions. I wonder if Vinay and Shivani will ever know the joys of belonging and attachment to a place that they can call home, the comfort of being members of a community, the innocence of a carefree childhood.

Vijay is clearly worried about his family's safety. They are unwanted, uninvited strangers in this place. The news of robberies and the sight of wayward unemployed boys roaming the streets worry him. There have been reports of a few assaults, some stray incidents of stone-throwing at nights and burglaries. Vijay does not have much to lose. There is no television or modern accessories such as a refrigerator in the house. But it is the violation of privacy, the sense of being violated, that worries people. Several fathers have formed an informal group and take turns to see the girls on to the bus every morning and wait for them at the bus stop after school. The safety and protection of girls especially is paramount with Indo-Fijian parents. It has always been that way.

Newtown is the first but will certainly not be the last stop for most refugees. Some have moved to larger plots of leased lands on the outskirts of Nausori — Korociriciri, Nakelo and Koroqaqa, while others have gone towards Navua. There they plant dalo and cassava and vegetables and sell them at roadside stalls to travellers on the Queen's Highway. I have talked to some of them. 'This is good life,' one of them said to me. 'We get *nagad paisa* [cash] everyday. We are our own boss. We sleep peacefully at night.' 'You won't get back to cane farming then?' '*Ganna men koi fayada nahin haye*,' a man says to me, there is no profit in sugar cane farming, repeating Vijay's sentiment. 'Pocket change' is how someone had described the earnings from cane. 'All that hard work: what for? You pay rent, Fijians demand kerekere all the time and before you know it, all the money is gone. No, this is good.' The reluctance to return to the cane farm was a familiar story throughout Fiji.

Vijay was considering moving to Nadi. He had met someone in Suva market who knew someone who was migrating. But he didn't want to sell his land. Would Vijay mind some share-cropping arrangement? 'I don't know what will happen,' he said to me, 'but I'm sure it will be better than this place.' Of that there was no doubt in my mind. 'There are many good schools there,' he said, 'I have seen them myself.' And he would fit in better in that environment anyway. '*Gaon ke admi log ke gaon hi acchha lagi.*' Village people will always be attracted to villages. Vijay was a true son of the soil who found Suva suffocating.

Shivani arrived after we had been talking for a couple of hours. She had a clutch of books and pads in her hands. 'Been studying, yes?' I ask. 'Yes, sir,' she replies. 'What subjects?' 'Science.' 'And what do you hope to become?' 'A nurse or a doctor, sir.' That kind of ambition from this sort of background sounds ludicrous: from the slums of Suva to the heights of the medical profession? But that, more or less, was how we all started — with nothing. 'One step at a time' was the motto of my generation. 'Why medicine?' I ask, knowing full well that it is the profession of choice for most people in Fiji, or anywhere else for that matter. 'Because I want to help people, sir,' she says. 'Yes, beta, making a difference and helping people is always satisfying. I am sure you will make a great doctor. Remember to look well after this uncle in his doddery old age.' She smiles and walks towards her mother.

Vinay has been in the background, serving us tea but otherwise listening intently to our conversation. There is a kind of sadness about him. As the older son, he knows that the responsibility of looking after his sister and his parents will fall on him. He helps out whenever he can. In addition to washing cars during weekends, he works at the local store down the road most evenings. The customer traffic is light at night, and he gets a free meal and a place to study as well as loaves of bread and occasionally a can of fish on the weekends. He frequently sleeps at the shop under the counter next to bags of onions and potatoes. I sense that Vinay will not talk freely in the presence of his family, and yet I am curious about his story. I have been at Vijay's place for longer than I had expected. I have already disrupted their schedule enough. I apologise as I leave, and promise to see Vinay during the weekend at the gas station.

The visit lingers in my mind for a long time. It is too close to the bone for comfort. I have travelled that route myself, as have so many others before and after me. It must have been some similar experience of disruption and dislocation caused by a prolonged drought, a death in the family, indebtedness, a quarrel, an act of rebellion, that led the *girmitiyas* to emigrate, with what hopes and fears we can only guess. They probably had no precise idea of their destination, but most thought they would be back one day. That day of reckoning never came. Now, a hundred years later, people are on the move again, uprooted, in search of a better life.

I take Vinay to the Victoria Arcade coffee shop on Saturday afternoon after he finishes work. 'Do you miss Labasa?' I ask him. 'Yes, sir, very much.' What particularly?' 'My friends, sir.' I wait for him to continue. 'All my friends I went to school with. We played soccer in the afternoons, swam in the river, walked in the mountains, played tricks on each other, stole mangoes and watermelon from our neighbours' farms. But then they all left one by one as their leases expired. I don't know if I will ever meet them again. I don't know where they are.' They had promised to keep in touch through letters, but they remained just that, promises, unfulfilled.

Once again, the *girmit* experience comes to mind. After a long traumatic journey lasting weeks in often rough seas, *girmitiyas* would arrive in Fiji and after about two weeks of quarantine detention at Nukulau would be allocated to plantations across the country. The officials made sure that people from the same locality in India were not sent to one place for fear of insurrection. The *girmitiyas* would cry and hug each other and promise to keep in touch. They never met again, starting afresh in new places with new people, old memories erased. I could understand Vinay's anguish.

'Anyone special you miss?' It is a kind of question only an older uncle is allowed to ask. It is very unlikely that anyone in the family would know about Vinay's private life. Children never talk about it to their parents, and Shivani was too young to confide in. 'Sir?' I smiled. Averting his eyes, Vinay looked at the ground. 'Daya, sir,' he replied after a long silence. 'She was my best friend. She used to bring me special lunches and sweets at Diwali. We used to do our homework together. I always wanted to be close to her, to protect her.' 'Your parents knew?' 'Yes, sir, they liked her.' 'Where is she now?' 'Don't know, sir. Somewhere in Viti Levu.' 'Father's name?' 'Rajendra Prasad, from Daku. People from Labasa know him as Daku Prasad.' 'I will see if I can find out.' One thing about Labasa is that nearly everyone knows everyone else. Daku had gone to Navua, I found out. One Sunday I went out for a drive to look him up. He had left the place some time ago, a stall keeper at the roadside told me. Try Sigatoka or Nadi, I was advised. 'Tracking him in those places will be like trying to find a needle in a haystack,' I said, if you pardon the cliché. 'God willing, I will find her one day, sir,' Vinay said.

I detected steely determination in Vinay's voice, and a trace of anger too. Enforced removal from the farm had embittered him deeply. To see his proud father reduced to impotent fury, seeking mercy from the officials of the Native Land Trust Board, unable to raise a loan to pay the rent, had hurt and outraged him deeply. No son wants to see his father humiliated. 'What wrong did we do, sir, that they took our land away?' he asks. 'It is not as if they are doing anything with it. You will see it for yourself, sir, that our cane land is now returning to bush.' That was certainly true in many parts of northern Vanua Levu. Non-renewal of leases was one cause of the decline of the sugar industry. 'They will take Fiji and all of us down with them, sir.' I understood Vinay's anger, but how do you explain to a hurt young man that we were always literal as well as metaphorical tenants in Fiji, tolerated as long as we knew our place in the broad scheme of things, that we were never allowed to belong?

'What are you studying, Vinay,' I ask. 'Science subjects, sir.' 'What would you like to study at university?' 'University, sir?' He reacted as if I had asked the most impossible question. 'Why not? It should be a natural thing for a bright boy like you.' 'I would like to become an accountant, sir.' 'Is that what you want?' Vinay hesitated momentarily. 'That is what *Pitaji* [father] wants me to do. He says it will be easier to find a job as an accountant.' 'And probably easier to migrate too, I should think.' 'Sir, but I really want to do history and politics.' That surprised me. No one I had spoken to had ever expressed an interest in those subjects. We historians were like dinosaurs, I thought, irrelevant, like deaf people answering questions no one had ever asked us. History could not make anything happen. The subject wasn't taught in schools, or was taught minimally as part of more amorphous social studies.

'Why history?' I asked. 'I like stories, sir, true stories about real people.' I wouldn't argue with that. It was a good description of the discipline. 'Sir, I don't want to migrate. I want to live here and make my little contribution.' 'Vinay, that's admirable, but have you thought about jobs?' 'I will become a high schoolteacher, sir. That's where all our problems start.' 'But that's not where you will end your career,' I said. 'No sir, God willing.' We parted with promises to keep in touch, and we did intermittently for a few years.

Vinay had gradually slipped from my mind until last year when I was invited to be the chief guest at the annual prize giving ceremony at Namaka Secondary in Nadi. Imagine my surprise to see Vinay there! He was the school's head of social science. 'Good to see you, sir,' he said at tea after the formal ceremonies. He had been at the school for a couple of years. 'So you kept your promise to become a teacher, Vinay.' 'Yes, sir,' he said smiling. Vinay was confident and articulate, not the shy, awkward young man I had met a few years back. Over dinner at his flat in Namaka that night, Vinay told me the details. He had done well in high school to win a scholarship to university. There he had excelled as well, winning prizes and awards all prominently displayed on the walls. He was encouraged to go on to graduate studies, but Vinay declined. 'I had to look after my parents and Shivani,' he said without a trace of bitterness. 'They depended on me,' he said. Responsibility was responsibility. Such an admirable spirit of sacrifice, so rare these days, but somehow with Vinay, I was not surprised.

'Still thinking about history?' I ask. 'Yes, sir, but now I want to make some history.' 'Is that so! Wonderful.' Vinay was doing by correspondence a law degree from Waikato University in New Zealand. He had already completed half the degree. Once it was finished, he would leave teaching to become a full-time lawyer and eventually enter politics. He was active on the local scene, as an elected member of the Nadi Town Council representing the Nawaka Ward. He was close to the powerbrokers of the local branch of the Labour Party and was one of its rising stars. I felt for him. His passion for public service had not dimmed, but I also knew of the bumps he would encounter on the road ahead. A political career in the Indo-Fijian community is not for idealists, or the faint-hearted. 'You cut steel with steel,' people say. It is as brutal as that.

'How is Vijay?' I ask. '*Pitaji* died two years ago. Heart attack.' I touched Vinay's shoulder in sympathy. 'Too young to go now,' I said. 'But that, sir, is not uncommon these days. The stress, the heartache, the glass ceiling in government service, the name-calling by religious bigots, the displacement of our farmers all take their toll.' Vinay had chosen his words carefully. 'Shivani?' 'She graduated last year with a nursing degree and then married and migrated to New Zealand. Mum is with her too, looking after their infant daughter.' 'Remind her of her promise to look after me in old age,' I joked.

'And Daya? Remember you said you will find her one day.' 'Well, sir, I found her at last in Nadi, but by then it was too late.' Daya's parents had settled in Votualevu as sharecroppers after moving from Navua. A family visiting from Canada looking for a bride for their son had chosen Daya. Vinay wasn't surprised: she was a beautiful young woman with fine, almost film star features. Her parents were ecstatic. Daya was going to be their passport to freedom finally. Everyone envied her, the first in the family to migrate. By the time Vinay found Daya working as a cashier at the local ANZ Bank, her marriage papers had already been signed and wedding preparations were well under way. Daya was distraught, but there was nothing she could do to extricate herself from the arrangements. Her parents had spoken for her, and that was that. Yes, *It was over all too soon.* Vinay was similarly helpless. He did not have the one thing that every struggling family in the community prized above all else: a foreign passport. With touching resignation, he said, 'Some things are not meant to be, sir.' 'Yes, son,' I said gently taping him on the shoulder in sympathy, recalling a couple of lines from Lord Tennyson: *Let what is broken so remain/ The gods are hard to reconcile.*

Yes, that Passport. That damned foreign passport. To anywhere.

9

An Australian Fusion

'Please Uncle, talk to Dad. You are the only one he will listen to.' Rani, my niece, sounded desperate. 'See you at the Black Pepper for lunch, Beta.'

Such calls are a regular part of my life. As the eldest male in the extended family in Australia, a community elder, I am contacted once a week or so about all kinds of favours: help with visa applications, advice about bonds for intending family migrants, scholarships for children, hostel accommodation. It's an obligation.

Ramesh, Rani's father, was my cousin from Labasa. He is from the wealthier branch of the extended family. I often stayed with him and his wife, Sharmila, whenever I visited Sydney to buy Fijian fruits and vegetables from the shops and markets in Liverpool. They were my window on the life of our community in the sprawling more affordable western suburbs, where most of the Indo-Fijian migrants settle.

Ramesh was a successful migrant. He had a house, a good job, two cars, his son was in high school and his daughter at university. Sharmila was a secretary in the state government. People looked up to Ramesh for the good standard he was setting for the new arrivals. He was a regular speaker at weddings and funerals and community gatherings. He was a good singer of *bhajans*, Hindu devotional songs. He played the harmonium well.

I noticed in a corner next to the bedroom in his house pictures of Hindu gods and goddesses and a place of prayer: *lota, thali,* dry flowers, a religious book covered with red cloth, a harmonium, *dholak, tabla* and *dandtal.* This side of Ramesh was new to me. I hadn't known him as a particularly religious type. Now he insisted that his children take language and cultural lessons at the local *mandir,* learn proper ways of doing things. I understood the impulse but knew that we were fighting a losing battle. Our world will go with us.

Once, expecting my visit, Ramesh organized a *havan* at his place. It was a full-blown affair, complete with solemn readings of *shlokas* from books I had never heard of before. The priest was from India and he insisted on doing things the proper way, the way they were done back home rather than the corrupted way they were done in Fiji. Everyone present recited the *Gyatri Mantra* and joined in singing verses that were completely unfamiliar to me. I had never heard them in Fiji. Some of the men wore Indian-style dress, while women were in sparkling *salwar kamiz* and *sarees.*

That evening, after the guests had gone and we were relaxing with a bottle of Black Label, I asked Ramesh, 'When did all this *sadhugiri* start,' this passion for religion? 'Since coming to Australia,' he said. In this, Ramesh was not alone. Religion was the eternal opiate. 'But why this obsession with doing things the Indian way?' I wanted to know. 'India is our motherland, Bro.' 'I thought Fiji was.' 'Fiji was where we were born. It is our *janambhumi* the place of our birth. It was never our spiritual home. India is our *matrabhumi*,' our motherland, the land of our religion and culture.

There was bitterness in Ramesh's voice when he spoke of Fiji. Many Indians spoke distressingly about racial discrimination back home, the glass ceiling in the public service, the regular trashing of temples, the burglaries and the assaults. The land problem was uppermost in their minds. 'We even have to bury our dead on leased land,' Ramesh said. The plight of Indo-Fijian tenants forced off land they had occupied for generations hurt. 'Our grandparents built the damn place through their blood and sweat, and this is the treatment we get? How can we call Fiji home?'

Nikhil, the teenage son, was listening to our discussion intently. 'What have we done to claim it as our own, Dad,' he said. 'We can't even speak the language. We don't invite Fijians into our homes. They were there first. Why blame a whole race as if all Fijians are the same?' Nikhil's maturity surprised and delighted me. Ramesh was short with him. 'Yes, but how many of them lifted their finger when we were hurt? Kicked in the gut? They were all rubbing their hands in glee, looking forward to taking our land, our homes, our jobs, our businesses.'

'We have to look at the larger picture, Bro,' Ramesh continued as I sat pondering Nikhil's point about home and belonging. 'Have you been to India recently?' Ramesh asked. I hadn't. 'India is going places. It will become a superpower in my lifetime.' He continued as if he was talking to himself: 'We can't escape our heritage, Bro. In the end, we are all Indians. That is the truth. When Australians ask you 'where are you from,' they think you are from India. When you say Fiji, they say 'but you are not a real Fijian. You don't have bushy hair. You don't play rugby. You don't smile.'

Ramesh had bought hook, line and sinker into the rightwing Hindu view of the world. He was an ardent supporter of the Vishwa Hindu Parishad, which sought to promote a pan-Hindu fraternity. He regularly visited the web sites engaged in wars of words about India and Hinduism. For Ramesh, the fount of all knowledge was the ancient Indus civilization. He supported the destruction of the Babri Mosque. He even bought into the argument that the Taj Mahal was built by Shah Jehan on the foundations of a destroyed Hindu temple. And unbelievably, he supported Bush's war on Iraq: one more Muslim country lacerated by the West, one less Muslim threat for Hindus to contend with. It was as simple as that for him: my enemy's enemy is my friend. On these matters, Ramesh always spoke with a calm, unswerving conviction.

Sharmila did not share his views. 'There you go again,' she would say whenever Ramesh launched one of his India lectures. 'We Indo-Fijians are the most hypocritical people in the world.' Indo-Fijian: that was how I described myself. Ramesh hated the word. 'I am an Indian, full stop, not some hybrid, hyphenated thing,' he used to say whenever the topic was raised. 'I hear they are trying to ban the word in Fiji. Identity theft, they call it. I rest my case. They won't allow us to identify with the land of our birth.'

'I am definitely not an Indian,' Sharmila continued, ignoring Ramesh. She was adamant about that. 'Do you know that these India Indians look down on us? We have lost our culture, they say, we can't speak the language properly, we are too Westernized. They snigger at the way we dress, the way we walk and talk.' She was right about that. I had once read an article by an Indian journalist that created a furor in the community. In the article *Blood Cousins or Bloody Cousins*, the writer said he was ashamed to be identified as an Indo-Fijian, low types beyond redemption. Indo-Fijians gave all Indians a bad name.

'Shami, I agree with you,' I said. 'But don't you think we are superior to them?' I answered my question, 'I mean, there is no question. Of course we are. Has it ever occurred to you that they actually envy us, our freedom, the way we get along with other people, not hung up on status and rank?' 'Yes, Bhaiya, that's what I keep telling Ram, but he won't listen. He hangs out with them, mimics their ways, tries to be more Indian than Indians. Look at the way he dresses.' Ramesh had long flowing Indian cotton *kurta* and pants on. 'It's all a sham.'

'Not all Indians are like that, Shami,' Ramesh countered. 'You and I know many who are concerned about Fiji. Take Suresh Batra and Vandana, or Ravi Palat and Malti.' Sharmila cut in abruptly. 'Yes, but most have contempt for us. Remember what they say: four coups and how many Indians have shed an ounce of their blood to defend their honor? Always expecting the world to do something but not lifting a finger themselves. What kind of *kayarpan*, cowardice, is this?' 'But isn't that true, Shami? Aren't we the most cowardly people on earth? *Ek dam darpok?* Look at India. People there die to defend their land. Look at Kashmir.'

'Exactly,' Sharmila retorted. 'Fighting over some thing that belongs neither to India nor to Pakistan! Fighting is such a terrible, stupid way of solving problems. Call them cowards if you want, but our people in Fiji are wiser. All the guns are on the other side, so what do you do? We protest with our feet.

It makes sense. *Darpok* maybe, but we are *samajhdaar* as well,' wise.

Ramesh and Sharmila were chalk and cheese in their attitude to Fiji. Sharmila was a graduate of the multiracial Dudley High in Suva. She had Fijian, European, Part-European and some Chinese friends. 'People complained to my parents that I was being bad by associating with my friends. *Kharaab ladki*: bad girl. They thought my friends had loose morals, sitting ducks for rape or whatever. I hung around them because they were more fun. Indian girls rarely played sports, always clinging to each other, gossiping all the time. They called me a tomboy, the worst thing they could say about an Indian girl.'

In Sydney, Sharmila had met up with some of her former schoolmates. They occasionally went out to parties, visited the usual haunts at Circular Quay, had picnic at the Botanical Gardens. 'With them, I have so much fun, Bhaiya.' Fun was not a word she associated with the community functions she attended. 'With Indians, you go there all dolled up, sit quietly in a segregated corner with other women, talk about children, how well they were doing at school, the Bollywood videos they have watched, the latest model of washing machines they have bought, who is seeing whom. The men expect us to cook and clean while they sit and drink grog and gossip. Nothing's changed, Bhaiya. *Ek dam ganwaar ke aadat*,' behaving like real country bumpkins.

Sharmila told me about a Book Club for Fiji women she had once started. Only Fijians and Part-Europeans came. 'Bhaiya, you go to Indian homes and you won't find them reading. There are no books around. Most will never read a book. They think reading is for school children. 'I did all my reading when I was in high school,' one woman told me the other day proudly. Grown-ups don't read, like grown up men don't cry. They can't spare time from window shopping or Tupperware parties or weddings and socials.'

Ramesh disapproved of Sharmila's social activities and the way she dressed — knee-length skirt, stylishly cut hair, the expensive perfume, but did not say much. Once or twice his friends had noticed her drinking wine at Darling Harbour with her friends, which hurt Ramesh. He was a leader of the community and expected his wife to have some respect for his position and status. 'I am married to you, Ramesh. I am not a doll that you dress up for show and then put back into the cupboard whenever you want. If you don't like it, you know what do.' Sharmila's sharpness had increased in the time I knew her.

When we returned to the topic of Fiji and the events there, Sharmila said pointedly, looking at Ramesh, 'We are quick to point a finger at others. How many of us can say we have really good Fijian friends? How many of us allow our children to go out with Fijian boys and girls? We look down at them. After all these years in Fiji, but how many of us can speak even basic Fijian, and understand Fijian culture? You can count them on the fingers of one hand.' Almost exactly Nikhil's words.

'That's not fair, Shami, and you know it, Ramesh responded indignantly. 'How many of us know our own culture and language? We are a bastard culture, if you ask me. And when were we ever allowed to learn Fijian? We were locked up in racial ghettoes all our lives. Race is a fact of life, we were told. We looked at each other through the glass curtain. Why wasn't Fijian taught in schools? Whose fault was that? It is not fair to blame our people for Fiji's mess.'

'Shami, Indians are not all peas in the same pod,' Ramesh said after some time although curiously, he saw Fijians in that way. 'They are not, although from your Christian perch, they might all appear the same.' Turning to me, Ramesh said, 'Bro, you know how it was in Labasa. North Indians thought the South Indians inferior. The Arya Samajis hardly mixed with the Sanatanis. And Hindus and Muslims lived apart on different planets. When did we ever have the time to reach out? We lived in a series of concentric circles, and by the time we reached its outer edges, it was time to kick the bucket.' 'Yes, divided by ancient prejudices and modern greed,' I added.

'Excuses and more excuses, as usual,' Sharmila replied dismissively. 'We were the immigrant community. We should have tried harder to adapt. We are repeating the same mistake here. We live in Australia, but how much of this country do we really understand? We congregate in our ghettoes and think this is Australia. Well, there's more to Australian culture than barbecues and beer and beaches. We must keep up with the Jones's, mustn't we? Yup, and never be backward in condemning Aussie lives as shallow and superficial. Never.'

'Shami, there you go again,' Ramesh said, trying to break Sharmila's onslaught. 'As I was telling Bro earlier, no matter how long you live here, you will not be an Anglo-Saxon, you will still have black or brown skin. They still ask 'Where're you from?' They say this is a multicultural country, but how much multiculturalism do you see in the government, in our schools and universities? When you apply for jobs, they talk about this gender equality thing. Does anyone talk about color?' Then, homing in to seal the argument, he said, 'Just look at New Zealand and see what they have been able to achieve. Even their Governor-General is a person of color, with Fiji Indian roots to boot. That will never happen here. Conformity and subjection is what they want.'

'That's being so unfair, Ram,' Sharmila responded. 'Yes, this is a white man's country, I agree. But things have changed since we came here twenty odd years ago. Just look at the number of ethnic restaurants around us, welfare programs and government-funded languages classes for migrants, grants for cultural things. Look at the Bollywood movies in local theatres. Look at the spice and video shops. It is everywhere, Ram. Your Mandir, of which you are so proud, was partly government-funded. You condemn this country but you still take its generous dollars when it suits you. You want to have your cake and eat it too. That's our problem, not theirs.'

'When will we ever learn?' Sharmila continued. 'Bhaiya, Ramesh and I had this huge argument when Pauline Hanson made that speech in parliament about immigrants swamping this country. Our church group took a strong stand against her. We signed petitions and protested. We even took a delegation to Bob Carr. What did Ramesh do? He just sat here and did nothing. Actually, he scolded me. 'Hanson is not against us,' he said. 'She is against the slit-eyed types, people who pollute Cabramatta and fight gang wars. I hate them too. Such hypocrisy, and we have the gall to complain about Australian racism?'

I knew of our lack of historical sense. In Fiji, we hardly knew our past and, worse, did not seem to care about it. For many, the past was simply past. In Australia, our sense of disengagement was obvious. We had nothing to say about the 'Stolen Generation.' Wik and Mabo we did not care about. Ramesh had once said to me, 'We were not here when the land was stolen from the Abos,' Ramesh said. 'Aborigines,

Ramesh,' I reminded him sharply. 'They are the first people of this land.' 'Whatever. We're not a part of all that. Why should we lose sleep over somebody else's problem?'

'We can't pick and choose, Ramesh,' I said. 'Australian history is our history too now. We can't ignore that history because we live within its structures and beliefs. We are implicated because that past lives in us.' 'My history in Australia begins the day I arrived here,' Ramesh replied calmly. And then he launched into a long diatribe about how Australians had terrorized the *girmitiyas* in Fiji, turned them into slaves on the CSR plantations. 'This country should apologize to us, just as the Americans apologized to the Japanese for interning them in World War II. And hasn't Clinton apologized for slavery?' 'Ramesh,' I said, 'if the government does not apologize to the Aborigines for decades of abuse and neglect and physical violence, do you think they will apologize to us. For what? Get real.'

I was puzzled. Ramesh had lived in Australia and did not seem to care about its past, but became a volcano of passion about India and things Indian. Kashmir concerned him, and the Babri Mosque, the Hindu chauvinist Bajrang Dal, the Shiv Sena as well. He was the local representative of the Vishwa Hindu Parishad and met regularly with visiting Indian cultural delegations and priests. Ramesh's religiosity did not impress Sharmila. On the contrary, she despised it. 'They read the *Ramayana* and the *Bhagvada Gita*, but do they truly understand their message?' she had once said to me. 'It's all to do with rituals and appearances, to see who does things bigger and better. It is all a huge competition thing. A *tamasha, dikhaawat ke liye*,' all for show.

I had noticed the proliferation of *mandalis* in Sydney. People from the same village or suburb in Fiji or one extended family had a *mandali* of their own. Unlike Sharmila, I liked the cultural rituals and ceremonies. They were fun, brought our people together and kept them intact, gave them a sense of collective purpose and identity. The elaborate celebrations of *Holi* and *Diwali*, of *Ram Naumi* and *Shiv Ratri* among the Hindus and *Eid* and *Milad* among the Muslims kept alive a culture that would otherwise flounder in the arid urban sprawl of Australia. Ramesh seemed glad that at least on this point, I shared his views.

Neither Ramesh nor Sharmila were prepared to concede an inch. Such conversations must take place in other homes as well, I reckoned, people torn between cultures, making inner adjustments, confronting the long painful silences that intersperse family conversations. This is the fate of the first generation of migrants everywhere, I suppose, having left one home but not quite found another in their own lifetime, caught in-between. The problem is especially acute for the 'twice banished,' such as our people for whom questions about belonging and attachment often take complex, contested shapes. We belong neither here nor there, like the washer man's donkey, *Dhobi ke gadhaa, na ghar ke na ghat ke*, or else everywhere all at once.

I often wondered how children of migrants coped with it. I had seen many in Liverpool who seemed lost. Many, I was told, had ended up in the local court on charges of drug abuse. I had seen many affecting Australian mannerisms, speaking the local lingo in broad 'Austraaian' accents, wearing trendily torn jeans and T-shirts with blush-making slogans to slap across the face such as 'Masturbation Is Not A Crime,' 'Smell My Finger,' 'My Other Name Is Cock Screw.'

Once or twice I tried talking to some of the boys. They seemed slightly embarrassed, uneasy, in my presence, apologetic about their shabby appearance. Proper deference to the elders of the community, acknowledgement of age, is still observed, even among the seemingly wayward youth. There is something warm and endearing about this. Some cultural habits are difficult to break. More often than not, I am addressed as 'Uncle' by Indo-Fijian children who are complete strangers.

Rani would have been in her mid-twenties, in her second year of university, working part-time. I had known her from when she was a teenager, when she first moved to Australia with her parents. She was more like her mother, feisty and opinionated, ready to take on the world. Rani was close to me. We could talk about things she couldn't with her own parents or even friends. Being an elder uncle has its advantages.

Rani was feeling her way around courses at the university, unsure of what she really wanted to do. This was a sore point with her parents, especially with Ramesh. 'Why can't you be like other girls,' he would admonish her, 'and do something useful, like accounting or economics? You have a future to think of. *Time barbaad nahi karo*,' don't waste your time. But Rani's heart was not in money making subjects. She was leaning towards primary school teaching.

'Primary school!' Ramesh exploded. That for him was the end of the world. 'Do you think we came here so that you could become a primary school eacher? *Padhaai koi khelwaar baat nahi haye*, education is not something to trifle with. Teaching is for no-hopers, and you know that.' 'But that's what I want to do. I love children.' More troubling than Rani's choice of profession was Ramesh's concern about what others in the community might think of him and his family. Their children were doing law, dentistry, and medicine, socially respectable, point-earning subjects like that. 'Oh God, where did we go wrong?' he wondered aloud in his lounge chair. 'We haven't gone wrong at all Ram,' Sharmila reacted angrily. 'If primary teaching is Rani's passion, why not let her do it? Who cares what others think? You seem obsessed with this status thing. That's your problem. Please don't take it out on Rani. Beta, ignore your Dad.'

It is not only Rani's choice of career, Shami,' Ramesh said after Rani had left the room. 'She is going off the rails everywhere.' He was especially dismayed that Rani showed no interest in things Indian. 'She seems to be ashamed of her background,' Ramesh said to me. 'She's not ashamed of being an Indian, Bhaiya,' Sharmila retorted, snubbing Ramesh. 'It is just that she doesn't find any meaning in them. It's not only Rani who feels this way. I do too. Their obsession with horoscope and hierarchy leaves me cold. You go to any function, and you will see how these people behave. It is all about who ranks where. The status thing is big with them. They can't figure us out.'

'I am not ashamed of who I am, Uncle,' Rani said to me later. 'But these fellows look down on us, they mimic our language. And just because we go to bars and night clubs and enjoy a drink or two, they think we are easy lays. Sorry about the language, Uncle, but that is the truth.' It was not only India Indians who did that. 'Fiji boys are not much better. Probably worse.'

Rani was like many children I had met over the years. They did not have the language, but they had the right values, I thought: respect for age, polite language in the presence of family and friends, refraining from Western gestures of love and affection in public, never calling older relatives by their first name. All this to me was important. I was proud of the way our children were negotiating their way around the perilous paths of Australian youth culture.

'Dad keeps putting Australia down, Uncle,' Rani said to me one day. 'What do you expect from a land of convicts,' he says. He seems to have no sympathy for the Aboriginal people. 'Abos' he calls them, '*Hafsis*,' whatever that means.' 'A put-down for 'half-castes.' 'But this is my country now. This is where I have grown up. This is all I know. Yes, it has faults, with all that stuff about the 'Children Overboard Affair' and the 'Stolen Generations,' but it has been kind to us. This is home. I hardly know Fiji and India I have visited only once. Dad can't understand where I am coming from, nor does he want to. That makes it so frustrating.'

'Don't be too harsh on your Dad, Rani,' I said. 'He is a product of his time and place. He has traveled a long way in his lifetime. His journey from Labasa to Liverpool has not been easy. Give the old man a break.' I talked about the difficulties of being a first time migrant. You have to start all over again, usually at the bottom of the ladder. The ambition to become something is gone; you are content just to make ends meet, pass your time until retirement. If you get promoted, it is a bonus. 'It hurts, Beta, all those years of hard work ending like this. A time comes when we want to hold on to things that matter, things that give us purpose and identity. We all have to change with the times, but sometimes you hang on to your past because that is all you have. Have you seen *Fiddler on the Roof?*' She hadn't even heard the name. 'Do, because then you might understand your Dad better.'

'I will, Uncle', Rani replied. 'I don't ask Dad to change his ways. I know he won't. But he should let me live my own life. I am an adult now. I didn't ask to be brought here. This is

Australia, not Labasa. They throw me in at the deep end and expect me to swim straight away. Well, it is not easy. If I don't hang out with my Australian friends, they call me names and keep me out. If I mix around with them, Indians look down on me. Dad thinks getting used to living here is a bed of roses. Well he is dead wrong.'

Rani had dated a few boys, none of them from Fiji or India. She had finally found an Australian boy, David. He seemed, when I met him, to be a decent person, level headed, clean-looking, who was working in the Australian public service. They were in love, holding hands, glancing at each other, making plans for a future together: thinking about putting a down payment on an apartment in Carlingford, taking a loan out for another car, buying gifts for a friend's wedding — the sort of things most young couples do.

Rani and David were completely at ease with each other. Rani's first language was English; she spoke Fiji Hindi haltingly. But her taste in music was totally Western, played by artists whose names I had never heard before. I thought 'Eminem' was a kind of lolly you kept in jars! Flabbergasted at my ignorance, Rani gave me an Eminem poster. 'Put it on your office wall, Uncle: I dare you to.' 'I will,' wondering what my ageing colleagues might think!

David was making a real effort to learn the basics of Indian culture. He was intrigued about the different kinds of uncles we have: Mama (mother's brother), Mausa (aunt's husband), Phuffa (father's sister's husband), Kaka (father's younger brother) and Dada (father's older brother). He would invariably get all this mixed up, causing mirth all around! *Bas Hangama*, enough of this confusion, he would plead playfully. *Ek Jhaapat maarega*, Rani would reply, I will give you one slap, and break into a giggly smile. David had taken to hot Indian curries, especially *Jungali mugli* (murgi), wild chicken, and was becoming a good cook too, learning to distinguish between different kinds of Indian spices: *jeera, methi, haldi, garam masala*.

Rani's circle of friends included many of her age from various ethnic backgrounds: Greeks, Lebanese, Indians, Sri Lankans, Maltese, Croatians. What brought them together, I realized, was a common predicament. They were all facing pressure from their parents to conform, to stay within defined boundaries, not to let the family down. They were all rebels with a cause, trying to create a niche for themselves in Australia, searching for an identity that reflected their complex cultural heritage. The circle was therapy as well as a counselling session, a network of shared sadnesses, frustrations and clouded hopes.

Sharmila accepted David, but Ramesh exploded when he found out. He felt betrayed. 'Why are you doing this to us? Can't you find someone from our own community?' he asked Rani. 'If you can't, I will. I know a few families with eligible boys. Good boys with education and careers and culture, too. We can go to Fiji, put an advertisement in the papers. Everyone is doing it. I will go along with anyone you choose as long as he is an Indian boy. Is that too much to ask?'

'No, Dad. There will be no advertisement in the papers. I will decide. As a matter of fact, I already have.' Then, all of Ramesh's prejudices came out. 'A *gora* [white man] will always be a *gora*. They are different. Look at their divorce rate. Don't be blinded by this so-called love of yours, Rani. Think about the future. Where will you be in ten years time? You will have no place in our community. Our relatives will shun us. Don't get me wrong. All I want is what is best for you.'

'Let me be the judge of that, Dad,' Rani replied instantly. 'In case you have not noticed, our own divorce rate is nothing to be proud of either. And I will not embarrass you with the names of all your friends, family friends mind you, who freely break their holy marriage vows. See it for yourself who goes in and out of the Sunshine Motel in Parramatta. You will be surprised. It is no point being holier than thou, Dad. At least Australians are honest enough. If things don't work, they don't work out, not like us who pretend everything is hunky dory when often the marriage is just a shell.'

Ramesh thought long and hard about what Rani had said. Her words made sense although he was not quite prepared to admit it. He feared that if he began to see things from another angle, he might lose his own convictions and cultural certainties. If he kept opposing Rani, he realized, he might lose Sharmila as well. Life had not been easy for them. Quarrels had become more frequent, and sullen silences even longer. Sharmila had begun to avoid Indian functions and went out shopping or doing some other errand when Ramesh's friends came home. Her deliberate absence was noticed. Once or twice, the talk of separation had come up in their conversations. Fearing the worst, Ramesh had begun to mellow.

Even so, he was not prepared for what lay ahead. One day, Rani mentioned casually to Sharmila, and within Ramesh's hearing, that she was moving with David into an inner-city two bedroom apartment. 'Why?' Ramesh had asked indignantly. 'What's wrong with this place of ours that you want to move out?' Rani refused to budge. Ramesh pleaded, 'Well, at least get married before you move in. Do the proper thing, girl. Get engaged so we can announce it in a proper way to our relatives. You are the eldest in our extended family. You should think of your nieces and nephews. You must set a good example for them.' Rani had become immune to such a guilt trip. She was not going to be a moral exemplar for anyone. She had her own life to lead, on her own terms.

Marriage kept recurring in family discussions, causing acrimony and heartache. 'What difference does a piece of paper make, Dad?' Rani said one day. 'What matters is how we feel about each other. We have to find out if we are compatible. I am sure we will get married one day, but at a moment of our choice, not anyone else's. David agrees with me. You should think about what David wants too sometimes' 'But if a piece of paper doesn't make any difference, then why not get it done and over with? All the getting to know each other will come later, as it does in marriages. Adjustment will follow.' 'Dad, please, *Bas*, enough.'

It was at this point that Rani had rung me to help break the impasse between her and her parents, especially Ramesh. 'All I can do is try, Beta,' I told Rani at our lunch at the Black Pepper. 'That is all I ask, Uncle. There should be no doubt in their minds about what I will do. I will not change my mind.' Two very stubborn people, I thought.

The next day, I sat Ramesh and Sharmila down and told them what Rani had told me, her plans for her future with David, her determination to go ahead no matter what. The usual arguments were rehearsed, with increasing temperature between the two of them. 'Rani is a beautiful child,' I said. 'You should be proud of the way you have brought her up. I love her as my own daughter. She is an adult now. You should trust her judgment. David would be a son-in-law you would be proud to have, I would be proud to have. I have met him. I like him.'

'I have bowed so much, Bro, I might just break the next time. First it was the drinking and the nightclubs and the endless late nights. Then, it was long breaks at the coast with boys whom I didn't know, had never met. Then it was all the 'dates,' and now this.' 'Why is it always about you, Ram?' Sharmila reacted angrily, 'How you feel, how hurt you are. Have you ever spared a thought for Rani? What she might want? You treat her like a little kid and she resents it bitterly. As for the *palwaar shalwaar*, extended family, where were they when we needed them, when we first moved to Sydney? No one wanted to know us, if you care to remember. Now, all of a sudden, they have become so important to you. You really are something else, Ram.'

'Ram, the choice seems clear to me,' I said emphatically. 'You can either stick to your views and lose your daughter, or you can bend a little and keep the relationship intact. David is a lovely boy, but if things don't work out, it's not the end of the world. As a father, you should stand in the background, ready to help when your children need help. You encourage and advise and support. You can't dictate. That's a sure recipe for disaster. When it comes down to it Ramesh, it's Rani's life we are talking about, not yours.' I was blunt. Surprisingly, Ramesh took my words calmly. Sharmila seemed quietly satisfied with my firmness.

I was harsher with Ramesh than I should have been or wanted to be. Much later, I found out how convulsed his inner culturally-ordered world was, although he never spoke about it to anyone, including Sharmila. The pettiness and bickering of his fellow community leaders was beginning to drain his spirit, people advancing their own private agendas at every opportunity, abusing the public funds collected for charitable purposes. *Chor-Chamar*, he called them, scoundrels. Many arranged marriages were floundering, infidelity was common. His own marriage, he realized, was in cold storage and could crack any time if he wasn't careful.

But it took a tragedy in his cousin's family to drive home the dangers of his stubbornness. The cousin insisted that his daughter marry a Fiji boy he had chosen for her, the son of his business partner seeking to migrate to Australia. 'I will hang myself if you don't do it,' he had threatened. The poor girl was in love with someone else, but would not dare to have her father's blood on her hands. Once safely in Australia and his permanent residence papers secure, the boy absconded and married his long-time girlfriend from Fiji. Some months later, rejected, depressed and with no one to turn to, the girl committed suicide with an overdose of sleeping pills. That jolted Ramesh. Robert Browning's words would have summed up his feelings: *This world has been harsh and strange; Something is wrong; there needeth a change.* But how? Ramesh was searching for a solution.

One day, still not making any headway, I had an inspired thought. 'Why don't the four of you go on a holiday together, away from all this *jhanjhat*, bickering? Give yourselves some breathing space. You will have time to consider things calmly, get to know David, see how things go. You can only go up from here.' Sharmila jumped at the idea, Ramesh was less enthusiastic. But in the end, they did go for a holiday in Fiji over Christmas.

'That was the best thing you ever did for us, Bhaiya,' Sharmila told me after they had returned to Australia. The trip was obviously a success. At Nadarivatu, the family had hiked in the forested hills and climbed Mt Victoria, mingled with the villagers from nearby *koros*, cooked food on an open fire, played touch footy and drank and talked long into the night. This was the first time Ramesh had 'met' David. They talked endlessly — like two chatterboxes, as Sharmila put it — about cricket. Both were passionate and knowledgeable about the game, together composing lists of the all-time great first eleven.

David shared Ramesh's interest in current affairs, more than any of his friends or even family. They both liked the bush and the outdoor life. Nikhil told Ramesh and Sharmila proudly that David was like the older brother he never had. That meant a lot to Ramesh. Rani could be impetuous and flighty, but Nikhil was the thoughtful, sober one in the family. The ice was gradually thawing though everyone gingerly avoided the topic of engagement and marriage. 'I told Ramesh to let me handle that,' Sharmila told me. Good advice, I thought to myself.

In between swimming and kayaking, there were endless hours of talk and tears between Sharmila and Rani. 'Meet your father half way, Beta. Get engaged now. Marriage can come later, at your convenience. We will have enough time for a formal announcement, invitations would be sent out, proper arrangements made. This way you will win Dad over. He will save face. You know how important that is to him.' And then she added, 'And to me, too, if I am honest with myself. I want to give you away in the proper style, in the presence of our family. It's every mother's dream. All that *Monsoon Wedding* stuff.'

'But Mum, we are not ready financially. Think of all the expenses involved, hiring a wedding hall, the reception, the gifts, accommodation for family members. We really can't afford it right now. David wants to complete his university course,

secure his job in the public service. I would like to complete uni. And we both want to travel a bit before we finally settle down.'
'Beta, hosting the engagement party is not your responsibility. It is ours. Dad and I will take care of everything. We have talked about it. That's what parents are for.'

Rani and David went for a long walk on the beach, mulling over Sharmila's proposal. Then, all of a sudden, it happened. Ramesh was swimming when David called out to him. Returning to the beach, Ramesh sat in the hammock under a coconut tree when David said to him, 'Ramesh, will you accept me as your son-in-law?' Rani froze as David spoke the words. Sharmila looked straight into Ramesh's eyes, unblinking. 'Who am I to stand in your way when Rani approves?' Tears were running down Rani's cheek as David hugged Ramesh. 'Rani is the queen of my heart. Cherish her.' Sharmila wiped a tear. 'Oh, I see, so Mother's permission is not required, is it,' she bantered, obviously delighted with the way things had worked out. Then, it was time for beers all around. 'Champagne will come later,' David said, relieved.

The wedding took place a year later at the Sydney Botanical Gardens. It was a grand affair, with nearly one hundred close friends and family in attendance. Rani looked exquisite in a cream sari with colored borders and David was resplendent in his *salwar kamiz*. It was fusion wedding, an eclectic mixture of Hindu and Western ceremonies. Rani and David exchanged wedding vows and rings in a delightfully, if minimally, decorated *mandap* under an ancient eucalyptus tree. I gave a short, light-hearted speech, 'Wedlock is a padlock,' I told David, to laughter. 'Marriage is like a lottery,' I continued to appreciative smiles, 'but you can't tear up the ticket if you lose!' And then a couple of lines from my favorite poet, Lord Tennyson:

> *Two lives bound fast in one with golden ease*
> *Two graves grass-green beside a grey church tower*

Ramesh and Sharmila were the happiest I had seen them in years.

Immediately after the formal ceremonies were over, Rani and David came over and said, 'Thank you, Uncle, from the bottom of our hearts.' Then, spontaneously in a traditional gesture of respect and affection and seeking my blessing, they both touched my feet in the quintessential Hindu way. Someone had been tutoring David. Perhaps he too was a cultural tutor.

10
One Life, Three Worlds

To be an Indian from Fiji is to be a complex bundle of contradictions. It is to be formed and re-formed by a unique mix of social, cultural and historical experiences. Although the Fijian constitution defines us as 'Indian,' we are, in fact, marked by a confluence of three quite distinct cultural influences: South Asian, Western and Oceanic. Generalizations in these matters are always risky, but the truth will be obvious to people of my age, the post-world war two generation growing up in Fiji. Our food and our religious and spiritual traditions, our dietary habits and general aesthetic sense (in music and cinema, for instance) is unmistakably South Asian. Our language of work and business and general public discourse, our educational system and legal and judicial traditions, our sense of individual and human rights is derived from our Western heritage. And our sense of people and place, our sense of humour, our less charged, 'she'll be alright,' 'tomorrow is another day,' attitude to life in general, comes from our Oceanic background.

A century of enforced living in a confined island space has produced overlapping and inseparable connections. The precise contribution of one influence over another on us, our world view, on the general shapes of our thought and action, would vary from time to time and from place to place. It would depend on our educational background, the degree of exposure we have had to external influences, the family circumstance and our network of relationships. There will be variation and diversity. We will accentuate or suppress a particular aspect of our heritage depending on the company, context and perhaps acceptance: more English here, less Indian there. Nonetheless, every Indian person from Fiji will carry within them the traces of the three primary influences which have shaped them.

Most Indo-Fijian people of my age would have three — sometimes more — languages: Fiji-Hindi, Hindi, English, and Fijian. Proficiency in the last three would vary. A person growing up near a Fijian village, or with extensive interaction with Fijians at work or play, would speak Fijian more fluently than one who grew up in a remote, culturally self-enclosed Indo-Fijian settlement. Likewise, a person from a rural area is likely to be more fluent in standard Hindi than his or her urban cousin who did not have the opportunity to learn the language formally in primary school. And someone who grew up in a town or city and went to a government or Christian school is likely to be more at home in English than a person from the country.

But every Indo-Fijian person, without exception, would be able to speak Fiji-Hindi without prior preparation. That is the language that comes to us naturally. It is the mother tongue of the Indo-Fijian community, the language of spontaneous communication among ourselves. It is the language that connects us to time and place, to our childhood. It was the language through which we first learned about our past and ourselves. It was the language that took us into the deepest secrets, stories and experiences of our people. Our most intimate conversation takes place in Fiji-Hindi. Our thigh-slapping sense of humour, earthy and rough and entirely bereft of subtlety or irony, finds its most resonant voice in that language. And its influence persists.

Whenever we Indo-Fijians meet, even or perhaps especially in Australia, we are very likely to begin our conversation by asking *Tab Kaise*, 'How Are You.' This is less an enquiry than an effort to establish an emotional connection. Yet, the irony is that we do not accord Fiji-Hindi the respect that it deserves. Purists tell us that it is broken Hindi, a kind of plantation pidgin, with no recognisable grammatical pattern, full of words with rough edges and a vocabulary of limited range incapable of accommodating complex thoughts and literary expression. We are slightly embarrassed about its humble origins and apologetic to outsiders, especially from the subcontinent. Its use is properly confined to the domestic sphere. It is not the language we use in public discourse. There is little Fiji-Hindi on Fiji radios, there is nothing in the newspapers. The media uses — has always used — standard Hindi. That is what hurts: the continued calculated neglect and the sniggering put-down of the language by the Indo-Fijian cultural elite. The startling gap between the reality of our private experience and the pretensions of our public performance could not be greater.

I cannot comment on the deeper structures and origins of the language, but common knowledge and popular understanding suggest that Fiji-Hindi is 'cobbled together' — as the critics would put it dismissively — from the dialects and languages of northeast India, principally Avadhi and Bhojpuri.

Formal Hindi was not the mother tongue of the immigrant population; these two languages were, which then merged into Fiji-Hindi, with subsequent words, metaphors, images from South Indian languages, and Fijian and English. This was the new *lingua franca* which emerged on the plantations. The plantation system was a great leveller of hierarchy and social status. The caste system gradually disintegrated, and with it the finely-regulated cultural order that the immigrants had known in India. The new regime rewarded initiative and enterprise, and individual labour. The living conditions on the plantations produced new cross-caste, cross-religious marriages. People of all ranks and social and religious backgrounds lived and worked together, celebrated life and mourned its passing communally. They had no other choice.

From that cloistered, culturally chaotic environment emerged a new more egalitarian social order, and a new language, Fiji-Hindi. Old ways had to give way and they did. New vocabulary and grammar had to be mastered, new ways of looking at the world acquired. The Indian calendar — *Pus, Saavan, Bhadon, Asarh, Kartik* — was, or began to be, replaced with the Roman calendar. English words entered the new vocabulary, names of institutions (town for *shahar*, school for *pathshala*, *binjin* for benzene, *kirasin* for kerosene, *kantaap* for cane top, bull for the Hindi word *baile*, *phulawa* for plough. And in areas near Fijian villages, Fijian words entered the language as well. This humble new language, levelling, unique, unadorned, a subaltern language of resistance, drawing strands from a large variety of sources, is the language that comes to me naturally.

Yet it is not the language that I would speak on a formal occasion, while giving a public talk in Fiji or an interview to a Hindi radio station in Australia. I am expected to use formal Hindi in public discourse. Everyone expects this of a cultural or political leader. It confers dignity and status on him, earns him (for it is rarely her) the people's trust and acceptance. To be able to use Hindi fluently is to be seen as someone who has not lost touch with the people, is still connected to his roots, can be trusted not to betray the interests of the community. Over the years, I have given dozens of public addresses in Hindi. People express genuine appreciation that I am still able to speak the language, after being away from Fiji for most of my adult life. 'Look,' they say to the supposedly wayward younger generation losing touch with their cultural roots, 'he lives in Australia but still speaks our language. He hasn't forgotten his roots. And nor should you!' Notice that Indo-Fijian identity in this quote is tied with Hindi. The same people who applaud me for speaking in Hindi would talk to me in Fiji-Hindi in private; to speak in formal Hindi with them in private, informal situations, would be the height of pretension. It is all *tamasha*, theatre.

I am glad I am still able to read and write Hindi. I would be the poorer without it, but for me it is a learned language all the same, with all the limitation learned languages bring with them. Those who hear me speak the language fluently have no idea of the amount of effort I put into preparing my speeches. Although I don't actually read the text in order better to connect with the audience (as all good teachers know), each word is written down, in *Devanagri* script, the speech rehearsed line by line several times over, virtually committed to memory. Proper imagery and metaphors have to be chosen with the help of a bilingual Hindi-English dictionary, because what is clear to me in English is often obscure in Hindi, and the forms of address are different. The disparity between the private, painful effort of preparation and the appearance of a polished public performance is deep.

For years, I unthinkingly accepted the need to speak formal Hindi. It was the expected thing to do. No other alternative, certainly not Fiji-Hindi, was conceivable. I could speak in English to Indo-Fijian audiences, but that would be pointless, talking over their often unlettered heads. I felt curiously elated that I could read and write and speak the language better than many of my contemporaries; it was my badge of honour and pride, my way of demonstrating that I could still connect with my people. But I now realise the futility of my action: a reluctance to acknowledge the 'game' I was playing, thinking that Hindi was my mother tongue. When it clearly was not.

Hindi was the medium of instruction in most Indo-Fijian community schools from the very beginning, and an examinable subject for the Senior Cambridge School Certificate in the post-war years. From the start, the colonial government was keen on Hindi. It encouraged the spread of English because it was the 'official and business language of the colony,' but Hindi — or Hindustani — could not be ignored. 'Hindus and Muslims alike will need it in different forms as the key to knowledge of their religions and literature and as the means of communication with their relatives and co-religionists in India. And for a considerable section too busy with their own affairs to undergo much schooling, and imperfectly equipped to use a foreign language as a vehicle of thought without danger to their practical relations with their environment, their 'mother tongue' must remain both their sole means of communicating with others and the sole means of expressing their thoughts and feelings.' Hindustani was important for administrative purposes, too, because 'an adequate knowledge of Hindustani must be needed by the European community in touch with the Indians, the more so because without it, it is, and will be, impossible for the European official or man of affairs to get into close touch with just those classes which to a large extent depend on him for help and guidance.' And finally, there was the broader consideration 'that Hindustani is the *lingua franca* of probably a larger number of inhabitants of the Empire than English itself and is spoken in a number of colonies besides Fiji.'

The government's agenda is understandable, but it is not entirely certain that Hindustani *was* the 'mother tongue' of the indentured migrants, who came principally from the Avadhi-Bhojpuri speaking areas of northeastern India and Telugu, Tamil and Malyali speaking regions of the south. For the South Indians, Hindustani was not the mother tongue at all, and in the north, Hindustani or Urdu was the language of business and administration and the cultural elite, a legacy of the Moghul era of Indian history; it was not the language of the mass of the peasantry. And it is not at all certain that Hindustani was the language spoken in other colonies whose immigrants, too, had derived from the same regions as the immigrants in Fiji. For administrative convenience, then, Hindustani was imposed as the 'mother tongue' of the Indo-Fijian community.

The government's position was supported by the Hindi-favouring Indo-Fijian cultural elite, although many of them preferred not Hindustani — which was a mixture of Hindi and Urdu — but a purer form of formal Hindi, and wished for an extension of English in primary schools. The preference for

Hindi or Hindustani (but not Fiji-Hindi), reflected a wider process of sanskritisation taking place in the community in the post-indenture period. For many Indo-Fijians, indenture or *girmit* (from the agreement under which the immigrants had come to Fiji) was viewed as a period of unspeakable shame and degradation. That ended upon the abolition of indenture in 1920. Community leaders sought to establish voluntary social and cultural organisations to erase the memory of a dark period in their lives, and to impart correct moral and spiritual values to their people.

This was evident in virtually every aspect of Indo-Fijian life. The Fiji-born discarded rural Indian peasant dress of *dhoti* (loin cloth) and *kurta* (long flowing shirt) and *pagri* (turban) for western-style shirt and shorts and slacks. In religion, animal sacrifice and other practices of animism of rural India gradually gave way to cleaner forms of Brahminical Hinduism. The caste system, with all the ritual practices associated with it, slowly disintegrated. Hindu children were given names after gods and goddesses — Ram Autar, Shiv Kumari, Saha Deo, Ram Piyari, Latchman — to erase caste distinction. All these represented a conscious, deliberate dissociation from a past understood as painful, embarrassing and degrading. The public embracing of Hindustani as the *lingua franca* was a part of that effort.

Both Hindustani and Indian history and culture were promoted in the colonial curriculum, and published in the *School Journal* edited by A W MacMillan. Stories of great men and women, of kings and queens, historical events of great antiquity appeared, all designed to make the Indo-Fijian children proud of their ancestral heritage, of their 'motherland': stories about Siddharata (Buddha), Rabindranath Tagore, Emperor Akbar, Pandita Ramabai, Raja Harishchandra, people like that. The *Journal* also highlighted the great achievements of the British Empire, and published pieces on important places and peoples in it. There was nothing — or very little — on Fiji and the Pacific, little beyond some amusing anecdotes on the Fijian people. So not only the language, but the mind and soul of the Indo-Fijians was nourished by stories from our two 'motherlands': India and England. The actual 'motherland,' Fiji, was left undiscussed, disregarded, confined to the fringes of the humorous anecdotes. Our immediate past was ignored not only because it seemed mundane but also because it was the site of deep contestation. Indenture was an indictment of the government, whom the labourers saw as having a complicit role in the atrocities which they endured on the plantations. India was safer. The emphasis on India and things Indian, hero-worshipping and frankly romantic, continued in the post-war years in the specially composed school texts, *Hindi pothis*, by the India-born Ami Chandra.

English was the second language taught in the Indo-Fijian primary schools. The aim was to give school children an elementary knowledge of grammar and vocabulary, the sort of rudimentary knowledge required to understand official instructions and notices, and occasional snippets from the great texts of English literature. The texts used in the post-war years were the *New Method Readers*, *Caribbean Readers*, *The Oxford English Readers for Africa* and University of London's *Reading for Meaning*. There was nothing in these texts about Fiji or the Pacific Islands. Here is the Table of Contents of *The Oxford English Readers for Africa, Book Six* for the last year of primary education: The Story that Letters Tell, How Messages are Sent, *The Island*, by Cecil Fox Smith, Farmer's Work, The Arctic

Wastes, *I Vow to Thee, My country*, by Cecil Spring-Rice, Sound and Light, Different Kinds of Buildings, The Bees by William Shakespeare, The Fight Against Disease, The Work of the Post Office, *The Discovery*, by JC Squire, The Men Who Made the World Larger, A Wonderful Little Builder, *Bete Humaine* by Francis Brett Young, Napoleon, Some Stories of Famous Men, Bridges and bridge-Building, Good Citizenship, A Famous Speech from Shakespeare, On Mercy by William Shakespeare and, finally, Some Business Letters.

The list needs no commentary: it is Anglo-centric and its intellectual orientation and purpose self-evident. Much the same trend continued in secondary schools where English texts and examples were replaced with examples from Australia and New Zealand. I suppose the intention of the texts was to inculcate in us a deep pride in the British empire (upon which the sun never set, we were taught to remember, and to remember, too, that Britannia ruled the waves, that 'we' had won the great wars of the 20th century, that London was the cultural centre of the world, that the best literature, the best of everything — the Bedford trucks, the Austin and Cambridge and Morris Minor cars — came from England), to appreciate the good fortune of being its member, to be grateful for what little tender mercies came our way because we had nothing, we were nothing.

I recognise the cultural bias of the texts now, and it is easy enough to be critical of their colonising purpose. But these large and troubling issues did not matter to us or to anyone else then. I recall the thrill, on a remote sugar cane farm with no electricity, no running water, no paved roads, of reading about faraway places and peoples as an enthralling experience, making imaginary connections with African children whose neat faces we saw in glossy imperial magazines that came to our school as gifts from the British Council. An acquaintance with them reduced our sense of isolation, expanded our imaginative horizon. And it is the appreciation of that enlarging, enriching, experience that has remained with me.

While we learned a great deal about the western and the Indian world, there was nothing in books about Fijian language and culture, beyond the fear-inducing stories about a cannibal (Udre Udre) who had eaten a hundred men and marked each conquest with a stone — which was there for everyone to see. There were a few innocuous stories about Ratu Seru Cakobau, the wise and great Fijian chief, who eventually ceded Fiji to Great Britain in 1874 and the Tongan intruder and challenger to his authority, Enele Ma'afu; but that was about all. Fijians remained for us objects of fear; many an unruly child was sent to bed with the threat that Seru (or Emosi or Sakiusa or some other Fijian with similar name) would snatch us away from our parents if we did not behave properly.

The Fijian ethos, as we understood it, often through the prism of prejudice, inspired no great respect. We valued individual initiative and enterprise, their culture, we were told, quelled it. We saved for tomorrow, they lived for now. We were the products of status-shattering egalitarian inheritance; Fijian society was governed by strict protocol. They ate beef; we revered the cow as mother incarnate. Our schools were separate. Fijians went to exclusively Fijian schools (provincial primary ones and then to the Queen Victoria or Ratu Kadavulevu), while we attended primarily Indo-Fijian schools. For all practical purposes, we inhabited two distinct worlds, the world of the *Kai Idia* and the world of the *Kai Viti*. Fiji has paid a very large price for its myopic educational policy.

This, then, is my inheritance, and the inheritance of my generation: complex, chaotic, contradictory. I have lived with it all my life and throughout the course of my university education in different countries over the past three decades. It enriches me even as it incapacitates me, complicates the way I do and see things, the way I relate to people around me, the way I see myself. There have been many moments of sheer agonising desperation over the years when confusion reigned in my linguistically fractured mind, when I could not find words in any language to convey precisely what I wanted to say, how I felt about a particular place or person, when I felt hobbled and helpless, like the washerman's donkey, belonging neither here nor there: *Na ghar ke na ghat ke*.

English is the language of my work. I am not closely familiar with its deeper grammatical structures and rules of engagement and composition: alpha, beta and coordinate clauses, auxiliary, infinitives and intransitive verbs, prepositions and subordinate conjunctions — these things confuse me even now. And its classical allusions to Greek and Roman mythology — Pandora's Box, Achilles Heel, Trojan Horse, Crossing the Rubicon, Cleopatra's nose, Ulysses, Cyclades and Cyclopes Medusa's Head; its references to the stories and people of the Old and New Testaments, to Job, John, Matthew and Abraham, the Wisdom of Solomon, to quotations from the *Book of Ecclesiastes* and *Ezekiel*; its borrowing of words and phrases from European literature — it was years after high school that I realised that the phrase 'to cultivate your garden' came from Voltaire's *Candide*, what TS Eliot meant by 'Hollow Men' and why 'April is the cruellest month,' what Heathcliff's windswept moors looked like — all this knowledge had to be acquired through surreptitious reading; they remain beyond my easy reach even now.

Yet, my professional competence in the language is taken for granted. The journals and academic presses to which I send my work for publication make no concession to my chequered linguistic background. That is the way the game is played in academia. It has taken many years of learning and un-learning, many years of doubt and desperation, to acquire some proficiency in the language. I try to write as simply as I can, which leads some colleagues, *au fait* with the lexicon of post-modern scholarly extravaganza, to equate simple writing with simplistic thought! I have sometimes been accused of writing fluently, but only if the readers knew the effort, the revision after revision and the deliberate thought that has gone into the writing. I recognise good writing when I see it; I envy the effortless fluency of writers who produce words as if they owned them. Essays and reviews in *The New Yorker*, for instance, with their wonderfully engaging prose, the breathtaking quality of images and metaphors, invariably provoke admiration in me. I readily accept my limitations, my inability to produce with words meanings and miracles like those for whom English is the mother tongue. That is the way it is, and always will be.

Some colleagues in the Pacific islands, non-native speakers of English, are more adventurous, less accepting of the conventions of the language, who are prepared to flout its rules, play with it in unconventional ways, bend it to meet their needs. They have 'indigenised' the language in interesting ways, encouraged, I suppose, by the liberating tenets of post-colonial and cultural studies. So what appears to me to be badly mangled English in need of a sharp, ruthless, editorial pen is avant-garde poetry for them. In an appealingly rebellious kind of way, they are unapologetic, defiant in their defence of idiosyncrasy. Clearly scholarly conventions, styles and expectations have changed in the last two decades or so. The diversity tolerated — perhaps even encouraged? — now would have been unthinkable when I was learning the alphabets of the academe. I recognise, as I see the younger generation, that I am trapped by a different past and different expectations. I am sometimes accused of being a part of the 'assimilationist' generation which paid scant regard to local modes of expression, local idioms, but slavishly embraced the ethical and intellectual premises of colonial and colonizing education and the English language. I suppose we are all products of our own particular histories.

Writing formal academic English is one thing, speaking it colloquially quite another. To be reasonably effective, one has to have some knowledge of the locally familiar idioms and metaphors, a grasp of the local lingo, as they say. These are not as easy to acquire for someone who came to Australia half-formed. I have had to educate myself on the side about Australian society and culture and history and its special vocabulary. This has not been easy in an academic life filled with pressure to create a refereed paper trail that government bureaucrats can see and understand (and, most importantly, reward). The task is made all the more difficult because we had nothing about Australia in school beyond the most elementary lessons about Lachlan Macquarie, John MacArthur and the merino sheep, the gold rushes of the 19th century, the convict settlement and the squattocracy, cramming exercises in geography (which was the longest river in Australia, its highest mountain, its capital city, its tallest building: that sort of thing) and the occasional novel (*Voss* and *To the Islands*) in high school. Not surprisingly, Australia remained for us remote and inaccessible, the *sahib's* country, a place to dream about, a land from where all the good things we so admired came: the Holden car, the refrigerator, the tram engine, the canned fruit, the bottled jam and the refined white sugar, so pure and so good, that we used it as an offering to the gods in our pujas.

Seeing Australia as a student from a distance was one thing; living in it, trying to get a handle on the texture of the daily lived life, was another. Its sheer size and variety: the hot, red featureless plains merging into the shrubbery desert in the distance, the remote, rural, one-street towns on the western fringes of the eastern states, dry, desolate spaces along highways littered with the decaying remains of dead animals and the rusting hulks of long-abandoned vehicles, places that lie beyond the certitude of maps, at the back of beyond, as they say. I had to get used to the idea that golden brown, not deep green, was the natural colour of Australia, that its flora and fauna were unique.

New words and phrases I had never heard before had to be learned and used in their proper context: Dorothy Dixer, Gallah, A peshit, Blind Freddy, R els, B ulldust, Coathanger, Dingbat, Wanker, Drongo, Tall Poppy, Scorcher, Ripper, Ratbag, Ocker, My Oath, Knockers, Bludger, Dinky Di, Fair Dinkum, Perv, Spitting the Dummy, words which locals use effortlessly, but which are strange to newcomers. Nothing can be more embarrassing than using a wrong word at the wrong time, or committing a *faux pas*, in the company of people who assume you are equally knowledgeable about the local lingo as them. At a party in Canberra many years ago, I used the word 'fanny' in what context I do not remember. In the United States, where I had lived for a decade, it means female buttock, but here it meant something quite different (you know what I mean!) Pin drop silence greeted my remark, to use that tired cliche.

Beyond vocabulary, I also felt as a new migrant that I should equip myself with the basic knowledge of this country's history. One cannot be a university academic in Australia and remain ignorant of its history, especially when I live in Canberra and have as neighbours colleagues who have had a large hand in shaping the way we see Australia: Ken Inglis, Bill Gammage, Hank Nelson, John Molony, Ian Hancock, Barry Higman. But it is more than the desire simply to be 'one of the boys,' 'to be in the know.' When new migrants enter a country, they enter not only its physical space but also its history with all the obligations and responsibilities they entail; to be effective and responsible citizens, they need to understand the inextinguishable link between the country's past and its present.

So I had to bone up on Australian history and folklore: Gallipoli, Eureka Stockade, Ned Kelly, the Anzac Tradition, the debate about Terra Nullius, the Great Dismissal, the Bodyline Series and Bradman's Invincibles, about Phar Lap, Mabo, Bob Santamaria and Archbishop Daniel Mannix, Dame Edna Everidge, Simpson and his Donkey, Kokoda Trail, Patrick White, Gough Whitlam, 'Pig Iron' Bob, 'The Australian Legend,' 'The Rush That Never Ended.' I now know the names of most Australian prime ministers in roughly chronological order. I am passionate about cricket. My summer begins the moment the first ball is bowled in a cricket test match, and ends when the cricket season is over (and when the agapanthus die out). And I read Australian literature and follow Australian politics as a hobby. Gaps remain, of course. There is much catching up to do. I wish, as I write this, that I — and the Indo-Fijian community generally — had made half as much effort to understand the culture, language, traditions, the inner world of the Fijian people, among whom we have lived for well over a century, but about whom we know so little. Sadly, the ignorance is mutual.

The curiosity and the thirst for new knowledge I have about this country, its past and its present, its vast parched landscape, is not matched, with few exceptions, by my colleagues and friends in Australia about *me* and *my* background, my history and heritage, the cultural baggage I bring to this country. I have sought to educate myself about the Judeo-Christian tradition, about the meaning and significance of Lent and Resurrection and the Last Judgement, for instance, or about the Sale of Indulgences, the Reformation, about Yahweh and the Torah. And I know a few Christmas Carols too (*'On the twelfth day of Christmas...'*). But my Australian friends, perhaps understandably, have no idea about my religious and cultural heritage, about the *Ramayana* and the *Bhagvad Gita*, about the festivals we celebrate: *Diwali* and *Holi* and *Ram Naumi*, about our ritual observances to mark life's journey or mourn its passing. It is not that they are incurious: they simply don't know. My inner world remains a mystery to them. I regret very much not being able to share my cultural life more fully, more meaningfully, with people whose friendship I genuinely value.

The process of understanding is a one-way street, I often feel. Perhaps they have no incentive to know about me; it is I who have the greater need to know. I am the one who is the outsider here, not them. Perhaps things will change when — it is no longer a question of if — multiculturalism takes deeper roots, when the public face of Australia truly shows its diverse character, when more of us become more visible in the public arena rather than remain as cartoon characters propped up for public display on suitably ceremonial occasions. The contrast with the United Kingdom is huge in this respect. There, as I discovered in my two extended trips there in recent years, multiculturalism is a publicly accepted and proudly proclaimed fact, in popular culture, in the universities, in the media. Multiculturalism is just starting its journey here. In Australia, in my experience, the primary line of demarcation is gender, not cultural identity. When we advertise positions, we are asked to make special effort to alert women candidates to potential employment opportunities. Universities require adherence to the principle of gender balance on committees. Few colleagues ask: why are there so few Pacific and Asian academics in my research School of Pacific and Asian Studies. Many would remark on the gender imbalance in it. But I digress.

English is my language of work, but it is inadequate in expressing my inner feelings, in capturing the intricate texture of social relationships which are an integral part of my community. There are simply no English words for certain kinds of relationships and the cultural assumptions and understandings which go with them. The English word Uncle denotes a particular relationship which most native speakers would understand. When finer distinctions are required, the words maternal and paternal are added. But it is still inadequate for me. We have different words for different kinds of uncles. A father's younger brother is *Kaka*. His elder brother is *Dada*. Mother's brother is *Mama*. Father's sister's husband is

Phuffa. They are all uncles in English usage. But in Hindi, each has its own place, its own distinctive set of obligations. We can joke with *Kaka*, be playful with him, but our relationship with *Dada* is more formal and distant. A *Dada* can be relied upon to talk sense to one's father, with some authority and effect; a *Kaka*, knowing his proper place in the order of things, cannot, at least not normally. Brother-in-law in English is pretty generic, but not in Hindi. Sister's husband is *Jeeja* or *Bahnoi*, but wife's brother is *Sala*. We have a joking relationship with the latter — he is fair game — but not with the former. Your sister's welfare is always paramount in your mind. A troubled relationship with Jeeja could have terrible consequences for her. Older brother's wife is *Bhabhi*, and younger brother's spouse *Chotki*. *Bhabhi* is treated with a mixture of respect and affection, more like a mother. With *Chotki* we have an avoidance relationship, and keep all conversation to the bare minimum. We don't call *Bhabhi* and *Chotki* by their names. Ever. And it would be unthinkable for them to call you by your name either. We relate to each other not as individuals, but as social actors with culturally prescribed roles.

Some of the cultural protocols and restrictions governing family relationships have inevitably broken down in Australia, and even in urban Fiji, succumbing to forces of modernity and the culturally corrosive effects of accelerated mobility. You have no choice but to speak to *Chotki* if she is the one who picks up the phone. But my younger sisters-in-law still do not address me by my name, not because this is something I myself prefer. On the contrary. I am still addressed respectfully as *Bhaiya*, as cultural protocol, or memory of cultural protocol, demands. And I take care not to be a part of loose talk in their presence. All the children invariably call me

Dada. It would be unthinkable for them to call me by my name. It is the same with my children when addressing their uncles and aunties. Even Indo-Fijian community elders and my friends would be called uncles and aunties though this convention or practice would not apply, on the whole, to my Australian friends. So, in denoting the complex maze of domestic relationships we have, I find English inadequate.

English has made greater inroads and makes more sense in other day-to-day activities though. When shopping for groceries, I often use English names. Watermelon, for example, not *Tarbuj*, Bananas, not *Kela*, Rice, not *Chawal*, Onion, not *Piyaz*, Potatoes, not *Aloo*. But some vegetables I can only properly identify with the names I used as a child: I always use *Dhania*, not Coriander, *Haldi*, not Turmeric, *Karela*, not Bitter Gourd, *Kaddu*, not Pumpkin, *Dhall*, not Lentils. I wish I knew why some names have remained and others have gone from memory.

I was once a fairly fluent reader and speaker in Hindi, although now the more difficult sanskritised variety is becoming harder to understand. It takes longer to read the script and decipher its meaning. Listening to the news, on SBS Hindi radio for instance, I get the meaning but miss the nuances; painfully, the gap increases with each passing year. My Hindi, now more stilted than ever, is restricted to the occasional conversation with people from South Asian background, from India, Pakistan and even Bangladesh. There is an expectation on the part of many South Asians that I would — should -- know Hindi because I look Indian and have a very North Indian name.

It is not an unreasonable assumption. And I use it, as best I can, to establish rapport with them, to acknowledge our common ancestral and cultural heritage, to establish a point of contact, to define our difference from mainstream Anglo-Australia. I cannot deny the enjoyment this gives me. Many weekend taxi drivers in Canberra are Pakistani university students keen to bolster their meagre incomes. When I travel with them, they — or I — would ask the obligatory question: Where you from? The taxi drivers would reply in English. *Achha*, okay, or *Theek hai*, that's fine, I am likely to say. If there is chemistry (about cricket, for example) we will continue in English-interspersed Hindustani. When words fail, or are unable to carry a conversation forward, we revert to English, but the connection has been made. That is the important point; that is what matters.

Hindi comes in handy in my private cultural life. The music that fills my house, to the bemused tolerance of my children — Dad is playing *his* music again! — is Hindustani or, more appropriately, Urdu: *ghazals*, romantic songs, by Mehndi Hassan, Jagjit Singh, Pankaj Udhas, Talat Aziz, Ghulam Ali, and sweet-syrupy songs from Hindi films of yesteryears by Talat Mehmood, Mohammed Rafi, Lata Mangeshkar and Mukesh. This is the music that arouses the deepest emotion in me, takes me to another world, can reduce me to tears. An even faltering knowledge of the language, often with the assistance of a bi-lingual dictionary, enriches my appreciation of the words in the songs.

It is the same with movies, though the language of the screen, designed to reach the masses and denuded of flowery literary allusions, is much more accessible. Most Hindi videos these days are dubbed in English to reach the non-Hindi speaking world (especially the Middle East and Southeast Asia) or young children of the diaspora who have no Hindi, but the pleasure is not the same as listening to and understanding the dialogue in the original language. Hindi enables me to enter a wider culture and connects me to people and places that would otherwise remain inaccessible. In that sense it is like English, minus the fluency.

I am glad I still retain some small knowledge of the language. But things of the heart, which give me meaning and deep pleasure, enrich my life, I cannot share with most of my Australian friends. The gulf is too wide; we are too different. Nor, to be fair, can I, try as I might, understand or truly enjoy the deepest aspects of their cultural and aesthetic life. I was on a remote pre-historic farm, beyond the reach of radio, when the Beatles were taking on the world! And the sporting heroes of Australia, with whom they grew up, are unknown to me.

In everyday life, though, I do not use formal Hindi at all. To do so would be considered silly and pretentious. At home with my wife, and sometimes with my children, I speak Fiji-Hindi. It is my natural language. There are no standard conventions which I have to follow. Its loose grammatical structure enables me to improvise, to incorporate into the vocabulary English words of ordinary usage. That freedom is exhilarating. I use Fiji-Hindi when talking to other Indo-Fijians, not necessarily to converse at length in it, but to establish a point of recognition. The nature and depth of the conversation would depend on the closeness I have with the speaker. With most Indo-Fijian men, I would have no hesitation using Fiji-Hindi. I would be more reserved with Indo-Fijian women though, so as not to give any signal or hint of intimacy. Indian cultural protocol even today demands a degree of distance between men and women who are not close friends or family: hugging, giving someone a peck on the cheek and other western forms of showing affection are out of bounds and considered improper. English would for me be the most comfortable medium of communication with them, neutral. It is the same with my wife when talking to Indo-Fijian men. With children of friends and family, I normally speak in English, conscious that they might not — and many don't — have Hindi or Fiji-Hindi.

The Fiji-Hindi I speak now is not the one I spoke as a child. Then, it had few foreign words. But now, my Fiji-Hindi is increasingly filled with English words and phrases. I suspect it is the same in many urban parts of Fiji too. *Drinks aur Dinner hai*: it is a drinks and dinner party. *Kafi late hoi gaye hai*: it is getting quite late. *Lunch kar liha*: have you had lunch. *Kutch trouble nahi*: no trouble. *Bada bad hoi gaye*, does not look good, *Us ke support karo*, support him, *Report likho*, write a report, *Walk pe chale ga*, will you join me for a walk, *Telephone maro*, ring. My Fiji-Hindi would sound strange, unfamiliar, to people of my father's generation back in rural Fiji. My children's precariously limited, English-accented Fiji-Hindi would be incomprehensible to them, just as their language, full of rustic references and vanished metaphors and words would appear vaguely strange to us.

There is some sadness in this perhaps inevitable change. It is the price we pay for 'progress,' I suppose, for living away from our place of birth. Fiji-Hindi was the language of my childhood. It was the only language of communication between me and my parents, both of whom were unlettered and are now dead. It was the language through which I saw the world once, through which I learned about our past and ourselves, told stories and shared experiences. That Indo-Fijian world, and my mother tongue, will go with me.

Fiji-Hindi is my mother tongue, not my children's, who have grown up in Australia. They have some faltering familiarity with it, but that will go with time. It is the same with other children — or young adults — of their age. There will be little opportunity or incentive for them to continue with the language. Fiji is their parents' country, they say, not theirs. For most of them, English will effectively become the only language they have. Some Indo-Fijian families in Australia and elsewhere, traumatised by the coups and the ravages of ethnic politics, have actively sought to erase their memories of Fiji and things Fijian, even Indo-Fijian. The rejection of Fiji-Hindi is a part of that process of denying the past. Others have sought actively to embrace aspects of Indian subcontinental culture. Their children learn Hindi or Urdu in community-sponsored language classes. They attend temples and mosques to learn the basics of their faith and celebrate all the most important festivals of the Hindu or Muslim calender. Classical dance and music classes flourish in many Indo-Fijian communities in Australia.

Hindi or Urdu, I suspect, rather than Fiji-Hindi will be the second language of choice for the new generation. Born or brought up in Australia, they will have their own contradictions and confusions to deal with. Their problems and preoccupations will be different from mine. I admire the way they are adapting to their new homeland in ways that I know I could not, did not have the skills to. Confident and resourceful and inventive, they are completely at home in cross-cultural situations. The cultural gulf between their world and that of their Australian friends in music, film and general aspects of popular culture will never be as great as it is for me and people of my generation. My fears and phobias, my confused and confusing cultural inheritance, won't be theirs. Mercifully, their destinies won't be hobbled by mine.

As for me? The words of Mary Oliver will do:

When it is over, I don't want to wonder
if I have made of my life something particular and real.

I don't want to find myself sighing and frightened
or full of argument.

I don't want to end up simply having visited the world.

Acknowledgements

My journey into 'faction' writing has benefited immeasurably from the support of many colleagues over the years. First among them is, must be, Ian Templeman, former publisher of Pandanus Books in the Research School of Pacific and Asian Studies at The Australian National University, who encouraged me to think about writing texts without footnotes, to be concerned about getting at the essential truth and meaning of an experience, not only its factual accuracy, and to appreciate the fine difference between the two. I have been fortunate in having a collective of colleagues who have read my words and offered valuable suggestions. Among them are Doug Munro, Hank Nelson, Vicki Luker, Paul D'Arcy and Tessa Morris-Suzuki. My gratitude to them is beyond words. Padma has suffered much from my absent-minded preoccupations over the years that far exceeded the call of indentured duty, while Yogi and Niraj learned a long time ago to leave their 'old man' alone when he was 'in that mood of his'. Some day, I hope, they will come to understand what it was all about. I thank Jan Borrie for her careful reading of several stories in the volume, and Chandra Dulare for his careful scrutiny of the text in its final stage. Dorothy McIntosh, the Divisional Administrator of Pacific and Asian History, is a gem beyond measure. And Emily Brissenden's elegant craftsmanship of the book is self-evident.

Some of these pieces have appeared elsewhere and are reproduced here in some cases with a few silent emendations for clarity and consistency and, yes, readability. 'The Road to Mr Tulsi's Store' began as a talk given to the National Library of Australia workshop on 'Travellers Tales,' and was subsequently published in the Australian literary journal *Meanjin* (62:4, 2003) 'Marriage' and 'Masterji' first appeared in *BitterSweet: The Indo-Fijian Experience* (Pandanus Books, 2004). 'In Mr Tom's Country' appeared as the sole essay 'Mr Arjun' in Bruce Connew's book of photographs on the cane cutters of Vatiyaka, Ba called *Stopover* (University of Hawaii Press, 2007). 'Three Worlds, One Inheritance' appeared in Mary Besemeres and Anna Wierzbicka's edited volume *Translating Lives: Living with Two Languages and Cultures* (University of Queensland Press, 2007). A slightly revised version of 'A Gap in the Hedge' will appear in *The Contemporary Pacific: A Journal of Island Affairs* (Honolulu).

Finally, a word to my readers, from all over the world — Mudit Jain, Ravindra Nanda, Shridhar Barve, Jenny Sattar and dozens like them — who have written to me over the years to express their appreciation for my efforts: your warm words have given me undeniable pleasure and sustained me in moments of assailing doubt. Thank You; Vinaka Vakalevu; Dhanyavad.

Brij V Lal
Canberra, 2008

www.ingramcontent.com/pod-product-compliance
Lightning Source LLC
Chambersburg PA
CBHW042145160426
43197CB00030B/2966